ONCE I HAD A COMRADE

ONCE I HAD A COMRADE

Karl Roth and the Combat History of the 36th Panzer Regiment 1939–45

R.W. Byrd

HELION & COMPANY LTD.

Helion & Company Limited
26 Willow Road
Solihull
West Midlands
B91 1UE
England
Tel. 0121 705 3393
Fax 0121 711 4075
E-mail: publishing@helion.co.uk
Website: http://www.helion.co.uk

Published by Helion & Company 2006

Designed and typeset by Helion & Company Ltd, Solihull, West Midlands
Cover designed by Bookcraft Ltd, Stroud, Gloucestershire
Printed by Cromwell Press Ltd, Trowbridge, Wiltshire

© Helion & Company Ltd 2006

ISBN 1 874622 58 2

British Library Cataloguing-in-Publication Data.

A catalogue record for this book is available from the British Library.

All rights reserved. No part of this publication may be reproduced, stored in a retrieval system, or transmitted, in any form, or by any means, electronic, mechanical, photocopying, recording or otherwise, without the express written consent of Helion & Company Ltd.

Covers: The 14th *Panzer* Division's emblem was the Teutonic rune 'Ethel' meaning 'homeland'. At first the rune meant the circular swath cleared around the family home, it grew to mean the territory of the clan, then land of the tribe, and finally the nation of the peoples, therefore, native land. The symbolic action it represented was a man ploughing a field with a yoked cow (viewed from above), and the emblem, a thatched cottage (viewed from the side). Karl Roth in parade full service dress uniform (Gesellschaftanzug). The purpose of the service uniform was to promote enlistments in the military by inducing soldiers like Karl to vie for the various awards they could display on it, representing certain skills, time in service, and rank held. The army national emblem, a silver or grey eagle, is worn on the right breast of the field and service coat and on the front of caps. Long trousers and high black shoes always are worn with this uniform (Courtesy E. Roth). Remaining picture shows a *Panzer* from 36th *Panzer* Regiment near Rostov-on-Don, winter 1941/42 (courtesy Bundesarchiv).

For details of other military history titles published by Helion & Company Ltd contact the above address, or visit our website: http://www.helion.co.uk.

We always welcome receiving book proposals from prospective authors.

Dedication

This work is dedicated to the memory of Karl Roth and to my wife Jutta, who spent countless hours translating German into English. Also to my mother-in-law Else Roth, and to the veterans I interviewed, whose recollections of past events (some they would have rather left forgotten) made this book possible.

Memorial dedicated to the German Army (1914–1918, 1939–1945) and located at the *Ehrenbreitstein* Fortress above the heights of Koblenz, Germany
(Author's collection)

Ich hatt' einen Kameraden
(Ludwig Uhland 1809, set to a melody by Friedrich Silcher 1825)

Ich hatt' einen Kameraden,
Einen bessern findst du nicht.
Die Trommel schlug zum Streite,
Er ging an meiner Seite
In gleichen Schritt und Tritt.
In gleichen Schritt und Tritt.

Translation:
In battle I had a comrade
You won't find a better one.
The drum called us to fight,
He always walked at my side,
In step through good and bad.
In step through good and bad.

Contents

Acknowledgements ix
Preface x

Part I: Introduction: Germany before the war
1 Fulfilling the Dream (1916–1939) 17

Part II: The 4th Panzer Division
2 Loss of Innocence: Operation White and the Polish Campaign
   (September–October 1939) 33
3 Triumphant Victory: Operation Yellow-Red, France (May–June 1940) . 42
4 English Invasion: Operation Sea-lion, France (Summer 1940) 53

Part III: The 14th Panzer Division
5 Campaign in the Balkans: Operation Punishment, Yugoslavia
   (April 1941) 59
6 Campaigns in the East: Operation Barbarossa
   (June 1941–November 1942) 64
7 Kharkov: Operation Fredericus I and II (May–June 1942) 78
8 The Dream is Destroyed: Operation Blue, Stalingrad
   (June 1942–March 1943) 83

Part IV: The New 14th Panzer Division
9 Rest, Recovery and Return to Russia (March–December 1943) 109
10 Year of Fate (1944) 119
11 Heroic Stand: Courland (August 1944–May 1945) 132

Part V: Conclusion: After the War
12 The Nightmare is Over (May 1945–present) 157

Appendices

I   Hans Niedt, the Photographic Journal of a Combat Pioneer 169
II   Karl Roth's Personal Records 174
III   Orders of Battle and Organisational Charts 177
IV   *Panzer* Recovery and Repair 183
V   Regimental Tanks 186

Notes 190
Bibliography 204

Acknowledgements

I would first like to recognize my mother-in-law, Else Roth, and my wife Jutta and her family including her cousins, without whose help this work could not have been completed. Also Gernot Loeffler, my brother-in-law, for driving me into France, Belgium, and Luxembourg, a great man now deceased. I also wish to thank Elfrieda Bock, and everyone at the Prince Eugen divisional remembrance room in Kuhlsheim. A special thanks to the late Paul Schmitt, a former 36th *Panzer* Regiment supply officer, and all the veterans of the 14th *Panzer* Division 'Traditional Association', including General Peter von Butler, Heinz Neuendorff, Erwin Jungkunz, Hans-Joachim Braun, Karl Brier, Klaus Voss, Leo Schwarz, Alois Weigand my step daughter's father, and anyone else not mentioned. Another special thanks goes to two military book publishers, Dana Lombardy and Arnie Dupuy, who provided critical analysis to the story. An important thank you goes to Frau Caspers and the staff at the Koblenz photographic archives for their valued help, as well as the staff at the still pictures department at the National Archives College Park Maryland. A last thank you goes to longtime Schweinfurt resident Wilhelm Boehm author of *Zwischen Schulbank und Kanonen*, and Bernhardt Strobl, director at the Schweinfurt photographic archives.

This book would not have been possible without the devoted support offered by my family, including my parents, sister, and brothers. A special note of thanks goes out to all my friends, for their unending words of encouragement, especially my brother Dan. Two former Allied veterans provided their inspiration, my Uncle, Les Houde, a former B-17 pilot with twenty-five missions completed in Europe who read the entire manuscript, and Robert Bowen author of *Fighting with the Screaming Eagles*, who was captured during the Battle of the Bulge. I could not end the acknowledgements without thanking all those who document history, making it a pleasure for me to study.

Preface

This project began in the fall of 1987 when I met my wife, Jutta Roth, while stationed with the United States Army in Schweinfurt, Germany. During our first conversation she mentioned that her father, who died in 1972, was stationed at the same barracks facility I was then residing in. Being interested in modern European history, I inquired if her father served in the military in the Second World War. Jutta said he was the top sergeant of a maintenance company assigned to a tank regiment during the war, and then produced his metal identification disk (that all German soldiers carried) from her purse, reading: *Stab* (HQ) 36th *Panzer* Regiment. She then said he was the only one not killed of three other step-bothers sent to fight and also survived the epic battle for Stalingrad in 1943.[1]

My father-in-law's story sounded fascinating and I decided to look into the history of his unit to find out where they were and what happened to them during the war. After consulting my mother in law, Else Roth, I learned his regiment early in the war was originally part of the 4th *Panzer* Division. I was impressed at the extent of combat experience the unit possessed, having fought in almost every major campaign and some of the most important battles of the war. Their history spans seven years, from November 1938 until May 1945, covering such major events as the rearmament of Germany and the four year plan, the *Blitzkrieg* campaigns, Barbarossa and the attack on the Soviet Union, Stalingrad and the encirclement of Paulus's Sixth Army, the bombing campaign against the German homeland, defense of the Atlantic Wall, the Dniepr River battles of 1944 and defence of the Courland peninsula, one of the last outposts still resisting at the end of the war in May, 1945.[2]

Returning to the United States, I began researching the 36th *Panzer* Regiment's history and found many sources written on the organizational structure and brief histories concerning Army, Corps, and Division level units. Researchers though will have difficulty looking for the original German regimental war diaries as most of the documents were either destroyed in the Potsdam fire outside Berlin in 1944, by the unit commanders themselves, or were captured by the Russians at the end of the war and are only now becoming available. After my preliminary research, I discovered Karl Roth's story and his regiment's war record was almost a model in microcosm of the history of the European conflict on a whole.

The only official history of the unit is found in Rolf Grams' book, *Die 14. Panzer-Division 1940–1945*. This first hand account of the war by a former unit commander published in 1958 is an invaluable source on the operational period 1941–45, but does not cover the vital *blitzkrieg* campaigns conducted early in the war, when the regiment was assigned to the 4th *Panzer* Division. Grams' book is also a broad division history that inadequately details the strength of the unit during certain periods, leaving out some of the fateful events surrounding them. And last, this book was only published in German and therefore no exclusive English combat history exists, that encompasses the full story of Schweinfurt's *Panzer* regiment. This book then provides a brief but concise chronological history of the unit encompassing from start to finish the tactical and strategic events affecting them, and the personal accounts of those who were there.

Starting with some generic order of battle charts and regimental daybooks the story was pieced together from various sources, where I discovered discrepancies in some of the official passages presenting the history of the regiment.[3] For instance after the battle of Stalingrad, most books report the 36th *Panzer* Regiment as totally destroyed during the encirclement and subsequent surrender. In fact nearly half survived, along with other units that provided the core around which the future division was built.[4] A.N. Shimansky writing about the battle of Cherkassy in 1944 for Liddell-Hart's, *The History of the Second World War* series, reported all the defenders of the pocket were either killed or captured trying to break out,[5] but the truth is more than half made it back to German lines.[6] And about the evacuation of Courland at the end of the war, Cornelius Ryan in his famous book, *The Last Battle*, reported that only a few boatloads of men were evacuated to northern Germany, when actually thousands were.[7]

So what made Karl Roth and his regiment so extraordinary and why was their story above average, when compared to other German soldiers and tank regiments? As for Karl Roth, the answer to these questions is the fact that he survived six years of war, and was assigned to a revolutionary new branch of service playing the central role in the European conflict. The goal of the German ground warfare planners was to defeat the enemy in large encirclement battles, using the tank to achieve the new *blitzkrieg* strategy. Karl participated in and escaped his share of these engagements, including the Kutno Pocket in Poland in 1939, the reduction of the Dunkirk Pocket in 1940, the two largest encirclements of the war at Kiev and Uman in 1941, the Soviet setback at Kharkov in 1942, the most famous at Stalingrad in 1943, escaped from the Cherkassy pocket in 1944, and was evacuated to freedom from the forgotten Courland pocket in 1945. His story then is not that of the infantryman, following in the steps of their forefathers in the Great War, but instead of a skilled maintenance sergeant, repairing the tanks used by the most powerful motorized army the world had ever seen up until that time.

What made the 36th *Panzer* Regiment unique can be summed up into one word, 'Stalingrad'. Of the thirty or so tank regiments that existed in the German Army during that time, only three (including the 36th) could claim to have fought the vicious street battles within the city. The 36th *Panzer* Regiment was always at the focal point of any battle and was involved in the advance on Stalingrad from the south in August (accumulating more miles in an advance than any other tank regiment in Russia at that time), the struggle for the factory districts in the center in October, and the desperate attempt to hold the northern line from the Russian onslaught outside the city in November. A battle group was then involved to a minor extent holding the jump off positions outside the pocket for Manstein's relief attempt to reach the city in December. The famous struggle for Stalin's city was the psychological turning point of the war, and arguably the most written about subject of the whole Russo-German conflict.

This book then does not attempt to glamorize, promote, or trivialize the war, but does seek to reconstruct a brief history of this unit to highlight their activities, and explore the personal path of a remarkable man who survived them. The most common question asked by others during the research process was, "was your father-in-law a Nazi?" What my research revealed was not a man who survived through blind devotion to National Socialism, but instead through his own resources and desires to see his homeland and family once again. A friend and fellow historian, Arnie Dupuy, wrote after reading the manuscript,

> This is a story that should be told. It further proves that the average German soldier was not a fanatical or superhuman warrior, as many would like us to believe. Karl Roth, like countless of his fellow soldiers in the *Wehrmacht*, was dedicated, resourceful and motivated when fighting a seemingly endless and hopeless war against the Soviets. What is also portrayed in this work is that he was a devoted father and patriot caught up in a series of events that were beyond his comprehension and clearly out of his control.[8]

The true physical and psychological suffering he and his comrades endured or inflicted will never be known or truly expressed into words, but his survival story and the history of the 36th *Panzer* Regiment is truly remarkable. If for no other purpose the research done and material covered helped my wife better understand her father, and the sacrifices he gave for a country he loved. In 1998 I was invited and attended a reunion of the 14th *Panzer* Division in Kuhlsheim, Germany. There I met Hans Braun, a former officer of the unit in the early days before and during the war. He replied to my wife a month later in response to a questionnaire I asked him and his comrades to look over. What follows is the translation of his brief but accurate description of the 36th *Panzer* Regiment, sent to me at the beginning of the research process:

29 Nov. 1998

Dear Miss Roth!

I met you during the meeting of the 'Traditional Association of the 14th *Panzer* Division' in October by the Pz. Btl. 363 in Kuhlsheim, and engaged in a conversation about your father, who was assigned to the workshop company of the 36th *Panzer* Regiment in Schweinfurt.

This letter is in response to the questions you gave me. The extensive questionnaire I cannot go into detail on because my memory of the road of the 36th Panzer Regiment only spans the period 1938–41. In this time frame I was together with Karl Roth in the same regiment, but cannot recall direct contact with him, although the picture of *Feldwebel* Roth, was fairly familiar. The reason I cannot recall him is that the regiment had 60 officers, 360–400 non-commissioned officers, and over 1000 enlisted men at that time.

On October 1st 1938 a new *Panzer* Regiment was established, the 36th, under the command of the 4th *Panzer* Division in Wurzburg. Out of the 4th *Panzer* Division emerged the leadership and troop personnel for the Regiment, and were moved to Schweinfurt.

The formation of the Regiment was not quite finished in the spring of 1939 despite the first warning orders for war. Under the leadership of the regimental headquarters staff in Schweinfurt, the tank battalions came from the 35th Regiment in Bamberg. The workshop company was established in Schweinfurt. In response to the first warning order for combat we moved from Austria to the training area of Doellersheim, then to Bohemia/Moravia, and reached the town of Iglau.

In the autumn of 1939 came the Polish Campaign, and after a short rest the Regiment was in January 1940 called to the West, in the area of Sauerland, and later we redeployed into the area around Julich. The road of the Regiment, inclusive the workshop company and *Feldwebel* Roth can be traced on the map included. After the French Campaign was over the 36th Regiment was moved with the 4th *Panzer* Division back to Schweinfurt, and in November 1940 was used to build the new 14th *Panzer* Division. The forming of the division took place in the beginning of 1941 in the training area of Milowitz, near Prague. From this point on the road of the Regiment can be found in Rolf Grams' *Die 14. Panzer-Division 1940–1945*.

Until August 1941 I was the Regimental Adjutant of the 36th *Panzer* Regiment, in December 1941 I commanded the 1st Company, and from September commanded the 1st Battalion until they took back the front by the Mius River Line. In December 1941 I was moved to command as the 1st Ordnance Officer in the III *Panzerkorps*.

I hope Frau Roth with these references you can trace the road of the Regiment from 1938–1941 and altogether highlight the steps of your father and the 36th *Panzer* Regiment.

With friendly greetings, yours,
Hans Joachim Braun

Richard Byrd
Phoenix, Arizona

PART I
INTRODUCTION: GERMANY BEFORE THE WAR

Karl poses for the camera in front of the 36th *Panzer* Regiment's headquarters building at the barracks in Schweinfurt, dressed in his black *Panzer* field uniform, and wearing the early black beret issued to the tank men in the Regiment prior to the winter of 1939–40. The field uniform was designed to retain as much flair as was possible, while at the same time providing a practical utilitarian wear for the troops. The beret was to serve as a crash helmet, but the headgear proved unnecessary, and was later replaced with a black wool-rayon field cap. The black double-breasted coat issued with the uniform is known as the field-jacket (*Feldjacke*) and is dyed black to conceal dirt and grease stains. *Panzer* troops wore a metal death's head on each collar patch. The black trousers are referred to as field trousers (*Feldhosen*) and are fitted with tapes, so they may be bound to the leg at the ankle. Standard black service shoes were worn with this uniform, as the use of boots was contrary to German army regulations. By the end of the war, the black *Panzer* uniform was standard for almost all tank and armoured car crews, cultivating an aura of *esprit de corps* within the regiment.
(Author's collection, courtesy E. Roth)

CHAPTER I

Fulfilling the Dream (1916–1939)

After the First World War concluded economic depression in Europe caused bitter social divisions to develop along ethnic, racial, and political lines. The enforcement of the Versailles Treaty, coupled with the worldwide depression of the 1930's, caused an environment to develop in Germany that placed into power Adolf Hitler and the Nazi Party.[1] His rise to power was promulgated by the fulfilment of early promises to the German people concerning employment, rearmament, and the restoration of nationalism.

Karl Wilhelm Roth was born illegitimate in 1916 and grew up during these tumultuous years in the Franconian city of Schweinfurt, located in northern Bavaria. The town, with a population of 60,000 at the time was situated among wooded hills through which the Main River flowed, and was a major regional centre for the middle Main area.

His mother, whom he lived with in the early years of his life, was a waitress and since his birth was married, having one son, Hans Niedt (see Appendix I). Karl's father, also remarried from his first wife and having two sons, belonged to a union and worked at the Kugelfischer ball bearing factory. The senior Roth was a Social Democrat, as were most of the city's industrial plant workers and not very sympathetic to the Nazi cause.

In the early 1930's heavy rioting broke out in Schweinfurt and other cities in Germany between the Socialists, National Socialists, and Communists. When the Nazi party took control in 1933, Hitler disbanded the labour unions replacing them with craft guilds, the Social Democratic party was outlawed, and conscription was reintroduced.[2] These new policies not only affected the older Roth's life, but that of his son and the future of the entire German nation as well.

The patchwork of federated states formed after World War One was perceived by Hitler to be a threat to his goal of national reunification and therefore he disposed the state leaders, replacing them with his own men. In 1936 he further reorganized the country into fifteen military districts, the aim of which was to prepare the new German nation for war within four years.[3] Next he reduced the unemployment rate significantly by introducing mandatory labour service and by 1938 rearmament was so successful workers were being imported from other countries.[4]

Germany's youth took a high priority in the 'four year plan' and young men regardless of class or status were forced into labour camps for two years. Karl was inducted into the organization at Bad Kissingen in 1936, and worked as an agricultural labourer. This programme consisted of hard work with long hours and miserable living conditions. It was designed to mould the young men into believing in a 'New Ideal', the purpose of which was to instil the discipline needed to obediently follow orders once they were further drafted into the military.[5]

The Nazi organization discouraged higher education and "by the late 1930's most students were dropping out of school to work as craft apprentices or industrial trainees".[6] The mandates and obligations of the Hitler Youth movement made

Schweinfurt's ornate *Rathaus* (city hall), originally built in 1572, was used to hold governing counsels, and the central square a farmers market. In Medieval times, the highest-ranking kings in Germany were the only ones who could counter the laws passed in these free city-states. (Author's Collection, courtesy E. Roth)

Schweinfurt is a factory town situated on the Main River in the region of Franconia. Its location in the middle Main valley and the ability to ship multiple goods out by barge and rail, led to major economic growth for the city in the 1930s. With the introduction of the motor engine, Schweinfurt's Main River factories converted to producing ball bearings. This image is from turn of the century era post card. (Author's Collection, courtesy E. Roth)

FULFILLING THE DREAM (1916–1939)   19

The city of Schweinfurt in the 1930s was typical of most other German cities, with the civil servants and middle class (*Mittelstand*) usually residing within the old city walls, conveniently located near shops and government buildings. The poor and lower class lived outside the walls in sub standard housing near factories and railroad yards. Royalty and the upper class, including some of the top Nazi leadership resided on the best estates, including castles (*Schloss*) and old fortresses (*Berg*) dominating the heights. (Author's collection, courtesy E. Roth)

it difficult to continue academic study and so Karl left school, moving in with his father. He registered as a plumber's apprentice at the Kugelfischer factory in 1937 and one of his first jobs was to install the gutters on the roof of the new military barracks being built in Schweinfurt. But his time on the job was short, lasting just over one year, when it became time to fulfil his military obligation.

Due to Hitler's conscription decree of 1936, labour training was followed by mandatory military service. Young men who were forced into this type of regimentation at sixteen years old and then were trained as skilled workers, produced privates more proficient than corporals and sergeants in other armies. The German military's greatest asset until the closing days of the war was their ready supply of these well-skilled non-commissioned officers. Beyond their training these young soldiers pledged their lives to Hitler and embraced the idea of dying heroically on the battlefield for the new German Reich.[7]

General Heinz Guderian demonstrated the operational capabilities of armoured mobile warfare as early as 1929 during field exercises at Doberitz, forty miles west of Berlin. He played a central role in the development of the *Panzer* Division concept, often struggling against a reactionary military establishment bent on retaining the horse cavalry. His theory centred on total encirclement of the enemy by fast moving armoured troops that exploited the enemy's communications and rear areas. By 1938 three *Panzer* divisions existed. Converting former cavalry and infantry units into mechanized forces formed most of the new tank regiments within these divisions.[8] In 1938, during the fifth phase of the German Army's rearmament programme, the newly built barracks in Schweinfurt was chosen to house the regimental headquarters and workshop company of the new 36th *Panzer* Regiment. This Regiment, along with a sister unit (the 35th *Panzer* Regiment) from the neighbouring town of Bamberg, both made up the 4th *Panzer* Division of the 5th *Panzer* Brigade.[9] Brigade and Division headquarters was located thirty miles away in the city of Wurzburg.

The *Panzer* division was a formation of combined arms trained for self-contained action and deployment in-depth, consisting of elite troops. The *Panzer* regiment was the nucleus of tanks around which everything else in the division revolved. The grenadiers, reconnaissance, engineers, artillery and flak regiments' main purpose was to support the armoured offensive of the tanks.

Guderian ensured that officers who displayed above average fighting spirit and dependability staffed the tank divisions. He was convinced that armour would play the primary role in the upcoming war and insisted that the tanks be kept together as one fighting unit and provided heavy air support. This strategy directly contradicted his allied opponent's doctrine of dividing up the vehicles along the entire front to support the infantry. This '*Blitzkrieg*' concept allowed the Germans to defeat superior enemy forces by outflanking and shocking their defences, ushering in a new type of warfare.[10]

Karl swore into the 36th *Panzer* Regiment as a private during a torchlight and bonfire ceremony on November 18th 1938. The induction ceremony was a surreal spectacle of which Else Schaub (Karl's girlfriend and future wife) witnessed firsthand, telling me, "This night I realized the war was inevitable, as the flickering

The gradual encroachment on the civil and human rights of the Jewish population by the Nazi leadership culminated during *Kristallnacht* (Night of broken glass) on November 9th 1938, with the destruction of their synagogues and shops, to confiscation of their property, setting the climate for the greater crimes committed during the Holocaust years. Schweinfurt's clock-setter and Karl Roth's neighbour after the war Paul Rosenkranz and his wife Marie lost their shop on this day, ultimately forcing them into hiding.
(Federal Archives College Park, hereafter referred to as FACP)

FULFILLING THE DREAM (1916–1939) 21

Nazi programmes and restrictions were not only taken against the Jewish race, as multiple 'undesirables' further segregated the German population, with intellectuals, homosexuals, political opponents, and Gypsies all herded into ghettos and concentration camps. (Author's Collection-Courtesy E. Roth)

shadows and glow from the bonfire made the soldiers outstretched arms look as if they were those from skeletons ".[11] He was originally assigned to the headquarters section of the workshop company as a mechanic and driver. Although small, the workshop company provided critical services needed to remain on the offensive of an attack. During the war company maintenance teams laboured continuously to keep the vehicles combat ready, exposing themselves to minefields, enemy tanks, shellfire and attacks from the air.[12] Karl could personally attest to these dangers as he was wounded on one occasion after being blown off the tank he was attempting to pull off the battlefield, and returned from the war with grenade fragments in his leg.[13]

Unit strengths varied during the war years, but the 36th Regiment originally comprised two battalions of four light companies each. The maintenance company was organized into recovery sections and directed by a vehicle command-staff at the regimental level. The mobile command staff (*Instandsetzung*) consisted of two officers and a senior non-commissioned officer (the later position eventually held by Karl at the end of the war). This headquarters command squad was equipped with a motorcycle and sidecar, two open cross-country trucks and an Opel *Blitz* heavy truck. Karl was responsible for his rifle, personal sidearm and the section's MG34 machine gun, as well as the upkeep and security of these vehicles and items.

At the regimental workshop level only heavy work was done and tank crews were expected to make their own minor repairs.[14] An example of this was recounted by one of the regiment's survivors who told me Karl Roth reprimanded him after getting his tank stuck on an icy road during a winter battle in Courland, telling him in not so polite terms to remedy the situation himself![15]

The divisional workshop companies performed repairs on wheeled vehicles mostly and worked on tanks in emergency situations only, while maintenance at army level undertook the heavier and more time-consuming work having the more specialized equipment. Early on in the war tank transporters were used frequently to return vehicles to assembly points in the rear, but as the war progressed towing

Even as a child, Karl Roth was a gifted metal worker, designing and building this kayak out of aluminium at the auto repair shop that he worked at when he was fifteen. Young men like Karl growing up before the war in Germany were encouraged to be competitive and physically fit, grooming them for military service beyond the youth and labour camps. (Author's collection, courtesy E. Roth)

machines were adopted to pull the heavier Panther and Tiger tanks.[16] Sometimes the need for returning battle-damaged tanks to the front became so great the command staffs formed *ad-hoc* repair teams on short notice, as occurred during the battle of Stalingrad. These regimental workshop companies and command staffs were a vital part of Guderian's independent mobile force being made ready for war in 1939.[17]

The final days of 1938 and those following the spring and summer of 1939 found the Regiment preparing for combat at the training areas outside of Schweinfurt, at Grafenwohr and Hammelburg. New recruits training in certain particular functions such as maintenance work were provided instruction at specialist training classes when not in the field. Special abilities developed during their apprenticeship years were put to use by the army, and some training was done in civilian establishments such as auto shops and schools. Basic infantry training was normally sixteen weeks long followed by advanced training that was on going.[18] Military discipline was rigid in the German Army and political affiliations other than the Nazi party were not tolerated. Those personnel not measuring up to regulations were severely punished. During parades for instance, harsh punishments accompanied anyone caught moving unnecessarily.[19] These parades were highly organized spectacles put on by the Army High Command, the first of which the Regiment attended on April 20th, 1939. All branches of the armed services paraded for four hours in front of a world delegation at Hitler's fiftieth birthday celebration in Berlin, putting on the greatest military demonstration in the history of the Third Reich.[20] Germany was no longer rearming in secret and the sheer weight of Germany's hidden might was now evident to all the foreign diplomats who attended the celebration.

Hitler addressed the *Reichstag* eight days later and delivered one of his longest public speeches ever. After attacking the unfairness of the Versailles Treaty he made known his concerns about the treatment of Germans in the Polish Corridor and port of Danzig, both ceded from Germany after the First World War. Because Poland rejected his restoration plan and mobilized their troops he went on, the

FULFILLING THE DREAM (1916–1939) 23

Before the war, Karl Roth, and friends return from swimming in the Main River. Most of these young men did not survive the conflict, including two of Karl Roth's stepbrothers. As a generation of young men like Karl grew into adulthood in the mid 1930s under the National Socialist agenda, they produced the core of non-commissioned officers that became the backbone of the German army.
(Author's collection, courtesy E. Roth)

National Socialist women's auxiliaries were founded as early as 1931, with their main task being to coordinate all the women's organizations into a National Socialist Women's Front. By 1936 more than 2 million girls were enrolled in the 'League of German Girls', including Else Roth's sister, photographed here.
(Author's collection, courtesy E. Roth)

The Headquarters Company of the 36th *Panzer* Regiment is pictured here in this pre-war photograph (August 1939) in Schweinfurt. Karl Roth is located third row up from the bottom, third man in from the left side.
4th *Pz.* Div.
Wurzburg
Commander Maj. Gen. Reihirdt
5th *Pz.* Bde.
Bamberg
Bde Commander Maj. Gen. Hartlieb
Pz. Rgt. 35 Bamberg Lt. Col. Eberbach
I batt. Lt. Col. Stenglein
II batt. Maj. Hochbaum
Pz. Rgt. 36 Schweinfurt Lt. Col. Breith
I batt. Maj. Von Hillebrandt
II batt. Maj. Stempel

(Author's collection, courtesy E. Roth)

The tank barracks as it first appeared upon completion in 1936. It was originally to house *Panzer* Regiment 4 of the 2nd *Panzer* Division (which moved to Vienna in 1938). Its official name was the Adolf Hitler *Kaserne*, but was better known to the locals as simply 'the *Panzerkaserne*'. (Schweinfurt Archives)

Karl Roth was originally assigned to the headquarters section of the workshop company in 1938 as a mechanic and driver. As a work garment for drivers a two-piece coverall of rush-green cotton or rayon, or a work suit, was issued. Generally, only one was issued each man, the work suit being reserved for those with heavy tasks such as motor maintenance. Here Roth poses with an officer and leans on a Mercedes Benz light command car. (Author's collection, courtesy E. Roth)

non-aggression pact of 1934 between the two countries now did not exist. Nevertheless, Hitler said he was ready to negotiate and remain peaceful, but secretly gave orders to the armed forces to prepare for 'Operation White', the attack on Poland.[21]

The campaign was set to begin no later than September 1st, 1939 and Britain and France vowed to protect Poland if attacked by Germany, while Stalin and Hitler secretly signed a non-aggression pact that deceivingly discussed dividing up their neighbour. On August 22nd Hitler called a meeting at the Berghof in Berchtesgaden issuing the campaign orders to his senior commanders.[22] On the same day the 36th *Panzer* Regiment and the 4th *Panzer* Division were officially activated for war.

The Class Struggle

Being born an illegitimate child in Germany in the early 1900's severely affected Karl Roth's prospects for the future. A rigid caste system where birthright was the determining factor for success in life affected everything from education to living conditions and was loosely translated into meaning, "you are as your father was".

The civil servants and middle class (*Mittelstand*) usually resided within the city walls of typical German towns like Schweinfurt conveniently located near the shops and government buildings at the city's core. The poor and lower class lived outside the walls, in substandard housing near the factories and railroad yards. Royalty and the upper class, including some of the top leaders of the Nazi organization, resided on the best real estate including the castles that dominated the heights and entire forest estates. This segregation system was further divided along ethnic, social, religious and gender lines. Jews, Gypsies and other 'undesirables' were denied employment and ultimately rescinded to the ghettos of major cities. Workers were given jobs but stripped of the right to form or join a union, to strike and negotiate wages.

On the other-hand women stood to gain some rights under the new Nazi leadership as Hitler placed the Aryan mother on a high pedestal within his new vision

Karl Roth's bunk area at the *Panzer* barracks in Schweinfurt. On the top of the wall locker is his M1935 field helmet, and below are two dress uniform visor hats. In the closet are his uniforms, overcoat, bayonet, and on the wall a portrait of Adolf Hitler. When worn the bayonet hangs from a leather frog just ahead of the entrenching shovel, and is held in place by a loop on the shovel case that holds the scabbard. (Author's collection, courtesy E. Roth)

of Greater Germany. She could provide the manpower needed to wage a war of expansion and he created numerous government subsidies to ensure mothers did not have to work and raise a family as well. 'The Honour Cross of Motherhood' medal was given to those women who nurtured multiple children.

But for a young average German male, Hitler's role as a former corporal in the German army underscored the fact that the military provided the best opportunity of breaking out of this caste system. Karl Roth's chances of being accepted to a university were limited because of his class standing, so for the illegitimate son of a factory worker, the military was close to his only option of breaking out of this social order.

The German Army though had its own rigid caste system dominated by the old Prussian Guard of the First World War. The new Army, fast and mechanized, set off on a course that was appealing to young men of varying status from all over Germany. Karl Roth's assignment to the headquarters company of the tank regiment was a better position than most new recruits could hope for. The small makeup of the maintenance command section helped to develop a comradeship and loyalty between the enlisted men and officers of the unit. The officer corps was not only open to men of elite background, but also to those who showed skill and leadership ability. But the creation of a cohesive and resilient band of fighters was aimed at something else as well: the transformation of the *Frontgemeinschaft* (front community) into a *Volksgemeinschaft* (national community), or a social unity that embodied the vital principle around which a new German society would be formed.

Hitler purposely began this practice of bringing together Germans from differing social, educational, and occupational backgrounds with entrance into the *Reichsarbeitsdienst* (Labour Service). In a speech in 1938 he stated that:

> These young boys join our organization at the age of ten…then four years later they move…to the Hitler Youth… then we are even less prepared to give them back into the hands of those who create our class and status barriers… If they… have still not become real National Socialists, then they go into the Labour Ser-

FULFILLING THE DREAM (1916–1939)

vice and are polished there... And if... there are still remnants of class-consciousness or pride in status, then the *Wehrmacht* will take over from there...

As a veteran went on to say:

The creation of that *Volksgemeinschaft* in which the workers would be fully integrated, the end of the destructive class struggle, the realization of the principal 'common good before individual good' was all... revolutionary to that which had been before. The motto of our organization (the Hitler Youth), was, "Down with class snobbery, we are all comrades of the new German Reich.[23]

After Karl Roth came to the realization of what sacrifice Hitler was asking of them, he must have agreed that a career doing what your father did might not be that bad an alternative. Whatever his thoughts, he turned down an officers commission in the new German Army and spent his next twenty-five years after the conflict working as a maintenance engineer, for the same factory his father worked.

Left: Karl Roth was responsible for the upkeep and security of his personal and section weapons. He was issued the standard army 98k bolt-action rifle.

Right: Once promoted to sergeant he was issued either the Walther P-38 or the smaller Walther PPK. A semi automatic pistol with a grip magazine feed, it can be carried with the hammer un-cocked, and the first shot fired by a double-action mechanism.

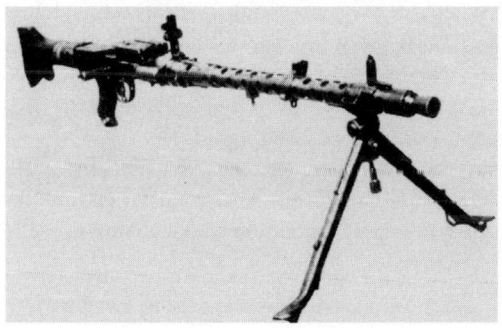

Left: The standard section weapon was an MG 34 machine gun, but later the MG 42 machine gun was adopted. Both were dual-purpose weapons that were used on a fixed bipod, a tripod mount, or an anti-aircraft mount. The gun was versatile and could be mounted on the section's light trucks and motorcycle as well. (Author's collection, U.S War Dept.)

28 ONCE I HAD A COMRADE

Two small children inspect the inside of a *Panzer* Mark I tank in this scene taken just before the war began in 1939. (FACP)

A cameraman takes a still photograph of a German square adorned in Nazi regalia. (Hans Niedt Collection)

Schweinfurt's market square before the war, gripped in Nazi Euphoria. (Schweinfurt Archives)

FULFILLING THE DREAM (1916–1939) 29

In the 1930s numerous Nazi rallies and military parades filled Schweinfurt's *Marktplatz* with marching columns and spectators. Here the 4th *Panzer* Regiment has just arrived, 1936. (Schweinfurt Archives)

New tanks of the 4th *Panzer* Regiment form up in front of the *Rathaus*. The third tank on the left is a *Befehlswagen*, or communication and command vehicle. Each platoon was originally supposed to consist of seven *Panzer* Mark I tanks, but was finally reduced to five. (Schweinfurt Archives)

In this photograph the same tanks are seen from a different angle. (Schweinfurt Archives)

PART II
THE 4TH PANZER DIVISION

CHAPTER II

Loss of Innocence

Operation White and the Polish Campaign (September–October 1939)

It was past midnight early in October in Schweinfurt as Else Schaub's girl friend ran up the cobblestone-street and upon entering her house exclaimed, "The Regiment is back already! But they're bringing them in on the side roads to town because they're all tore up!"

It was true that the campaign in Poland was swift, not lasting more than thirty-six days, but it also hadn't come without loss. The Regiment's sixth company was destroyed almost to a tank during the fighting on the Bzura River, and the loss of innocence to the horrors of actual combat affected Karl and his comrades for the rest of their lives. Long after the war passed he remembered his baptism of fire stating, "that was our toughest fight, I should have died in Poland on several occasions".[1]

After the 36th *Panzer* Regiment was activated for war towards the end of August, they moved to assembly areas in Silesia (near the city of Oppeln) along the border with Poland. Each *Panzer* battalion was instructed to leave one light company behind in Germany as a reserve, reducing each to three companies. All tank units were then issued four times their normal amounts of ammunition. This put the Regiment's total inventory on September 1st 1939 at 84 *Pz* I's, 66 *Pz* II's, 0 *Pz* III's, 6 *Pz* IV's, and 8 support vehicles, a total of 156 tanks.[2]

The 4th *Panzer* Division along with the 1st *Panzer* made up the XVI Motorised Corps, commanded by General Erich Hoepner, which in turn was assigned to the 10th Army (v. Reichenau).[3] The 36th *Panzer* Regiment's objective was to thrust into southern Poland, smash through the Lodz Army and push on towards the capital, Warsaw. The infantry would follow behind the fast moving armour, clearing out by-passed enemy pockets. After a delay of four days, 'Operation White' began at 4:34 a.m. on September 1st, with heavy air raids on strategic Polish command and control networks including rail and road bridges. Hitler specified as early as April that there was going to be no formal declaration of war and the Germans achieved complete surprise. By the second day of hostilities the *Luftwaffe* forced Polish aircraft to abandon their main forward airfields in favour of minor airstrips further behind the lines, which proved decisive by the end of the campaign.[4]

The weather in the south was clear when the Regiment crossed the border of Poland, racing between the Warta and Pilica rivers. Contact was made in the forests with rearguards of the Polish 28th and 30th infantry divisions. At 08:00 hours the Wolynska Cavalry Brigade ambushed the 4th *Panzer* Division near the town of Mokra.[5] Polish cavalry operated as mounted heavily armed infantry equipped with anti-tank rifles, and 37mm anti-tank guns, both of which could penetrate most

On September 1st, 1939, three quarters of Germany's ground forces were unleashed against Poland. Here tank crews wait for the orders to continue their advance. (FACP)

Dispatch riders were an important link in the dissemination of information sent from regimental headquarters down to the companies in the field. (FACP)

LOSS OF INNOCENCE 35

Karl Roth was a motorcycle dispatch rider for the regimental headquarters assigned to the maintenance section when Operation White began, and here stops for a brief meal. The three men to his right eating are standing in front of a *Panzer* Mark I tank. The 'H' stands for headquarters and Roth is seen next to a Zundapp KS750 with sidecar, which was issued early in the war. Motorcycle drivers were issued special clothing including a raincoat, a pair of goggles, and a pair of gauntlets. The special long rubber raincoat could be buttoned in a variety of ways to improve protection and facilitate operation of the motorcycle. Once, Roth travelled alongside the regimental band, and at some point his motorcycle stalled at a crossroads. Without success he continually tried to restart the bike, but only until he moved onto the alternate side road, and in another direction, did the engine start. He found out later the entire band section he was travelling beside was ambushed later up the main road, and all were either killed or taken prisoner by the Polish army.
(Author's collection, courtesy E. Roth)

German armour in 1939.[6] The resulting engagement was the most intense battle in this sector, exposing shortcomings in the new *Blitzkrieg* doctrine.

After an initial direct attack on the town with 25 tanks of the 35th *Panzer* Regiment was held off, the 36th *Panzer* Regiment was ordered to outflank the village to the south. This assault on the forest area between Mokra and Klobuck was broken up by Polish artillery at 10:00 hours that day, with significant loss to the unit. An hour later *Panzergrenadiers* were thrown into a renewed attack on the Mokra clearing, pushing them back to a railway line behind the town. Three hours later, tank companies that penetrated the Polish defensive lines were taken under fire by anti-tank and artillery fire from an armoured train positioned on the rail line. The train's 75mm turreted guns knocked out a few regimental tanks at point blank range, causing the division commander to call in *Stuka* dive-bomber attacks on this sector. Severe damage was done to the Polish rear areas by these air attacks, but a final drive by the *Panzers* was stopped by light tanks of the 21st Armoured Troop. By the end of the day Polish losses were so high they withdrew from their defence line, with the XVI Motorised Corps tanks in hot pursuit.

Polish Army equipment destroyed along a road during the drive on Warsaw. Their ineffectiveness against the Germans was not for lack of courage to fight as it was for faulty intelligence and poor equipment. This French built UE ammo carrier was ambushed on a cobblestone brick road before they could even respond.
(Hans Niedt Collection)

A *Panzer* Mark IV, of which few were available to the 36th *Panzer* Regiment in 1939, enters the outskirts of Warsaw. (FACP)

Both regiments of the 4th *Panzer* Division were tied down with street fighting after assaulting the city head on during September 9th and 10th. Dismounted German motorized troops try and use the cover and protection of the tanks. (FACP)

After the attack on Warsaw bogged down in early September the 36th *Panzer* Regiment was pulled away from the city, and sent towards the only major counter-attack made by the Polish Army during the campaign at the Bzura River. (FACP)

In this photograph a *Panzer* Mark I tank braces for the impending Polish breakout attempt from the Kutno Pocket. (Bundesarchiv)

After the heavy street fighting in Warsaw experienced early in September by the *Panzer* regiments, reduction of the city was left up to the infantry and Stuka dive-bombing attacks. (FACP)

Karl, posing as a Polish prisoner, stands amongst the crew of a *Panzer* Mark I tank and comrades from his regimental section. The man on his right holds a Luger pistol, and the one on his left a machine pistol MP-40. The machine pistols were designed for issue to parachute troops but their compact size made them perfect for *Panzer* crews as well. The white crosses on the turrets of these tanks were found to be dangerous as aiming points by the enemy and were subsequently painted over after the campaign ended. French helmets, uniforms, and vehicles made up a great majority of the Polish Army's equipment. (Author's collection, courtesy E. Roth)

The fighting lasted for two days in the forests north of Klobuck until the Regiment broke through the border defences, overrunning several more uncoordinated units trying to stem their advance.[7] Enemy tanks were engaged at Petrikau, and after they were defeated, all the key road nets leading to Warsaw were secured.[8] In eight days they advanced 140 miles, driving a deep wedge between Army Group Lodz opposing Reichenau, and Army Group Krakow further south. Polish armies were now falling back all along the line, and the Regiment was the first to reach the outskirts of Warsaw. Although exhausted, they were ordered to capture the city at dawn on September 9th, and followed the 35th Regiment into the city.[9]

The assault moved forward from the southwest into the Ochota and Wola suburbs at 0700, after an initial artillery barrage. The tanks advanced unhindered across a road bridge followed closely by motorised infantry. Soon the infantry were separated from the tanks, as anti-tank and machine gun fire began to make it difficult to maintain contact. The main train station was almost reached, but heavy anti-tank fire and desperate attacks by Polish sappers turned back the attack. Two hours later another attack was ordered along a different avenue of approach. At first significant gains were made, but again the motorised infantry received heavy small arms fire, forcing them to leave their vehicles and find cover. At 1100 hours the order was given to disengage, and after a half days fighting only 57 tanks out of 120 that began the attack that morning were operational. The maintenance-company was brought up the following day to do repairs and Karl and his comrades went to work repairing the damage.[10]

LOSS OF INNOCENCE 39

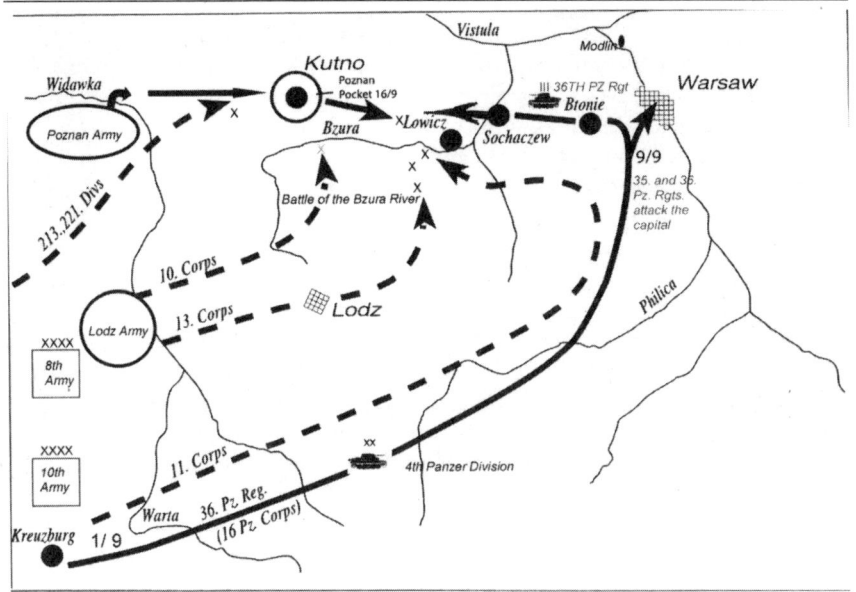

Operation White: Poland

In their rush to take the capital the Germans by-passed General Kutrzeba's Army Group Poznan, entrenched in a bend of the Bzura River, 30 miles west of Warsaw. Here unfolded one of the most-bitter fought battles of the campaign, and the only major counter-attack made by the Polish Army. The Poznan pocket represented one-third of the Polish Army left in the field, including four infantry divisions and two cavalry brigades. At 1200 hours on September 10th, the Poznan Army attacked the exposed left flank of the German 24th and 30th Infantry Divisions. This counter-attack seriously threatened all of Army Group South's plans, and attacks on Warsaw were postponed.[11] For two days the attack continued into the German flank while General Rundstedt, commanding Army Group South, consolidated his position. The Poles were surrounded and herded towards the tanks of the 4th *Panzer* Division and XVI Motorised Corps, recalled from the assault on Warsaw. It was during this assault that the 36th *Panzer* Regiment lost nearly all the tanks in the sixth company.[12] This 25-mile cauldron was known as the Kutno Pocket and now included twelve infantry divisions, and three cavalry brigades.[13] It was the Germans who were on the offensive after September 12th, squeezing the Kutno defenders into a smaller and smaller pocket.

My mother-in-law told me the following account of a disturbing engagement experienced by her husband, while serving in Poland. Karl moved forward on his motorcycle but was bogged down in soft sand near a village during the advance. He and his assistant driver decided to wait out the night in the clearing they were in, and dig the bike out the next morning. It was a full moon and they thought they were alone in the forest. But around midnight, a local militia group accompanied by a few regular Polish Army officers rose up only yards from their position and charged them, screaming and yelling. Karl and his comrade barely made it to their machine gun, but within seconds had cut down the advancing men. That night they stayed on the gun, fighting off continued attacks at point blank range that were perfectly lit up in the moonlight. The following morning, when support arrived, they advanced forward to inspect the perimeter and found dead farmers and civilians armed with only pitchforks and sickles.

General Kutrzeba led a breakout attempt in the direction of Modlin, on the outskirts of Warsaw on the night of the 16th, with almost two divisions. Some, including Kutrzeba himself, managed to fight their way into the forests between Modlin and the capital. But most of the Polish troops were driven back or destroyed by German air attacks.[14] The German air force ceaselessly bombed and strafed the pocket on September 17th, and it is estimated over 328 tons of bombs were dropped.[15] Some 170,000 prisoners were taken by the time the elimination of the pocket ended on the 19th. With this threat to their flank eliminated, the regiment now turned once again towards the final goal of taking Warsaw.[16]

Warsaw was surrounded and faced the same fate as the Kutno Pocket. The Germans decided storming the city was not worth the losses and opted for a siege instead. The German *Luftwaffe* attacked the city's power and water supplies on September 18th, as artillery hit the city itself. This time the infantry divisions attacked and probed slowly into the southern and western suburbs. Warsaw's civilian population were hemmed in and subjected to merciless air and artillery bombardment, causing at least 40,000 dead. Hitler ordered 420 bombers to destroy the city on September 25th, 'Black Monday', forcing total capitulation two days later.[17]

The Soviets attacked Poland from the east eight days earlier on September 17th, ensuring its final destruction. This made Hitler feel confident enough on October 5th to declare 'Operation White' officially over, and reviewed a victory parade in Warsaw.[18] During the ceremony Karl wore the campaign decoration he was awarded after the fighting was over, and was promoted from Private to Private First Class.[19]

Else finally saw Karl, her fiancé, the night the regiment returned to Schweinfurt and recalls his clothes smelling of smoke, oil, and diesel fuel. Vivid memories that lasted Karl and his comrades a lifetime related the haunting scenes of his moonlit forest fight, cleaning body parts out of tank treads after the campaign was over, and the suffering endured by the Polish army and civilians.[20]

The cost to the civilian population by Hitler's campaign and especially atrocities committed against Polish prisoners of war cannot be understated. Alexander Rossino states in his book, *Hitler Strikes Poland*, that,

> Some German soldiers showed restraint and mercy when dealing with civilians caught in the fighting, and in certain cases *Wehrmacht* officers demonstrated the willingness to intervene when it appeared that their men were committing crimes against noncombatants. Unfortunately, it is just as clear that many German military and SS personnel were quite prepared to behave with incredible brutality toward Polish and Jewish civilians.

Polish authorities determined later that after the battle on the Bzura River concluded, the 4th *Panzer* Division was complicit in the murder of civilians and Polish prisoners in four towns occurring as late as September 21st, two days after a formal surrender was signed. Poland was the testing ground for Germany's policies of genocide and ethnic cleansing against the Slavic populations of Eastern Europe, evolving into the brutal 'war of annihilation' implemented during the campaigns in the Balkans and in Russia.

The 4th *Panzer* Division incurred the most significant vehicle losses of the campaign reporting 85 damaged tanks, but many of these were repaired later at assembly plants, or by the workshop companies themselves and did not become total write-offs.[21] As far as Hitler and the German High Command were concerned, the Polish campaign was a huge success sustaining losses much lower than anticipated: 8,082 men killed, 27,278 wounded, 5,029 missing in action.[22] The achievement of these successes was attributed to Guderian's flexible *Blitzkrieg* strategy and the overwhelming power of the *Luftwaffe*.[23] Considering the Germans superiority in numbers and technological advantages in weaponry, the Polish Army cannot be faulted for not offering more resistance than they did.

CHAPTER III

Triumphant Victory

Operation Yellow/Red, France (May–June 1940)

In the eight months preceding the attack on the West the German Army reorganized their tank and mobile forces from lessons learned during the Polish campaign. It was evident from the street fighting in Warsaw that the motorised troops needed additional armour protection and the tanks upgraded to higher velocity guns. Also made apparent was the need to eliminate the white crosses painted on the turrets of the armoured vehicles (used as targeting points by Polish anti-tank gunners), and replace them with a black version.[1] In response to these and other problems, the *Panzerkampfwagen* I tank was being phased out, and the Mark II & IIIs had extra armour plating added to their hulls. The 36th Regiment gained 20 Mark III tanks when before they had none, and doubled their inventory of Mark IV medium tanks to 12.[2] Further changes were envisioned but not completed before the Battle of France commenced in May 1940.

The original German plan of attack mimicked the opening manoeuvres of the First World War, with the Army sweeping through central Belgium and the Low countries. But after this plan was compromised by the capture of a German paratroop major, Erich von Manstein conceived a new daring strategy to deal with the problem. His plan had the main thrust punching through the Ardennes Forest, the weakest point of the Franco-British line, between Sedan and Namur.[3]

Karl Roth's command section was tied up in the traffic snarl that built up on the German side of the river on May 10th. The truck is camouflaged against enemy air attack and has tow cable attached to the front grill. The symbol on the driver's side door represents the maintenance section. (Author's collection-courtesy L. Schwarz)

The Belgians succeeded in destroying the bridges over the Maas River in Maastricht and the one at Kanne, in front of fort Eben Emael as well. The lack of useful bridge crossing sites caused a twenty-four hour delay in getting the *panzers* over the river. (Author's collection)

Hitler is seen congratulating Captain Koch's glider commando officers, who helped capture the fort in eleven hours. (FACP)

Fort Eben Emael on the famed Maginot Line was intended to thwart any German move from the area into Belgium. Known as the world's strongest fort, it fell to German glider commandos, allowing the tanks of the 4th *Panzer* Division to exploit their success. (Courtesy F.E.E.)

Eben-Emael looks today much as it did sixty years ago, and is now a museum and military post. Signs warn of minefields and the roof of the fort is still off limits to civilians. (Author's collection)

The Allied plan to stop the Germans on the other hand developed based on defence of the Dyle River, along the French and Belgian border. It was devised to deal with the problem of Belgian-Dutch neutrality, and also the expected German attack against these countries. Even though the Maginot Line in the south already provided heavy border protection, the French theory of "continuous line" resulted in forces (including tanks) being distributed evenly throughout all sectors.[4]

The Dyle plan's concept had the whole Allied left wing moving forward, but only in a defensive mode to support Belgian and Dutch cooperation. The British Expeditionary Force was to move up to the Dyle position from Wavre, to a few miles north of Louvain. To the British left the Belgians defended to the Dutch border, as the French 1st and 9th Armies planned to move up on the right. Along the Dutch border a shorter line was held along the Albert Canal. The fall back position was the Escaut River Line, should reaching the Dyle Line prove impossible. The Belgians did not think they could defend the Albert Canal for more than two days without Franco-British support, and therefore, the whole plan depended on how quickly the Allies deployed their troops forwards.[5]

An Allied advance is exactly what the Germans hoped for, as this would provide the situation needed to sever the Allies best divisions between Belgium and the North Sea. Even though outnumbered in men and tanks, the German Army achieved numerical superiority in the breakthrough area, since its entire *Panzer* weight was concentrated in the north. To start the invasion and bait the Allies into moving forward into the Dyle positions, the 3rd, 4th, and 9th *Panzer* Divisions would attack Belgium and Holland. Before these attacks could begin however, a special detachment of glider commandos had the mission of capturing Western Europe's strongest fort, at Eben Emael.[6]

This obstacle was sitting directly in the path of the 4th *Panzer* Division and the 36th Regiment's planned advance, and guarded the bridges over the Albert Canal. The fort is situated approximately three miles south of the city of Maastricht and was built between 1932–1935. The purpose of the fort was to support the troops in the field, and because of its strategic location on the Albert Canal, to take the road bridges coming out of Maastricht under fire. The British high command expected the fort to hold out for at least five days, but as stated earlier, the Belgians thought they could last only two. There was a garrison of 1200 men billeted in local villages behind the fort, but communications with other units outside was poor and moral generally low. Wary to threaten Belgian neutrality, the fort held nothing higher than guns of 120mm, out of range of both Maastricht and Aachen. The superstructure was not protected from assault from the air, and in fact was an ideal landing place for gliders that even held a soccer field. Air defence on the fort consisted of four anti-aircraft machine guns positioned on the roof.[7]

The Germans created a storm detachment *(Koch)* that used gliders and a new explosive to crack the gem of the Maginot Line. Each glider held approximately eight to ten men. Transported to their targets in gliders towed by *Junkers* 52 transport planes, the two special action companies were given four targets on the fort to capture or silence. The parachute-company was given 30 gliders and held responsible for capturing the three bridges that the 5th *Panzer* Brigade needed to cross over the Albert Canal at Veldvezelt, Vroenhoven, and Canne.[8] The pioneer company in 11 gliders and armed with flame-throwers and special hand-grenades would use newly developed shaped-charges to attack and destroy the fort. The cavity charge came in different sizes and could penetrate armoured domes up to 28cm thick. Both units were to hold their positions in the fort until relieved by the 51st Combat Engineers of the 4th *Panzer* Division. The 36th Regiment meanwhile was expected to be in Maastricht by ten o'clock on May 10 and prepared to move across the captured Albert Canal bridges.[9]

After training in strict isolation for half a year, Storm Detachment Koch finally received orders to assemble at airfields near Cologne and then pre-empt the ground war against the West. The *Ju-52*'s took off on the morning of May 10th, cutting their tow cables at 04:25 just above the city of Aachen. Out of 11 gliders, 9 landed quietly and unseen on the roof of the fort. Each glider unit received a primary and secondary target, to ensure that all the objectives were silenced.[10]

As for the parachute company, two out of three bridges over the Albert Canal were seized without damage at Veldvezelt and Vroenhoven. The Belgians managed to destroy the bridge at Canne, and also those in Maastricht. This forced a twenty-four hour delay in getting the regiments into the city, as pontoon bridges were erected, and alternative crossings built over the Meuse River. Fortunately for the German sappers inside Eben Emael, they destroyed their first objectives in ten minutes and by nightfall were attacking the intermediate levels with cavity charges.[11] At 0600 hours on May 11th a sergeant with the 51st Pioneer Company of the 4th *Panzer* Division was the first man to link up with and relieve Captain Koch's men. Eben Emael surrendered at 12:30 that day and the assault became known as the most successful pioneer air raid in the history of war.

The fall of the fort and the capture of two intact bridges over the Albert Canal allowed General von Reicheneu (commander of the 6th Army) to release Erich Hoepner's XVI Motorised Corps (3rd and 4th *Panzer* Divisions) to expand and exploit the bridgeheads.[12]

Not until May 11th and under Allied air-attack did the 36th *Panzer* Regiment move over the military bridges and begin their attack southwest towards the Gembloux Gap. Breaking out of the confines of the built up city, the 5th *Panzer* Brigade (The 35th and 36th *Panzer Regiments* made up the Brigade, known as Breith Group) crossed over the Veldvezelt-Vroenhoven bridges, deploying into a classic wedge formation once they reached the wide fields and excellent tank country of the French plain. By that evening they were poised west of Tongern, tired and exhausted but ready to resume the pursuit in the morning.[13]

As the 5th *Panzer* Brigade tanks raced forward the following day, the first major tank-versus-tank battle of the war erupted at Hannut, twenty miles in front of Gembloux. The Regiment collided with armoured cavalry units of the French 1st Army (3rd Mech. Div.) consisting of two light mechanized divisions equipped with 140 Hochkiss and 90 Somua heavy tanks, who rushed forward to defend the Dyle defences. During this engagement on the afternoon of the 12th the 35th *Panzer* Regiment moved forward into action with the 36th *Panzer* in reserve, temporarily halting the French 1st Cavalry Corps between Tirlemount and Huy.[14]

The *Panzer* Mark III tanks the division received just prior to the start of the campaign accounted for most of the enemy vehicles destroyed that day. The commander of the 35th *Panzer* Regiment, Oberst Eberbach, commented on the action in his after action report:

The swiftness of the fall of fort Eben Emael stunned the French, who found that their fixed fortification system was woefully inadequate to deal with this new *Blitzkreig* strategy. After the tanks crossed the Maas River, they pressed on further into the Gembloux gap. (FACP)

A tank company rests before engaging French tanks at Hannut on May 12th in what was the first large-scale tank-versus-tank battle of the war. (FACP)

Karl Roth takes a quick break for lunch during the brief reorganization period between the end of Operation Yellow and the beginning of Operation Red. These four days were anything but inactive as the workshop company worked around the clock in the city of Peronne, repairing as many vehicles as possible before the second phase began. Small detachments like Roth's command section were issued 29-pound cooking outfits that were fitted on the back of the truck, consisting of three nesting pots of 2 to 2 1/2 gallons capacity, complete with ladle, plates, and fork-spoon dining ware.
(Author's collection, courtesy E. Roth)

The 5th Company was sent to the west of Hannut to set up a defence. Upon leaving the village the 5th Company encountered 11 enemy Hotchkiss tanks. During the ensuing engagement 8 enemy tanks were knocked out, many with the 3.7 cm tank guns of the *Panzer* Mark III's.

Due to this type of action, after the campaign was over the *Panzer* commanders requested that the Mark III's be up-gunned to the 50mm, and the armour on both the III and IV be improved, as the *Panzer* force lost 35 percent of these tanks in combat and to write-offs.

The following day the 36th *Panzer* Regiment joined the battle south of Merdorp, mixing it up in the same fashion as their sister regiment did the day before, engaging enemy tanks at point blank range.[15] The French tanks proved better armoured than their German counterparts, but not as fast, manoeuvrable, or as well led resulting in equal numbers from both sides being knocked out.[16] The French then inexplicably withdrew two of their divisions out of the gap, giving the German regimental repair workshops valuable time in restoring their significant combat losses.[17]

Reicheneu gave orders to attack the enemy between Louvain and Namur, and the regiment forced its way into the Gembloux Gap on the 13th after being supported by heavy *Stuka* dive-bomber attacks. The following day the French 15th Motorised Division halted the 36th *Panzer* regiment temporarily, but opposition was overcome by that evening.[18]

Both regiments of the 5th Brigade were attacking the Dyle Line directly at Gembloux and fighting developed in the northern districts of the town on the 15th. But this stubbornness in Belgium was all to no avail, because Rundstedt's Army Group A was already out-flanking the Dyle positions from the Ardennes region in Luxembourg, further south. French and British units still holding positions on the Dyle River Line in Belgium were told to begin a four-day retreat on May 16th to the Escaut Line in northern France.[19]

The campaign in France was characterised by multiple river crossings. To ensure that its two *Panzer* divisions had the ability to jump across any river barrier, the XVI Motorised *Korps*, of which the 4th *Panzer* Division was attached, requisitioned almost all of 6th Army's bridging equipment. This photograph depicts a roadway pontoon bridge with double decking and double raft connectors being crossed by an 8-ton halftrack prime mover. (Hans Niedt Collection)

The French campaign was an even bigger success than Poland, with much in captured equipment falling into German hands. After the campaign for France was over, Karl and his comrades are seen aboard a French UE armoured weapon carrier. Roth is located third man in from the right, sitting in the middle on the rear deck of the vehicle. (Author's collection, courtesy E. Roth)

The day the Allied retreat began, the 36th *Panzer* Regiment was directed to move south and assist Army Group A with the major breakthrough being made in the center.[20] Their orders were to link up with General Hoth's XV *Panzerkorps* (5th and 7th *Panzer* Divisions) moving towards Arras.[21] They crossed over the Seneffe and Dendre Rivers after breaking through the Charleroi canal defences, supporting the 5th *Panzer* Division fighting in the Mormal Forest. Here a fierce battle then ensued and the attack west was postponed until the 22nd.[22]

During the time of this engagement, General Erwin Rommel's 7th *Panzer* Division was counter-attacked and he used 8.8cm flak guns to stop the assault on the 21st, destroying half the attacking force. This incident proved the lethality of 88 flak guns as a tank killer resulting in this calibre weapon being adopted as the main gun armament for future heavy tank designs.[23]

Panzer expert Guderian's reconnaissance units of the 2nd *Panzer* Division reached the coast at Noyelles-sur-Mer on the following day, the 22nd. Even though Guderian's armour was held back on the 15th because of flank and bridgehead concerns, he still put a solid Panzer corridor between the one million Allied forces trapped in the north and those still operating in the south (nine British and 45 French divisions, plus what remained of the entire Belgian Army). While the British planned the largest naval evacuation in history at Dunkirk because of this situation, Hitler was confident enough in victory that on the 21st he began composing his surrender terms.[24]

The Germans closed in on the surrounded Dunkirk pocket with no less than nine *Panzer* divisions, and were only a day and a half from the port by the 23rd.[25]

The Regiment was now fighting stiff resistance between Arras and St. Omer. Their tanks were overextended and worn down though, with 50 percent of their vehicles out of action due to maintenance needs. Hitler was also worried about the gaps in the lines that existed between the infantry and the armour, and the terrain was marshy and unsuitable for the tanks. Because of these reasons and because he wanted his mobile troops to begin the repairs necessary so that they were up to strength for the second phase of the campaign (Plan Red), he suspended all attacks against the Dunkirk pocket on the 24th.[26]

The air chief of staff, Herman Goering, persuaded Hitler that his *Luftwaffe* could clear the beaches of Dunkirk and stop the evacuation. To the protests of most of the Army General Staff, Hitler agreed to this plan and did not rescind the order to advance until the 27th.[27] During this break in the fighting the Allies organized their perimeter defences for a final evacuation effort. The day the attacks resumed the Belgian king, Leopold, informed the Allies that his country and its army would surrender the following day. This reduced the strength and perimeter of the Dunkirk pocket even further.[28]

The same day the Belgians surrendered a major Allied counter-attack occurred against the German bridgeheads south of the Somme, near Abbeville and Amiens. The 2nd and 29th Motorised Divisions, along with the 4th and 9th *Panzer* Divisions in reserve, defended these bridgeheads.[29] Late on the night of the 26th the stop order was rescinded and the order to continue the advance given. They met the British counter-attack with savage and confused fighting for two days along the La Bassée canal. The canal looped the city of Bethune, but an extended strip of land meant that it had to be crossed twice, and the ensuing battle was considered the heaviest combat of the campaign.[30]

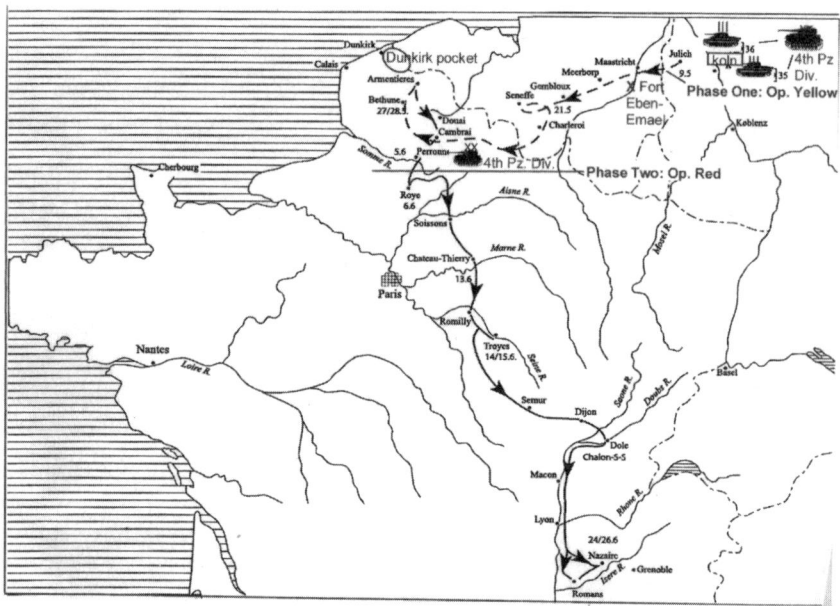

Operation Yellow and Red

As the Allied counter-attacks ground themselves to a halt on the 29th, Hitler again brought the tanks to a standstill. He ordered further reduction of the pocket be performed by the infantry and *Luftwaffe*. The Dunkirk port and beaches were heavily attacked from the air between June 1st and the 4th, and then the infantry closed in on the perimeter.

Goering's unfulfilled promise to win the day through air power was not to be his last to effect the German Army and the 36th *Panzer* Regiment during the war (the others being during the Battle of Britain and at Stalingrad), allowing the Royal Navy the opportunity to evacuate 330,000 British and Allied troops to fight another day. Because of his meddling in the affairs of the ground forces he was mistrusted and loathed by the soldiers. The port of Dunkirk capitulated to German infantry forces on the 4th ending the first phase for the Battle off France.[31]

The exhausted *Panzer* troops needed a deserved rest and their equipment was in dire need of repairs. The 36th *Panzer* Regiment only received nine replacement tanks by the end of May (5 *Pz* Mark I's, 2 III's and 2 IV's) but still maintained 80 percent strength by the time Operation Red began on the 5th. During this period the German forces were reshuffled and redeployed, with the 4th *Panzer* Division again assigned to the 6th Army, at the Somme bridgehead of Peronne.[32]

The second phase of the campaign called for both German Army Groups A and B to cross the French river defences of the 'Weygand Line'. They would then swing south into the interior of France, pinning the remaining defenders of the Maginot Line against Army Group C. The French General, Weygand, no longer could place his troops in a continuous line and instead he tried to group all existing forces into fortified hedgehog defences.[33]

Just such a defensive position was encountered south of the Peronne bridgehead as the 36th *Panzer* Regiment broke out east of the city and tried to avoid enemy strong points, slipping in between the French lines. Outdistancing their infantry by six miles, with their supply lines cut and artillery support out of range, they spent the next two days fighting a desperate battle of survival against the French 3rd Army Group. Without infantry support and low on ammunition the 36th *Panzer* Regiment was caught in a devastating crossfire and after losing a third of their tanks they were forced to retreat back across the Somme River.[34]

Their neighbour to the south, the XIV *Panzerkorps*, also experienced heavy opposition west of Amiens (9th and 10th *Pz* Divs, *SSLAH*). Therefore, Hitler redeployed both corps to the east of the line on the 8th. Serious opposition failed to materialize on other parts of the Weygand Line and as early as the 6th, both sides could see that the defence line was crumbling.[35] Reentering the line on the 10th to the right flank of Group Guderian (9th Army sector) the 36th Regiment made immediate gains towards a crossing of the Marne at Chateau-Thierry.[36] Battlefields that were fought over for years during the First World War were now overrun in hours as the Germans broke through the Weygand Line on either side of Paris.

For the next three days the 36th *Panzer* Regiment made up for lost time and reached the Seine River Bridge at Nogent, southwest of Romilly.[37] The bridge was destroyed, but after the delay they experienced in Maastricht, the Division's pioneers had requisitioned almost all of 6th Army's bridging equipment and they were across in record time on the 14th.[38] The same day Paris the capital fell, resulting in the British decision to order the evacuation of their last fighting units from France.[39]

Meanwhile, Army Group C advanced out of their defensive positions forcing the withdrawal of most of the French forces guarding the Maginot Line.[40] The 36th *Panzer* Regiment was ordered south towards Dijon and Lyon, assisting the Italians who by now were also at war with France. 50 to 60 miles per day were gained as the pursuit continued towards Côte-d'Or. The enemy troops who were trapped between the two Army Groups surrendered on the 21st when the regiment entered Dijon.[41] They were then again reassigned, this time into the 12th Army's advance front threatening the rear of the French Army of the Alps at Grenoble. During the closing days of 'Operation Red' only occasional resistance was encountered between the west Alps and the Saone and Isere Rivers, where the 36th *Panzer* Regiment ended their attacks.

The 36th *Panzer* Regiment witnessed and took part in the opening gambit of the French Campaign at Eben Emael, fought the first tank-versus-tank battle of the war at Hannut, and advanced further south than almost any other unit in the German Army during Operation Red.[42] The armistice was signed partitioning France into an occupied and unoccupied zone on the 24th and in 39 days during May and June 1940 the British, French, Belgians and Dutch were defeated in a swift campaign that refined the skill of the *Panzer* troops, making Germany's combined arms strategy now look invincible.

CHAPTER IV
English Invasion
Operation Sea-lion, France (Summer 1940)

The German troops stationed in France during the summer of 1940 were intoxicated with their recent victory, and made the most of pleasure before the ground war resumed. After division field-parades were conducted at the end of June (Karl was awarded the Campaign Victory Cross 2nd-Class), the 36th *Panzer* Regiment was rested. They received leave and visited the museums, cafés, dance halls in their area, and naturally Paris as well.[1] Some troops received an allowance of paper currency to buy French goods (Karl returning home with cheese, wine, sweets and champagne) and even the French population was at ease with the early conduct of the German troops.[2] The only worry the soldiers contended themselves with that summer was the talk from their officers about plans for a seaborne invasion of England. Hitler submitted a directive for such an operation in the middle of July, specifying that to be successful, all three branches of the armed forces had to be able to achieve their individual missions.[3]

The plan at first was to land on a broad front, but later this changed due to disagreements developing between the Army and Navy. The Navy argued they could not meet the needs of the invasion as the Army proposed them, due to the lack of proper troop transport. This convinced Hitler to choose a narrower front across the Straights of Dover.[4] Most of the invasion force planned to embark at Calais and Le Havre and land between the mouth of the Thames and Portsmouth. A smaller force would leave Cherbourg, land near Weymouth and then advance on Bristol.[5]

Assault infantry and paratroopers in the front waves preceded four *Panzer* divisions and two motorised infantry divisions in the second. The 36th *Panzer* Regiment was attached to XV *Panzerkorps* (Hoth with 4th, 7th and 20th Mot. Divs) and prepared to spearhead 9th Army's landing near Brighton.[6] New submersible tanks (*TauchPanzers*) would accompany the first waves onto the beaches, followed by a battalion of flame-throwing armoured vehicles to destroy the barricades and coast defences.[7] After consolidating in the Brighton area, the regiment was supposed to isolate London and occupy southeast England.[8] The invasion date for "Operation Sea-lion" was set for mid-August.[9] The British planned to repel this invasion by using flaming barges and oil to stop the German forces before they landed, and if all else failed, lethal gas.[10]

The *Luftwaffe* was the strongest air force in the world in the summer of 1940 and held the key to determining whether the invasion of Britain ever got underway. Germany needed to achieve air-supremacy before any invasion armada could venture into the Straights of Dover; therefore their planes and crews relocated to bases nearer the English Channel. The air offensive began in earnest during the beginning of August, as a war of attrition developed between fighter forces of equal size.[11]

36th *Panzer* Regiment troops combat loaded on their barge at the height of the cross-Channel alert, in July 1940. The *Panzer* crew on the left in the photograph stands on top of a *Panzer* Mark III tank. On the right is an 8-ton halftrack, and vehicles of the workshop company. Karl Roth's biggest fear during this time was the threat of British commando style raids against the transports. Behind them is a destroyed expansion bridge in the channel.
(Author's collection, courtesy E. Roth)

The *Tauchpanzer* was a submersible *Panzer* Mark III tank intended for the invasion of England, but when Operation Sea-lion was cancelled at the end of the summer of 1940, they were instead used to ford river barriers during the attack on the Soviet Union in 1941. The giant snorkel was used so that the vehicle could 'swim'. (Bundesarchiv)

ENGLISH INVASION 55

Karl is smiling as this was the "happy time" during the summer of 1940 and the pre invasion period.
(Author's collection, courtesy E. Roth}

While the German aircrews tried to clear the skies and win the Battle of Britain, the Army trained for the amphibious assault all along the French and Belgian coastline. The Navy was critically short of landing craft and drafted all types of boats into service, including barges, pleasure yachts and fishing trawlers. The German armada looked more like the flotilla the Allies used in May to evacuate Dunkirk, especially when compared to the invasion force sent over at Normandy in June 1944. Even so, morale was remarkably high in the Regiment as they conducted relentless tank up-loading and off-loading techniques in the landing craft.[12]

Hitler was still planning for an English invasion by August, but let it be known that he considered the Soviet Union to be the true enemy.[13] Because the Navy declared they were still not ready for the landing, the deadline was moved back to mid-September.[14] At this point Goering once again proposed to achieve total victory through air power, destroying the RAF and securing the skies for a safe landing on the beaches by the Army. Hitler agreed in the middle of August to let Goering try to achieve this victory, and ordered operation 'Eagle Attack' to begin on the 13th, the main air assault on Britain.[15]

The *Luftwaffe* targeted RAF airfields during the first phase of the operation, but later switched tactics to bomb British cities instead. This was an irreversible mistake that allowed the RAF to recover from almost total annihilation in the beginning of September, and resulted in *Luftwaffe* losses twice those to which the British sustained.[16] 'Operation Sea-lion' quickly faded as a military option when Goering failed to win air supremacy over the skies of Britain, and Hitler's focus turned to the East.[17]

Hitler was obsessed with the idea of attacking Russia and decided that the Panzer force must be increased to meet the needs of such an ambitious campaign. Each *Panzer* division was ordered to give up one of their regiments so that the force was doubled.[18] The invasion was postponed again, but this time indefinitely, and the new deadline was never fulfilled. The 36th *Panzer* Regiment was transferred to Poland on the eastern frontier, along with Army Group B on October 12th to begin training for an attack on the Soviet Union.

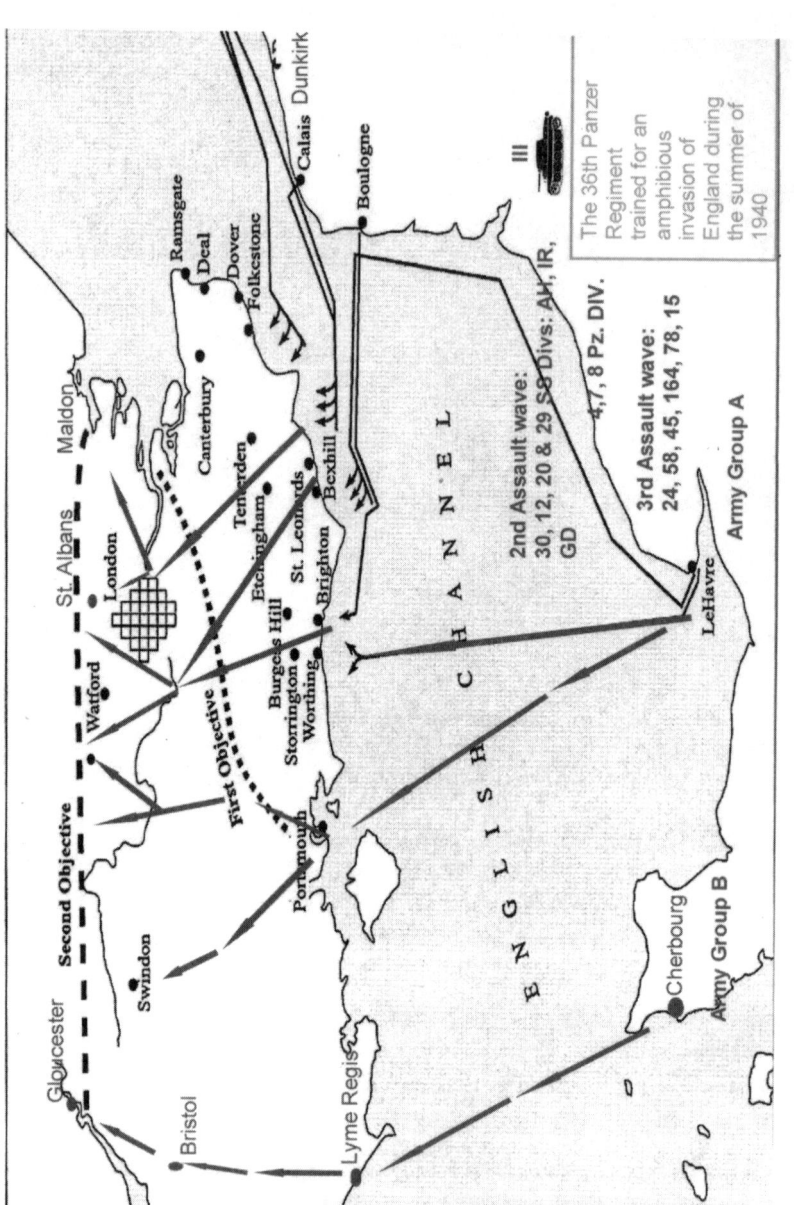

Operation Sea-lion: Invasion of England

PART III
THE 14TH PANZER DIVISION

CHAPTER V
Campaign in the Balkans
Operation Punishment, Yugoslavia (April 1941)

Hitler ordered ten more tank divisions created at the end of the summer of 1940 in anticipation of the great land war with Russia. Converting former infantry divisions into motorised grenadier formations created more than half of these new *Panzer* divisions. The 14th *Panzer* Division was authorized on August 15th, but besides a major reorganization of the existing formations, only four new tank regiments were added to the *Panzer* force during this phase.[1]

The 35th *Panzer* Regiment remained with the 4th *Panzer* Division, but in the autumn of 1940 the 36th *Panzer* Regiment was ordered combined with the 4th Infantry Division (out of Dresden) to formulate the 14th *Panzer* Division.

The 36th *Panzer* Regiment was led by Major Jesser and known in the division as Group Jesser, maintaining two battalions of three companies each. Within these battalions the *Panzer* Mark IV medium tank inventories were increased (to 35), and lost were almost all the obsolete Mark I's.[2] By January they were training at Milowitz in the protectorate of Bohemia, and in the spring they practiced combined arms operations near Breslau.[3] At this time Karl was promoted to corporal under six years, assuming more responsibility within the headquarters section.

After an anti-Hitler coup overtook the Yugoslavian government during the night of March 26th–27th, the Regiment was hastily redirected away from the eastern border where they were stationed. Hitler was furious at the uprising and also at Yugoslavia's delay in ratifying the Tripartite Treaty, making him decide the Balkans should be secured before any attempt to invade the Soviet Union was

Near Nagakaniza, Yugoslavia, two Hungarian border guards meet the advance party of the 36th *Panzer* Regiment. A major reason for the quick and smooth repositioning of forces by the Germans before the campaign was the help of the Hungarian government in opening up the borders with Yugoslavia, expediting rail travel into the country.
(Courtesy L. Schwarz)

The victory in the Balkans campaign was won more against the weather and bad roads than in battle with the enemy. Narrow snow-covered mountain passes and flooded river valleys proved a challenge to the *Panzer* troops. As early, as April 6th German shock troops were capturing intact bridges over the rivers into Yugoslavia before the enemy could destroy them, this obviously not being one of them.
(Hans Niedt Collection)

Bread-time. Karl Roth, flanked by two of his officers cuts into a loaf of bread provided by one of the local Croatian townspeople, who along with most of the population of Zagreb, welcomed the Germans. The *Panzer* crewman in the photograph wears the standard black tanker uniform, with Karl and the other man in regular grey issue field uniform.
(Author's collection, courtesy E. Roth)

CAMPAIGN IN THE BALKANS 61

The city of Sarajevo as seen by the men of the 36th *Panzer* Regiment after arriving on the heights dominating the city. The campaign was virtually over after only a week. (Courtesy L. Schwarz)

The effectiveness of the Yugoslavian Army was hampered by factional infighting within the armed services, made up of Croatians, Serbians, and Muslims. Here Muslim villagers are friendly and musically entertaining the men of the workshop company. Foreign signs and faulty maps made navigating the countryside difficult for the *Panzer* troops. (Courtesy L. Schwarz)

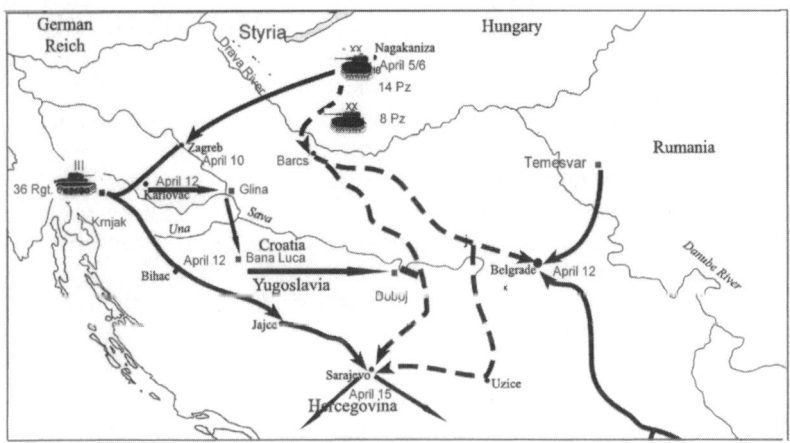

Operation Punishment Yugoslavia

made. Within twenty-four hours the German general staff altered its transport routes for an attack east (with orders given to 14th *Panzer* Division to re-deploy as early as March 23rd) improvising a *Blitzkrieg* campaign to attack Yugoslavia and Greece from Austria, Hungary, and Bulgaria.

The campaign order (Directive 25) to destroy Yugoslavia as a nation was issued the next day on March 27th to all three branches of the armed forces and was aptly nicknamed 'Operation Punishment'. According to Hitler's own words he was going too, "Destroy Yugoslavia as a military power and sovereign state".[4]

Marching from northwest of Vienna across the Hungarian border, Group Jesser road marched through heavy rain, arriving at their staging area in Nagykaniza, Hungary, on the evening of April 7th. They linked up with the rest of the 14th *Panzer* Division who arrived in town by train. They were attached to the XLVI *Panzerkorps* (8th, 4th *Panzer* Divs. and 16th Mot. Div) commanded by General von Vietinghoff, and assigned to the 2nd Army (Weichs).[5]

The 14th *Panzer* Division planned to split apart from the other Corps divisions after crossing the Drava River (at Barcs) to converge on Zagreb, acting as a diversion to the main attack on Belgrade.[6] Operations were to begin by April 10th, although small unit actions to take bridgeheads over the Drava were conducted earlier. The 36th *Panzer* Regiment's orders were to attack over the seized bridgeheads to take Zagreb the Croatian capital, and then assist the main attack on Belgrade; the Yugoslavian capital. The bridge at Zakany fell on the 7th and another at Barcs was captured the following day. The 36th *Panzer* Regiment and the Motorised 103rd Regiment attacked the morning of April 10th on a northwest route, and engaged elements of the Yugoslavian 4th Army in the town of Bjelovar. Although the fighting was fierce at first, the enemy was brushed aside, revealing the weaknesses of the Yugoslavian Army.[7]

The 36th *Panzer* Regiment marched more than 100 miles this day through very cold weather, securing a bridgehead on the Sava River, south of the capital. By seven o'clock that night, the Division headquarters was firmly established in a suburb of Zagreb. The Regiment arrived in the city the next day, after being delayed by the fighting at Bjelovar, and surprised an enemy regimental officers party that was in progress.[8] This celebration was only interrupted long enough to sign a quick surrender of the unit as the pro-German Croatians gave up mostly without a fight. Almost 15,000 prisoners were taken, including 300 officers and 22 generals. *Wehrmacht* infantry relieved the armoured units within the city the following day, so that operations against Serbia and the advance against Sarajevo could begin.[9]

After Belgrade fell on April 12th, the 36th *Panzer* Regiment spearheaded the western drive south, through the heart of Yugoslavia towards Sarajevo. They linked up with Italian units the same day in the city of Karlovac, but navigating the roads proved difficult because of faulty maps and foreign signs. The weather was pleasant when the advance began, but the route was over steep inclines, inclement mountain passes, and flooded river valleys. To better facilitate the narrow outdated roads, the 2nd Army split itself, planning to converge on Sarajevo with two *Panzer* divisions.[10]

Dealing with the Balkan terrain and weather proved the most difficult aspect of the operation for the *Panzer* troops.[11] Snow and very cold temperatures were encountered in the mountains, resulting in heavy wear and tear on the vehicles. The maintenance teams of the workshop companies struggled to replace broken tracks, torsion bars, and repair completely worn out brakes. After the campaign was over the 36th *Panzer* Regiment reported only one tank as a total write off, compared to an average of 14 reported by the other regiments, attesting to the highly skilled mechanics of the workshop company.[12]

The pursuit south continued at a quick pace as the Germans tried to wrap up the operation and re-deploy east. The 8th and 14th *Panzer* Divisions entered Sarajevo on April 15th simultaneously from both east and west.

By this time open hostilities were erupting between Croat-Serb factions and on April 17th, a formal armistice was signed with General von Weichs in Belgrade, officially ending the campaign.[13] It only took the Germans twelve days to subdue Yugoslavia and had cost a low casualty rate of 151 killed and 392 wounded. They had captured 254,000 prisoners, and for the next week the 2nd Army performed occupation duty in the conquered areas.

The Punishment

After the fighting was over in Yugoslavia, the German Army and *SS* were instructed by Hitler to carry out severe reprisals against the former government and military. The March *Putsch* conspirators, anti-Nazi government officials, and the majority of the former Slavic officer corps were either executed or sent to concentration and labour camps. Hitler's Commissar Decree of March 1941 laid out how the war against the Bolsheviks would be conducted, with "unprecedented, unmerciful, and unrelenting hardness". Yugoslavia was used as a precursor to the Barbarossa campaign, where mobile killing units formed under the SS and utilized for committing crimes behind the lines in conjunction with regular army units, were ordered to enforce the directives.

The 14th *Panzer* Division and other formations were instructed to perform 'cleansing operations' in the occupied territories of Yugoslavia in the last days of April 1941, and a 36th *Panzer* Regimental supply officer confessed during an interview in 1998 that he still was haunted by this action, and felt that this was the unit's darkest chapter during the war.[14]

CHAPTER VI
Campaign in the East
Operation Barbarossa (June 1941–May 1942)

The 36th *Panzer* Regiment began retracing their steps over the primitive roads out of Yugoslavia at the end of April. They stood up well during the campaign considering the operation was improvised from the start and the terrain was treacherously dangerous. Although the country fell quickly, the Balkan Campaign postponed Hitler's attack on the Soviet Union by five critical weeks.[1]

Moving into northern Germany by train via Breslau, Liegnitz, Frankfurt/Oder, the 36th *Panzer* Regiment arrived at the training area of Doberitz (near Berlin).[2] At Doberitz they were further equipped for the coming Soviet offensive, being issued a number of *TauchPanzers*. The submersible tanks, originally scheduled for the amphibious invasion of England, were now to be used to ford Soviet

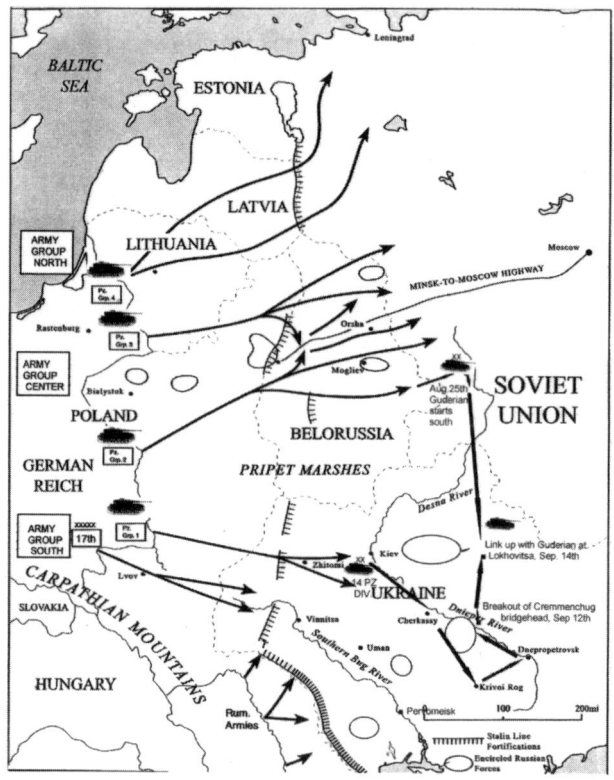

Operation Barbarossa: Attack on the Soviet Union

CAMPAIGN IN THE EAST 65

river barriers.[3] After recovering here for three weeks they moved east towards Lublin[4], two hours drive southeast of Warsaw, in the occupied territory of Poland.[5]

Hitler's Directive 21, the plan for Operation Barbarossa, was issued on December 18th 1940, and divided the German forces into three Army Groups - Group North (v. Leeb), Centre (v. Bock), and South (v. Rundstedt). The *Panzer* troops were again formed into four powerful groups, independent of the infantry. Each Army Group had a specific city to seize as an objective: Group North - Leningrad, Group Centre - Moscow and Group South - Kiev. The plan's main objective at first was Moscow, but later this changed to Leningrad on Hitler's orders, (and was ultimately changed back to Moscow again in the autumn). The main goal of the entire operation was to destroy the Soviet Army in massive encirclement battles, before they could retreat into the vast interior of the country.[6] Because Hitler expected such a lightning defeat of the enemy, only minimal winter clothing was issued to the troops. He set the date for the greatest land battle in history for June 22nd, the shortest night of the summer, stating, "when Barbarossa opens, the whole world will hold its breath".[7]

The 36th *Panzer* Regiment was assigned to Army Group South commanded by Rudolf Gerd von Rundstedt (nicknamed "the Field Marshal who never lost a battle"). A professional soldier of the old school, he warned Hitler against attacking the Soviet Union, only to be told that the Soviet armies would be destroyed before winter, west of the Dnepr River.

The 14th *Panzer* Division was assigned to *Panzer* Group One, led by a skilled young Colonel-General, Ewald von Kleist (later promoted to Field Marshal)[8] who displayed exceptional skill and initiative later in the campaign at encircling Soviet forces at Uman and Kiev.[9] They assembled in the area of Cholm on June 6th and were attached to the III *Panzerkorps* (v. Mackensen). This Corps contained four divisions including the 13th and 14th *Panzer*, and two Motorised *SS* Divisions (*Leibstandarte* and *Wiking*), with the 54th *Nebelwerfer* (Rocket) Regiment assigned.

Panzer Group One was ordered to cross the Bug River, breech the Stalin line at Zhitomir, and then advance on Kiev encircling the Soviet forces between the Pripet marshes and the Carpathian Mountains. The vital mineral and agricultural resources of the Ukraine were to be seized and a bridgehead over the Don River taken at Rostov.[10] After this, the *Panzer* force was ordered to ready itself for any additional task that should arise.[11]

Moving up to the frontier on June 18th the Regiment travelled at night to avoid being detected by enemy aircraft. The infantry were already in place ready to seize the bridgeheads over the Bug River, followed closely by the motorised units and later by the tracked vehicles.[12] Karl and his command staff were at their start positions by the 21st and consumed their last delicacies left over from the French campaign. Again morale was high, but most of the soldiers felt uneasy about embarking on such a monumental campaign, and what was to become the greatest and most tragic event of their lives.

The attack on the Soviet Union opened at 3:15 a.m. on June 22nd as a heavy bombardment from all calibres of weapons, including 300 artillery pieces assigned to III *Panzerkorps*, pounded border positions. Five river barriers needed to be forced before the Regiment reached their primary objective of Kiev. The bridgeheads, bridging equipment and infantry needed to secure these obstacles were of vital

A *Panzer* Mark IV of the 14th *Panzer* Division storms across the border into the Soviet Union on June 22nd 1941. The 25-ton *Panzer* Mark IV was the workhorse of most regular German tank divisions. It stayed in use throughout the war when most other early tank designs had become obsolete. A regimental survivor, Leo Schwarz, provided this photograph and said it was taken just after the 36th *Panzer* Regiment crossed the border, on the opening day of Barbarossa. (Author's collection, courtesy L. Schwarz)

The following pictures depict exercises and maintenance conducted by the workshop company of the 36th *Panzer* Regiment at Doberitz training base near Berlin, just before the attack on the Soviet Union. New equipment was tested here such as this amphibious jeep, or *Schwimmwagen* as it was known. A total of only 150 four-wheel-drive amphibians were manufactured (this being one of them) for tests and trial runs. The truly unique feature of the type 166 *Schwimmwagen* was the amphibian's retractable water propeller, and the single-welded, sheet-steel hull that gave the vehicle its buoyancy. (Courtesy L. Schwarz)

Upon arriving at a take-out point, the *Schwimmwagen's* propeller was disengaged from the drive shaft and hauled manually up and over the rear of the jeep. The four-wheel drive was then reengaged and the vehicle drove itself out of the water and onto dry ground. The Porsche design won over the competition and between 1942 and 1944, 14,276 *Schwimmwagens* were built, serving on both the Eastern and Western Fronts. (Courtesy L. Schwarz)

importance. Supported by heavy mortars the infantry captured an intact bridge over the Bug River early that morning and the tanks crossed over around one o'clock, running into heavy resistance on the opposite bank. Losses to enemy air attacks were suffered almost from the outset and on the 24th–25th the Soviets conducted a flank attack with cavalry and artillery. The 36th Regiment's 1st Battalion beat off a counter-attack by Alexandrovka the following night that resulted in 156 enemy tanks destroyed by morning, and their first great victory.[13] The second river barrier, the Styr, had its bridge blown just before the infantry got to the town of Lutzk.[14] A serious engagement ensued against the 1st Anti–tank Brigade as the pioneers prepared a pontoon bridge for the crossing. New enemy armoured reinforcements arrived in the town, further strengthening their positions under heavy air support.

Resistance broke down on July 1st as the regiment pushed on towards Rovno, and a crossing of the Horyn River (Goryn).[15] After being held up temporarily again by the 1st Anti-tank Brigade at Klevan, the Horyn was then breached easily. The Regiment immediately went over to the offensive, supporting an infantry attack against a twenty-four mile long Soviet column. A second crossing of the Horyn was made on July 3rd over pontoon bridges again constructed hastily by the pioneers.

Kleist ordered the capture of the Zwiahel Fortress, the Eben Emael of the Stalin Line in early July, because the concrete and stone obstacle was directly blocking the path of his mobile units. The Soviet soldiers were expected to stop the German advance along this defensive line, but their commanders knew that the fortifications were not properly maintained and couldn't hold out for long.[16]

Heavy artillery, Pak, and flak guns softened up the fort on July 6th and at 4:30 a.m. the next morning, the infantry assault began against the bunker line. Enemy air raids were again encountered and no progress against the fortress made that morning. Later that day, a *Stuka* dive-bomber attack was called in to destroy the structure, allowing shock troops, pioneers, infantry, and *Panzergrenadiers* to get the upper hand in the fighting. Entire infantry divisions were now involved in clearing the bunkers, and losses were high. The fort was firmly in German control by the 9th, and a bridge built over the Sluczk River.[17]

Zhitomir, the largest city yet encountered on the drive to Kiev, fell into Division hands on the 9th and the Irpen River was reached two days later, with Kiev now only nine miles away. The 36th *Panzer* Regiment probed the outskirts of the city but determined that it was too strongly held for a frontal assault. Rundstedt agreed with his commander's assessments and sent his forces streaming south towards the west bank of the Dnepr River, instead of attacking Kiev directly.

Meanwhile a critical situation developed in the great forest region northeast of Zhitomir, as parts of five Soviet armies assembled for a counter-attack.[18] These enemy forces were going to attempt to retake Zwiahel, re-establishing a defence on the Stalin Line. Although the Soviets launched a valiant counter-attack, it was contained and destroyed. The 36th *Panzer* Regiment was sent north along with the *SS Leibstandarte* Division to turn back the counter-attack at Makarov and Korolevka. After a tremendous artillery barrage, a second enemy attempt to break through on the night of the 17th was only just beaten back. All enemy attacks were stopped the next day and the offensive was contained.[19] This bold enemy stroke lured the Regiment twenty-four miles beyond Division support to win a major engagement.

The counter-attack also persuaded Hitler in his decision to suspend the momentum of the attack on Moscow, re-deploying the *Panzer* troops of Army Group Centre to coordinate with Army Group South. Group Guderian now formed the northern pincer of Army Group South and after a series of intense arguments with Hitler, was ordered to assist Group Kleist in enveloping two enemy pockets at Kiev and Uman.[20]

The 36th *Panzer* Regiment received orders to move south on the 26th, bypassing Kiev and moving towards Pervomaisk. The plan was for 1st *Panzer* Army to provide the anvil for 17th Army to close the door on the Uman pocket.[21] After being reinforced on the 29th with an additional three *Panzer* Mark III tanks, and one *Panzer* Mark IV[22], the regiment fought stubborn battles against heavy Soviet resistance at Swenigorodavka-Schpola, Novo-Mirgorad and ending on August 4th with an attack on Kirovograd.[23] The city fell the following night and unbeknownst to Karl, he would see this area of the Ukraine behind the Dnepr River again, although in another two and a half years under far worse conditions.

The inner pincers of Kleist's encirclement linked up south of Uman on the 3rd. The Regiment established itself at a bridgehead spanning the Dnepr River at Cremmenchug three days later, the area being lightly held due to the width of the river. With the capture of Cremmenchug, the Red Army's supply line behind Uman was also severed. The Uman pocket was now closed, causing the surrender of almost 100,000 Soviet troops on the 11th.[24]

Hitler by now was convinced the mineral and agricultural rich Ukraine was the great prize to be achieved above the objectives of the other two fronts. Therefore, the 36th *Panzer* Regiment was attached to the XL *Panzerkorps* (Including the 9th, 16th, & 60th Mot. Divs.) for an attack on the iron ore centre at Krivoi-Rog, and assisted the 60th Motorised Division in taking the town. Moving into the city from the southeast, it fell the next day.[25] This was the beginning of Hitler's obsessive interest in the great resources of the east Ukraine and planted the seed in his

At Doberitz training area the workshop company was busied preparing for Operation Barbarossa by repairing tyres, re-painting and servicing the vehicles, and training in manoeuvre areas. Here it looks as though two tanks and a command vehicle need servicing. The truck is the mobile repair shop of the company.
(Courtesy L. Schwarz)

CAMPAIGN IN THE EAST 69

Multiple river barriers needed to be crossed by Kleist's tanks during Operation Barbarossa and their drive to Kiev. A 36th *Panzer* Regiment tank (14th *Panzer* emblem on back of turret) was driven off a dilapidated bridge and is stuck. Usually the crew was responsible for remedying the situation themselves, and here they prepare to get towed across the bridge by another tank on the far side. (Bundesarchiv)

A column of trucks carrying infantry is stopped on the far side of the road as Leo Schwarz encounters the first German graves along his advance in June 1941. Division losses up to this point were already a staggering 600 dead, wounded, and missing. It was apparent that this *Blitzkrieg* campaign was going to be far more difficult than those gone before. (Courtesy L. Schwarz)

mind of a grand expansion to the Volga River, to seize the oil-rich Caucasus Region.

The 36th *Panzer* Regiment was back under control of III *Panzerkorps* by the 16th and ordered to advance on Dnepropetrovsk. The members of the Division found Dnepropetrovsk to hard to pronounce and nicknamed it *Kneppersdorff*. This city on the Dnepr River of a half million inhabitants was a major transport and communications centre, and the largest yet encountered. The advance went by way of Alexandrovka (not to be confused with the earlier one of the same name), until enemy armour was engaged on the 19th. Heavy KV tank designs were encountered for the first time here, and assistance from assault guns were needed to defeat them. By evening the attack was driven off, with 16 out of 21 tanks destroyed. Soviet troops now retreated into the bridgehead at Dnepropretovsk, only nine miles away.[26]

More inspections and additional duty came later in the day. Schwarz said about these pictures that any free time at all was taken up by spray painting and stencilling the vehicles. (Courtesy L. Schwarz)

The attack on the city began on the 25th. The main road crossing over the Dnepr was destroyed, but a pontoon bridge was still left intact. Enemy artillery, air and ground attacks continued all day long until 60th Motorised Division secured the far side of the river. German, Hungarian and Italian pioneers then repaired the bridges to accept motorised traffic, and a foot plank was built for the infantry. Six battalions were across by the 26th and the bridgehead was secured. At 8 p.m. that evening, the word came down that Dnepropretovsk was in German hands.[27]

With tank strength in the Division down to 50%, a rest period was needed, and for several days they repaired and reorganized inside the Dnepropretovsk bridgehead. The effects of the rapid advance began to take its toll on the condition of the vehicles with dust and dirt clogging the engines, along with the normal wear and tear of such a long drive, not to mention the battle damage sustained.

During the lull in the fighting German reconnaissance sections secured bridgeheads all along the Dnepr River. The 36th *Panzer* Regiment crossed over one of these bridgeheads on September 12th, halfway between Cremmenchug and Dnepropetrowsk. Moving 40 miles northeast the following day they secured the Division objective of Mirgorod, resistance being light and unorganised.[28]

The full weight of Guderian's *Panzer* force was now bearing down from the northwest, behind the static Soviet lines built up in and around Kiev. The move south by Guderian took the Soviet commanders totally by surprise and by the time they reacted a ring was already drawn tight around 43 of their divisions. The link up of the north and south pincers happened on the 14th at Lokhivitsa, and three

CAMPAIGN IN THE EAST 71

The maintenance crews were again called on to perform monumental tasks of improvisation and skill repairing the engines, drive gears, track sprockets, grousers and turret traverses, which were all choked up and overworked from the advance. Here a 36th *Panzer* Regiment workshop mechanic stands next to the chassis of a destroyed tank in a scrapyard from von Kleist's *Panzer* Army. (Courtesy L. Schwarz)

Since Hitler expected the Soviets to be beaten by the end of the first summer, orders were given for the troops to live off the land as much as possible. As the Germans moved farther into Russia supplies became scarcer for the spearhead troops. In this photograph, something obviously has been found to eat in the barn.
(Courtesy L. Schwarz)

Not long thereafter, the animal is roasted on a spit over a fire, behind the barn.
(Courtesy L. Schwarz)

days later Kiev was abandoned. Soviet troops were now panicking but fought stubbornly until the 26th, when the battle ended with over 500,000 soldiers taken prisoner.[29] The encirclement of Kiev in 1941 is considered by some historians to be the greatest feat of German arms, resulting in the highest numbers of troops surrounded by either side during the war.[30]

Kleist's command (now designated 1st *Panzer* Army) launched an all out drive south in the beginning of October towards the Sea of Azov. After receiving reinforcements in Dnepropetrovsk, the 36th *Panzer* Regiment entered the coast city of Mariupol (Melitopol) on the 11th, trapping another Soviet pocket to the west of the city. Squeezing the pocket between the infantry of the German 11th Army approaching from the Perekop Isthmus forced the capture of 11,000 more prisoners.[31]

III *Panzerkorps*' next order was to drive on the city of Rostov, gateway to the Caucasus. The last major obstacle before it was the port city of Taganrog and a crossing of the Mius River. The Mius was crossed north of the port on November 12th as stubborn fighting raged inside the city. The *SS Leibstandarte* Division, (operating next to the 36th *Panzer* Regiment) took especially heavy losses during the battle and was brutal in combat, but these *Waffen SS* divisions won the loyalty of most regular army units and commanders. During the advance on Taganrog six *SS Leibstandarte* soldiers who surrendered were found butchered in the city, and as a reprisal the Division took no prisoners for three days, executing some 4,000 Soviet POWs.[32]

The Soviet T-34 tank was being encountered in ever increasing numbers.[33] Resistance from enemy infantry, armour, and cavalry attacks were so heavy on the

As the 36th *Panzer* Regiment approached the great city of Rostov-on-Don, the temperature began to drop and the first snow frosts were felt. This was also the beginning of the Soviet Army's first major counter-attack of the war and the first military setback for Hitler, forcing von Rundstedt to pull back and establish a winter defensive line on the Mius River Line. When Hitler denied his request to fall back, he did so anyway, another first for the war, and then resigned. (Bundesarchiv) (Courtesy L. Schwarz)

CAMPAIGN IN THE EAST   73

In the winter of 1941–42, almost everyone in the Regiment came down with dysentery or frostbite and became sick. Leo Schwarz (on the right) went home to Germany on sick leave back to Ipsheim near Wurzburg, and also spent time performing light duty at the replacement battalion located in Bamberg. In this photograph, he is seen with another soldier (both wearing Tank Assault badges) as they guide a horse drawn wagon down the street in Bamberg. The wagon was filled with beer, wine, and *schnapps* for an all night party they held for themselves, before returning to Russia. They were so sick the next morning they slept for two days! (Karl Roth was separated from his convoy during this winter in 1941, and was also so ill he sought refuge in a peasant woman's house, next to an army ambulatory care facility and with her aid was nursed back into good health). (Courtesy L. Schwarz)

northern front that Corps headquarters responded with support from the rocket batteries, destroying 17 enemy tanks and 36 assault-guns.[34]

Meanwhile, heavy rain slowed the mechanized units advance to 1–2 miles a day, and they were still only a few miles past the Mius River Line in early November. The horse drawn *panje* wagon now proved its usefulness in supplying the tanks with petrol as the roads turned to mud and the regiment bogged down. For another week they fought through two outlying cities until the first heavy frosts and snow began, the Soviet winter arriving in force. Due to severe cold temperatures and high winds, the final attack on Rostov was postponed.[35]

Rundstedt reorganized his forces for a frontal assault on the city. Four unfinished defensive belts under construction by the local population ringed the city, consisting of minefields, anti-tank ditches and strong points. The attack went forward on the 21st with SS Division *Leibstandarte* deployed right, the 36th *Panzer* Regiment (14th Pz. Div.) in the centre and the 13th *Panzer* Division on the left. Desperate enemy fighting developed as the Germans drew closer to the centre of the city. A new plan had the *Leibstandarte* Division taking bridges over the Don to the southeast of the city, while the mobile forces backed by infantry tried to outflank the defences inside. Group Jesser (36th *Panzer* Regiment) moved into the northern portions of the city, destroying 17 enemy tanks in the process, but continued heavy resistance forced them to break off any attempt at capturing the city that evening.[36] The Soviet defenders suffered tremendous losses, including 12 more tanks destroyed and almost all their ammunition expended.[37]

The final attack was launched at eight o'clock the next morning and by midday the defensive inner ring was penetrated. Enemy aircraft bombing runs continued throughout the day's fighting, but for all intents and purposes the first battle for Rostov was over. The 36th *Panzer* Regiment opened the way for the assault gun brigade to seize the great bridge over the Don, and the city fell into German hands over the next few days.[38] This victory was to be short lived though because on the 17th the first seriously planned counter-attack against the German Army in the Second World War was already underway.[39]

The main goal of the Soviet counter offensive mimicked the German attack on Rostov of a few weeks earlier, only with the roles reversed. The Soviets planned to leap one army over to the coast as far as Taganrog, trapping Rundstedt's forces between two other armies advancing from the east and southeast. The first counter-attack was against the northern flank of 1st *Panzer* Army on the 17th, forcing back the *SS Wiking* Division. The weight of this attack was not fully felt by the Regiment until two other armies joined in on the 23rd, and in response to this threat the bridge over the Don River in Rostov was destroyed.[40]

After the Soviet northern group was half way between Taganrog and their start positions, they were joined by attacks all along the Tuzlov River Line south of Rostov. These attacks included a charge of Cossack cavalry that swarmed across the river at the entrenched positions of the 36th *Panzer* Regiment. Leo Schwarz, an eyewitness to the spectacle, said he could never forget the scene of hundreds of horseman armed only with carbines and sub-machine guns slung behind their backs, charging across the river yelling and swinging their sabres. His only explanation for the assault was that they must have been drunk, or very courageous and obedient to following orders. Nevertheless they were no match against the Regiment's dug in tanks and artillery, and were cut down almost to the man.

The Soviet counter-attack was so serious Rundstedt's army was in threat of being encircled. Losses to combat and the bitterly cold weather were high as the German troops tried to survive without adequate clothes or blankets. Hitler promised air re-supply, but this amounted to only 25 JU-52 transport planes landing on the 25th.[41] The front was shortened on the 28th and a small corridor held open for the trapped units inside the cauldron to escape from on the following day.[42] By this time the 36th *Panzer* Regiment was down to only between 12 and 24 operational tanks (half being repaired and out of action).

Faced with the first major defeat suffered by the German army to date, Rundstedt took matters into his own hands, and ordered a full retreat on the 30th during the critical moment of the battle, without informing Hitler. When he was ordered to rescind the order and stand fast, he resigned in protest.[43] This was the first of several strategic and personal decisions altering the historical course of events affecting Karl Roth and the unit as a whole. Had Rundstedt followed orders and not moved his troops, the 14th *Panzer* Division might have been encircled a full year before Stalingrad, and the outcome of Karl's fate may have turned out very different.

Winter War on the Mius Line

The beginning of December 1941 saw the end of offensive operations for the 36th *Panzer* Regiment as they settled into winter quarters on the Mius River Line, under control of the XIV *Panzerkorps*.[44] Tank inventories were at an all time low after almost six months of continuous fighting and driving over bad roads.[45] The condition of the *Panzer* companies demanded a major effort be made by the repair workshops to restore the force before the resumption of expected Soviet attacks. The unit reported only 5 tanks operational on December 10th, with total write-offs at the end of October amounting to more than 46, and replacements only equalling 11.

Karl's command staff now operated out of the large supply and rail centre at Stalino requisitioning parts, equipment, and supplies, from the various centres all the way back in Germany. Protecting this supply base and holding off continued enemy assaults to sever the rail lines was the primary mission for the division during this period.[46]

The most severe winter in years set in with record low temperatures ranging from -22°F to -40°F [47] and lice, dysentery, typhus, frostbite and hunger decimated the units all along the front, many being quarantined.[48] Supplies from Germany were slow in coming due to increased partisan attacks, but Karl was able to secure extra food and other commodities by making use his good friendship with the ration control officer.[49] The most appreciated of these perks Karl received was a steady supply of airmail stamps he gave to Else, so that she could keep the care packages coming to him.

Karl contracted gastrointestinal dysentery that winter and writing a letter for pension purposes just before he passed away in 1972, he describes how he acquired his illness and what the symptoms were. [This is the only written document concerning the war I acquired that was actually authored by Karl Roth]:

> In November 1941 after the retreat from Rostov towards the Mius River I was driving a motorcycle and sidecar in a maintenance section of command cars and trucks towing a column of vehicles by Taganrog to the repair shop of the 36th *Panzer* Regiment. We were following the retreating workshop company towards Mariuopol. Due to severe cold temperatures, a biting wind chill, and constant snow showers, I could not maintain contact between the motorcycle and vehicles in the convoy. I was only dressed in my uniform, light motorcycle coat, and boots. After half the way there I fell back but cannot remember the name of the closest village with a hospital, but believe it was near Prokowskoje. At this aid station I was only treated locally for my illness, but across the street from the hospital I found local quarters.
>
> The recollection of the symptoms of my illness were pain while urinating, with blood in my urine and stool. My treatment was steam over a bucket, tablets, and suppositories.
>
> I contest under oath that as an *Obergefreiter* [Corporal] of the 36th *Panzer* Regiment I suffered these ailments.   Signed, Karl Roth.

According to Else Roth, Karl recovered from his illness in this town ("local quarters") with the help of a Soviet peasant woman, who nursed him back to health with a local natural healing remedy that was vapour induced. He was always indebted to this woman and did his best to develop a trust with the local population, learning some of their language, and keeping tight discipline on the men under his command. As a former workshop company soldier stated during a 1998 division reunion in Kuhlsheim, "your father was very strict, and never allowed any pillaging" and, "we didn't talk to your father, he talked to us."

During this illness Karl Roth's identification disc was lost when he was doubled over with pain in a latrine in Prokowskoje. Sometime later, after he was gone, an enemy shell destroyed the stall. The nametag was sent home to Else claiming that the body found next to it was that of her fiancé! This was the first of two such incidents involving his identification disc claiming that he was dead during the war.

The miserable conditions during this unplanned first winter affected both the health and morale of the unit. Karl wrote to Else explaining that he was all right and still alive but that he needed foot warmers for his boots and that they had inadequate clothing. She misunderstood his request and instead sent him dusting rags to fit into his shoes! Karl wrote back and angrily explained that what he needed were insoles. Once Else understood this, she and her girlfriend knitted these sought-after items for the whole maintenance section. Many soldiers on the Eastern Front opted to use their leave time up that first winter in 1941–42 to escape their precarious position.[50] Fortunately for Karl, he suffered through that first severe winter and conserved his leave time, which proved instrumental in helping him survive the Soviet encirclement of Stalingrad the following year.

A surprise Soviet winter offensive began on January 18th from both north and south of the town of Izyum (near Kharkov) that drove 16 miles into 17th Army on the first day. The attack was fifty miles deep by the 24th and the town of Barvenkovo was captured. The Kharkov-Dnepropretovsk railway line was now cut at Lozovaya, with the Dnepropretovsk-Stalino line now only 35 miles away.[51] Disruption of this supply route meant a timely delay in restoring the regiment to fighting strength, therefore all further leave was cancelled and any retreat was strictly forbidden.[52]

Two days earlier the 36th *Panzer* Regiment was ordered north by road and rail to join *Kampfgruppe Mackensen*, an amalgamated battle group from 1st *Panzer* Army trying to shore up the southern flank of the breakthrough area.[53] Due to the defensive nature of the fighting, the division was broken down into battle groups, with the highest commending officer's last name ('Kohlermann', 'Sanne') being the force designator and leader within each. The 2nd Battalion of the Regiment was used to form *Panzer Abteilung* 60 on January 4th, but were so under-strength at this point they could only support these groups in limited numbers. By the end of the month parts of the 14th *Panzer* Division along with the 16th *Panzer* and 100th Light Division, made up 'Advance Group Hube', situated to block the Red Army counteroffensive.[54]

The 14th *Panzer's* 'Special Battalion Grams' made up of *Panzergrenadiers*, assault guns, and anti-aircraft artillery, were dug in on the Samara River (by Alexandrovka) resisting the main enemy attack from behind heavily defended hedgehog positions. These hedgehogs were supported independently from the rear or were supplied by the air if totally encircled. Their use against heavy Soviet penetrations proved so effective that winter they became standard battlefield doctrine for the Germans by the end of the war. The Soviet offensive was contained by February gaining little more ground, but the salient created (55 miles wide and 70 miles across) was a thorn in the side of Army Group South for the rest of the winter and into the spring.[55]

1st *Panzer* Army was called on to plug the gaps of the attempted enemy breakthroughs throughout the remaining weeks of winter as extremely cold weather and deep snow prevented either side from gaining the offensive. By the end of March though the temperature rose, the snow melted, and spring brought on the muddy season. The sacrifices of the German army that first winter did not go un-rewarded, and anyone serving more than 14 days on the Eastern front during that period was given the, 'Winter Battles in the East' decoration, becoming one of the most revered until the end of the war.[56] Morale was boosted by the change in weather and the misery of winter faded away, prompting Hitler to immediately begin planning his great summer offensive of 1942.

CHAPTER VII

Kharkov

Operation Fredericus I and II (May–June 1942)

The Soviet commander, General Timeshenko, planned to launch a two-pronged offensive out of the Barvenkovo-Volchansk salient created from the preceding winter offensive. The ultimate aim of the Soviet attack was to encircle Kharkov and Dnepropretrovsk, disrupting the German supply lines.[1]

By May the Germans were planning their own offensive against the salient in an operation (*Fredericus I*) to converge two pincers on Iyzum where the Soviet counter-attack originated. 6th Army (Paulus) would attack from the north, with 1st *Panzer* Army (Kleist) providing the armoured force in the south.[2] The 14th *Panzer* Division and 36th *Panzer* Regiment were concentrated in the south by Andrejevka, and reinforcing with elements of III *Panzerkorps* for the coming offensive (the 5th company loaned out to form '*Gruppe Montfort*' was now returned to the regiment).

The Soviets struck first on May 12th again taking the Germans by surprise. They advanced 12 miles from Barvenkovo, and 16 out of Volchansk. The 6th Army in the north took the brunt of the attack as Group Kleist fought to hold the southern flank. The Soviet advance made it to within a few miles of Kharkov, but then began to stall. The Soviet high command worried about the build up they observed on their flanks, and withheld their mobile troops at exactly the time when it may have made a difference.[3]

The Germans held firm and offered stiff resistance. Plan *Fredericus* was still a possibility in their minds and it now looked as if the Soviets were racing forward to fill up the bag. Careful preparations were made not to counter-attack prematurely before the enemy advance was given time to expend itself. The Regiment launched their attack along with the rest of III *Panzerkorps* on the morning of May 17th. Heavy fighting was encountered after the artillery lifted their barrage and 15 miles were gained, preceded by air attacks made in direct advance of the ground forces that proved especially devastating to Soviet units.[4]

By the next day the 36th *Panzer* Regiment was fighting into Barvenkovo and overran the headquarters of the Soviet 57th Army, capturing the city at 5 p.m.[5] The Soviets were slow in realizing the force of the German counter-attack and all requests to disengage were denied by Stalin. The Regiment moved forward being engaged by enemy tanks at Protopopovka as the drive moved north on the 20th and 21st. The mouth of the pocket was now only twelve miles wide to Balakleya, and a major effort was under way to close it. 16th *Panzer* Division, 60th Motorised, and 1st Mountain were all ordered to follow 14th *Panzer's* lead north, while two *Panzer* divisions from 6th Army were diverted south to implement the *Fredericus* plan.[6]

Combining the armour of both the 16th and 14th *Panzer* Divisions the assault ground northwards towards Balakyeva, reaching 6th Army tanks at Bayrak on the

78

Leo Schwarz (standing to the far left) was conscripted into the military in 1940 and sent for infantry training at Ansbach, Germany. After basic training he was assigned to the *Panzer* arm and sent to join the 36th *Panzer* Regiment in Schweinfurt-Bamberg. He was for a short time involved in the French campaign, but only for training purposes and did not see combat. Later, he was assigned to the I-staff (*Instandsetzung*) or the mobile maintenance section of the workshop company, where he served under Karl Roth. Schwarz was a commander and driver on the *Panzer* Mark II, IV, and Panther tank during the course of the war in Russia, and later in Courland. In this picture during the autumn of 1941, Schwarz is graduating to command a *Panzer* Mark IV tank that will have a four-man crew. Within two weeks of this photograph being taken, his former tank in the background was destroyed, and the man on the far right and the other closest to him (his replacement) killed. He survived the Battle of Stalingrad while assigned to the XLVIII *Panzerkorps* and gives his personal account of the Soviet counterstroke on November 19th (see Chapter 8). Fighting until the end of the war, he evacuated from Libau harbour in Courland to northern Germany, in May 1945, aboard the same cruiser as his comrade, Karl Brier (see Brier's biography in Chapter 9). (Courtesy L. Schwarz)

northern Donets River. Timeshenko's chances of escape were now over and the pocket was sealed shut. The 36th *Panzer* Regiment braced itself for the desperate breakout attempts that were expected to follow, and for a week the Soviets poured eastwards towards their Donets bridgehead at Ssavinzy.[7] But Kliest's wall of steel allowed only one in ten Soviet soldiers to get through, including four Soviet generals who were killed trying to breakout, attesting to the heroic and sometimes suicidal ferocity of the Red Army assaults.[8]

Isyum fell and over 214,000 prisoners were captured after the first *Fredericus* battle concluded. Hitler was so pleased with the outcome of the failed Soviet attack, and successful German counter-attack, that awards and promotions were forthcoming. III *Panzerkorps* commander Mackensen was awarded Oak Leaves to the Knight's Cross for his achievements.[9] His soldiers were also promoted, Karl making the rank of Sergeant on June 1st.[10] General Paulus of 6th Army was the most impressed by Hitler's steadfastness through the battle and his loyalty to the *Führer* proved a shortcoming later on.[11]

A *Panzer* Mark IV platoon. The Kharkov offensives began when the Germans were thrown off guard by a major spring attack out of the Barvenkovo salient, created from the prior Soviet winter offensive. The Soviets were allowed to outrun their supply lines just before reaching Kharkov, and then the Germans unleashed their reserves to cut them off, including the 14th *Panzer* Division. (Bundesarchiv)

Hitler was at Army Group South's headquarters on June 1st preparing the final details of Operation Blue, the summer offensive to take the Caucasus oil region and city of Stalingrad. He was going to bet everything on developments in the south and orders to strengthen the *Panzer* units in the region were given. The 36th *Panzer* Regiment was given a third battalion of tanks (transferred from 2nd Batt. 7th *Pz*. Rgt.) on the 2nd, consisting of two light *Panzer* companies and one medium *Panzer* company each. He also ordered two more small-scale offensives in the Kharkov sector to straighten out the lines and to provide jump off points for the drive south.[12]

After transferring north, the 36th Regiment was engaged in the battle to eliminate the remaining Soviet salient at Volchansk and to secure a bridgehead on the opposite bank of the Donets. A heavy enemy tank attack was beaten off on the 14th and two days later the Donets was reached, although a crossing was not made.[13] Army Headquarters ordered a new attack eastwards towards the Oskal River in the Kupyansk area, and from the 16th until the 21st the Regiment redeployed once again. Three divisions, the 14th, 16th *Panzer*, and 44th Infantry Division made up 'Group Hube', a battle group responsible for clearing the area east of Izyum between the Donets and Oskol Rivers (Operation *Fredericus* II).[14]

Most of the Soviet shock forces were defeated in the battles the month before and the Soviets were easily forced behind the Oskol River. An additional 47,000 prisoners were taken by the time the Kupyansk pocket fell[15] and the entire Soviet Southwest Front was now vulnerable to attack after these two setbacks with tank strength in the south now weighing in the Germans favour ten to one.[16]

As reinforcements began to arrive from the rear in June for the big summer offensive, German morale was high, and some believed that an end of the war was even possible before the next Russian winter.[17]

Leo Schwarz explained these two battle photographs: They were repairing tyres using gummy cement to seal the rubber, which they had to make. The enemy was close to them, but couldn't be seen because of the cornfield, and a mound surrounding a ditch.

Shortly after the picture was taken, Schwarz got on top of the truck to see into the cornfield, and noticed the glint of light on the barrel of a Soviet sniper's rifle. He and the other men tore off into the cornfield after the sniper. Schwarz ran so fast it startled the Soviet, even though he got off a shot at them, but missed. The sniper didn't know from where in the cornfield the Germans would emerge, when Leo landed on him, and began to choke him (They had no weapons because of the way they were dressed). He realized it was a boy maybe fifteen or sixteen years old, and released his grip. They took the boy prisoner, but a few hours later they didn't know what to do with him, as they moved out, so they released him. (Courtesy L. Schwarz)

Karl Roth and an unidentified comrade display a captured Soviet battle flag. The 14th *Panzer* Division overran the headquarters of the 57th Army during their attack north towards Barvenkovo, during Operation *Fredericus* I. After these two operations concluded, tank ratios in the south were 10:1 in favour of the Germans.
(Author's collection, courtesy E. Roth)

CHAPTER VIII

The Dream is Destroyed

Operation Blue, Stalingrad
(June 1942–March 1943)

The 36th *Panzer* Regiment was exhausted after the *Fredericus* operations concluded and reformed for eight days at the workshop depot in Stalino.[1] During repair operations the ordinance crews of the workshop company increased the firepower in the tanks by adding longer barrels of higher gun velocity to the *Panzer* Mark III's and IV's. Karl was also promoted to sergeant on June 2nd during a time of field parades and award ceremonies, recognizing the unit's success the preceding month. This psychological and material preparation of the *Panzer* forces in the south was for a great summer offensive that was meant to break the back of the Red Army west of the Don River, take the city of Stalingrad under fire, and move forces into the Caucasus Region.[2]

To achieve this plan Hitler divided Army Group South into two forces, A (List, 1st *Pz* Army with III and XIV *Panzerkorps*), and B (Bock, 6th Army with XL *Panzerkorps*, 4th *Panzer* Army with XXIV and XLVIII *Panzerkorps*), with the ultimate result being that neither group was strong enough to accomplish the tasks given them. Group A was to advance into the mountains of the Caucasus and secure the oil producing cities there, while Group B advanced on the city of Stalingrad through the Kalmucken steppe (a vast area of open space broken up by *balkas*, much like the wadis of the desert) threatening the Soviet supply line on the Volga River.[3]

At first the Caucasus was only to be invaded after Stalingrad was firmly in control of Army Group B, and their main function was to protect the southern groups supply lines through Rostov. But as events progressed, both of these plans changed; Stalingrad became a psychological obsession with Hitler that doomed Army Group B to encirclement, and Group A had to be pulled north from their incursion into the Caucasus, before their flank was turned by the great Soviet winter offensive.[4]

On June 28th, almost exactly a year since the invasion of Russia began, the German army lurched forward once again; launching one of the most infamous operations of the war code-named 'Plan Blue'.

The 14th *Panzer* Division moved north attached to III *Panzerkorps* under command of von Kleist's 1st *Panzer* Army, with orders to occupy the industrial centre of Artemovsk (east of Izyum). The 36th *Panzer* Regiment was sent ahead of the infantry on July 11th to take the Donets Bridge at Schachta-Tomascha before the enemy could destroy it. This attempt failed and the Division combat engineers had to set up a pontoon bridge to cross the river, after troops of the 103rd *Panzergrenadier* Regiment secured the east bank.[5] Light resistance was encountered on the other side prompting the Regimental headquarters intelligence officer to

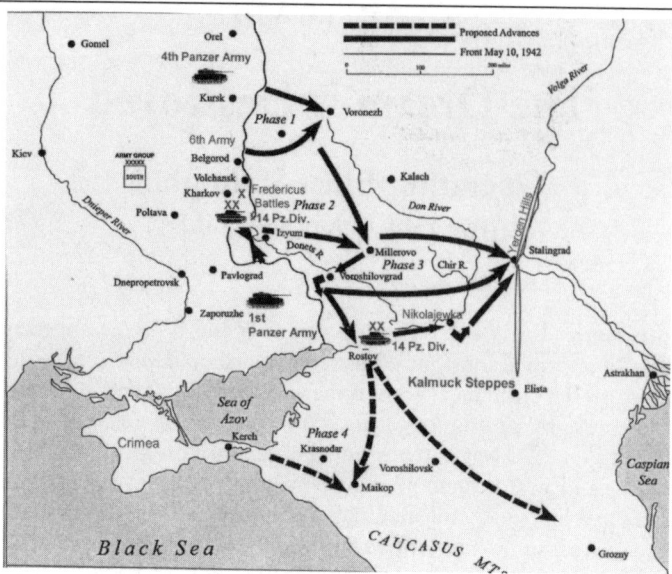

Operation Blue

wonder why the enemy was not stopping their retreat to fight. The Red Army's former combat doctrine was to meet most river crossings with fierce opposition, but instead the enemy was melting farther and farther away into the vast interior of the country. Two more river barriers (the Aidar and Derkul) were crossed in just three days but the Regiment captured little in the way of enemy prisoners or material. The weather and ground conditions were perfect for tank operations that summer and the *Panzer* columns rolled east.[6]

25 miles south of Millerovo one of the 36th *Panzer* Regiment's companies destroyed parts of two enemy tank brigades and 25 more Soviet tanks were destroyed on the 15th, west of Tarassovka, with 3,000 prisoners captured. The oppressive heat took a heavy toll on man and machine alike, halting them for a rest and refit the following day.[7]

1st *Panzer* Army's drive turned south on the 16th after reaching the heights overlooking the western-styled city of Forchstadt, at the fork of the Don and Kalitva Rivers. The sky let loose a downpour two days later and the unit was again delayed, due to the mud and rain. A river crossing was then taken over the Don at Kalitwenskaja (to the west of Forchstadt), and the Regiment crossed here the following day. Their orders were to head south and attack Novocherkask, a northern suburb of Rostov.[8]

Novocherkask was Manstein's headquarters upon his appointment during the crisis days of the Stalingrad relief attempt (but was abandoned when the Soviets almost took Rostov during the second phase of their counter-attack). The move on Novotscherkask came from the east of Schachty early on July 21st. Armour secured a bridge leading directly into the old city, but stubborn resistance was encountered inside. Heavy enemy fire poured from behind thick masonry walls and archways, making movement by day nearly impossible.[9]

The following night the Regiment disengaged and redeployed west of the town. With the support from the Corps artillery and combat engineers a crossing was secured over the Tuzlov River, 20 miles west of Novoscherkask. Later that night *Kampfgruppe Langkeit*, of the 36th *Panzer* Regiment, crossed over the bridge and drove into the city, fighting over anti-tank ditches, through field fortifications and around barricades.[10] The city fell the day after, and Rostov was now within reach of 1st *Panzer* Army.[11]

By the 23rd Hitler was still not pleased with the number of Soviets surrendering in the Don basin and in an attempt to capture more of the enemy, made the most fateful decision to affect Karl, the unit, and the course of the war up until that point. This far-reaching decision was encompassed in Hitler's Directive 45, outlining the next phase of the campaign. Describing the Soviets as virtually defeated, he now changed the schedule and objectives of the original plan.[12]

Instead of driving on Stalingrad in front of 6th Army, General Hermann Hoth's 4th *Panzer* Army was ordered to move south into the Don Basin.[13] Hoth was to assist 1st *Panzer* Army in forming a classic pincer envelopment meant to destroy the Soviet Army in the large bend of the Don River. So sure was Hitler that the Soviets were broken, he felt confident enough to pull eight divisions out of the southern theatre of operations. The most damaging effect of the directive though, as far as the regiment was concerned, was that it ordered simultaneous drives on Stalingrad and the Caucasus, effectively eliminating any mutual support the two groups relied on.[14]

The orders were implemented on the 25th along with a total mix up of divisions in the order of battle. After a delay built up outside the city of Voronezh early

Peter Neuendorff was the adjutant of the 36th *Panzer* Regiment, and his brother, Heinz Neuendorff, the commander of the 14th *Panzer*'s 108th *Panzergrenadier* Regiment. This photograph depicts the drive on Stalingrad in the summer of 1942. Peter Neuendorff did not survive internment as a prisoner of war after the debacle at Stalingrad. His brother, Heinz, survived the war and ran a pharmacy in Schweinfurt until retiring later to Munich. Heinz Neuendorff is a key contributor to the '*Traditional Association*' of the 14th *Panzer* Division, and also to the unit's division history, written by Rolf Grams. Herr Neuendorff provided this picture of his brother and a copy of memoirs made during the 50th anniversary of the Stalingrad battle. (Courtesy H. Neuendorff)

The summer of 1942 was extremely hot on the Kalmuck steppe in southern Russia and much of the advance was done at night to avoid the stress put on the engines of the vehicles. Here 36th *Panzer* Regiment tank crews await re-supply from light aircraft providing much needed water and fuel. (This photo is from a German newsreel taken of the 36th *Panzer* Regiment during the advance that summer) (Bundesarchiv)

in the campaign, Hitler began to shuffle his *Panzerkorps* like a deck of cards. For example, XL *Panzerkorps* began the operation with 4th *Panzer* Army but was given to 6th Army for the Voronezh battle, and was ultimately transferred down to 1st *Panzer* Army for the drive into the Caucasus. Some explanation is therefore necessary to understand how Karl and the 36th *Panzer* Regiment ended up four months later besieged at Stalingrad as members of 4th *Panzer* Army, instead of being involved in the relatively stable operations conducted in the south with their old unit, the III *Panzerkorps*.[15]

The III *Panzerkorps* (with 14th *Panzer* Division attached) drove into the lower Don bend next to and intermingled with, forces of 4th *Panzer* Army. Hoth gained control of the XIV *Panzerkorps* during this pincer envelopment, but the 14th *Panzer* Division was placed in operational reserve, and remained with 1st *Panzer* Army. Later, Hoth was ordered to relinquish the XIV *Panzerkorps* and another *Panzerkorps* (the XXIV) to Paulus, refreshing some mobility to 6th Army's drive on Stalingrad. This now left Hoth commanding one *Panzerkorps* (XLVIII with only one *Panzer* division attached), therefore the 14th *Panzer* Division was taken out of reserve status and assigned to bolster this unit.[16] With this new order came another redirection of forces by Hitler, and 4th *Panzer* Army was told to disengage with the drive south into the Caucasus, assisting instead 6th Army's slow march towards Stalingrad.[17]

So the 14th *Panzer* Division was now fatefully ordered to re-deploy northeast with 4th *Panzer* Army to attack Stalingrad from its southern flank. Field Marshal von Kleist, long-time commander of 1st *Panzer* Army, spoke personally to the Division just before their transfer and bid farewell to the 36th *Panzer* Regiment, expressing his gratitude of commanding the unit during the prior battles the year before.[18] After spending two days regrouping on the Don River, the Regiment caught up with the headquarters of Kempf's XLVIII *Panzerkorps* at the crossing of Nikolajewskava. A sergeant with the 14th *Panzer* Division described what it was like when they arrived at the Don:

> We got to the river [Don] to find most of the bridges down, but very little sign of the enemy...the whole length of the right bank was smothered in dust clouds as more and more vehicles began to pile up there. Soviet resistance was so slight that many of us were able to take off our clothes and bathe - as we had in the Dnepr exactly a year before. Let us hope that history does not repeat itself!

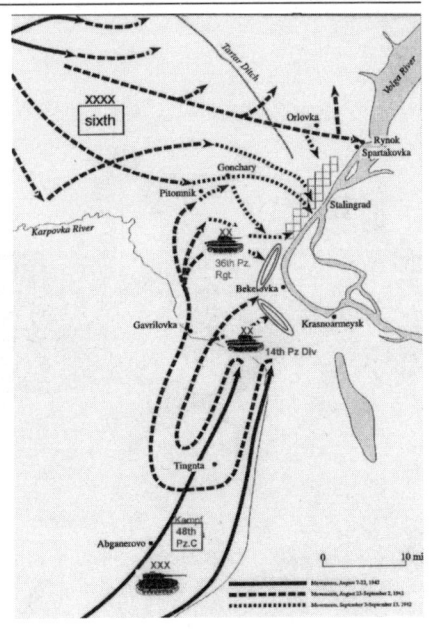

Advancing on Stalingrad

The weather was stifling hot as they struck out across the Kalmuck steppe towards Stalingrad. The 2nd Battalion encountered enemy tanks at approaches to the Sal tributary but Soviet resistance was light and brushed aside easily.[19] The 36th *Panzer* Regiment was supposed to be on the outskirts of Stalingrad by August 3rd, but instead the advance was delayed because of the heat, engine stress, and problems navigating across the endless steppe. Even so, they racked up more driving hours and miles then any other tank regiment in Russia at the time, most of it done at night due to the soaring temperatures and limited resources of water. After being refuelled by air, the advance continued northeast, paralleling the Stalingrad-Caucasus railway that ran through Kotolnikovo, bypassing isolated pockets of dug-in Soviet infantry.[20]

A small airfield on the Aksay River was taken on August 4th by other Division units, resulting in 200 prisoners captured and over 50 vehicles destroyed.[21] This and other small airfields taken on the approaches to Stalingrad proved invaluable later on when the siege began and airlift became the only means of re-supply. Even now, the Regiment and other units were supplied fuel and water by *Luftwaffe* transport aircraft, either dropping parachute canisters, or landing on make shift runways built on the steppe.[22] They moved ahead towards Stalingrad was goaded on by Paulus, whose 6th Army was already assembling outside the city.

Heavy fortifications constructed to the east of Abganerovo halted them on the 5th, and the long drive in pursuit of the enemy was now over as opposition steadily increased.[23] That evening the Division was counter-attacked from three sides, and all the regiments of the Division were engaged in the fighting. By the time the attacks were over, 70 T-34 tanks were destroyed. But the 36th *Panzer* Regiment suffered as well, with only 24 tanks reported combat operational, the others being

Fighting around the grain elevator in September was fierce and brutal. Here a tank commander is on the watch for Soviet anti-tank gunners and snipers. (Bundesarchiv)

The cramped quarters inside the tank complicated the ability to respond to the urban warfare tactics of the enemy. (Note that the side hatch is open to provide ventilation, but also making it dangerous for the crew inside). (Bundesarchiv)

THE DREAM IS DESTROYED 89

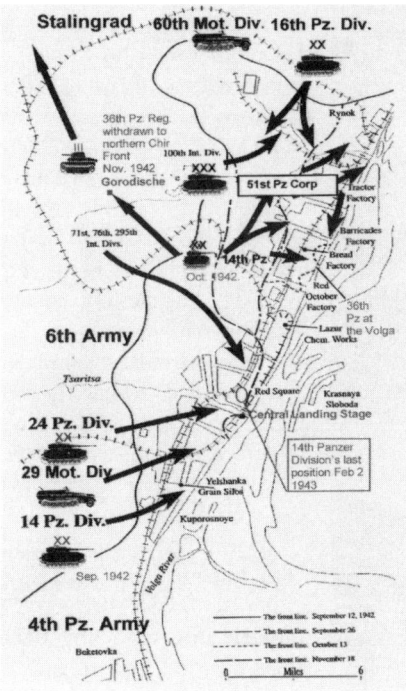

Stalingrad

repaired at the workshop centre in the town of Aksay. This was the first major setback for the Germans since the start of the campaign.[24]

Because Hoth was so under strength, Hitler ordered the 24th *Panzer* Division reassigned from 6th Army and sent on a 60-mile journey south to double the tank strength in XLVIII *Panzerkorps*. Both the 14th and 24th *Panzer* Divisions then attacked north on the 20th towards Tundutovo, but again ran into stiff defensive positions. Costly head on attacks against an enemy dug in on the heights resulted in repeated failure and heavy loss for the tank regiments. The attacks were called off five days later and a new axis of advance planned.[25]

Hoth pulled his armour out of the line unit by unit during the night of the 26th and replaced them with his infantry formations, reassembling the regiment the next day south and west of Abganerovo. A fresh attack northwest had the advantage of surprise and was also a quicker link up with 6th Army, but at the expense of seizing the heights between Beketovka and Krasnoarmeisk. This area of high ground in southern Stalingrad was possibly the most important vantage point of the entire battlefield, as it overlooked and anchored the whole Soviet defence line.[26]

After taking on ammunition, fuel, and rations during the 28th the Regiment attacked northward the following day, assisted by the 24th *Panzer* and 29th Motorised Divisions. The Soviets were caught totally off guard as they tore 20 miles into their lines. The Karpovka River was crossed at Gavrilovka on the 30th, with only 25 miles now separating 4th *Panzer* Army from 6th Army.[27] Paulus was urged by von Weichs to send an armoured pincer south to exploit the breakthrough being made. The goal was to split the 62nd and 64th Armies defending the northern and southern portions of Stalingrad respectively. Heavy attacks on Paulus's northern flank however kept all his forces occupied, and no strategic move or decisive defeat of the enemy was achieved.[28]

Having never commanded troops in combat, Friederick Paulus was put in charge of the 6th Army just prior to 'Operation Blue' and the advance on the city. He was an accomplished staff officer, serving under von Reicheneau in Poland and France, but lacked the quick thinking and experience of other commanders, such as Mackensen, Manstein and Hoth. While conducting operations during the *Fredericus* battles in May 1942, he was impressed by Hitler's accurate assessments of the enemy's intentions

Willi Langkeit, the 36th *Panzer's* Regimental commander, accepts a birthday gift in October 1942 given to him from Peter Neuendorff, adjutant 36th *Panzer* Regiment. This photograph was taken a month before the great encirclement of 6th Army. (Courtesy H. Neuendorff)

and weaknesses, developing a dangerous loyalty to him that influenced his decisions after 6th Army was encircled.

The 36th *Panzer* Regiment was ordered to move rapidly on Pitominik airfield on September 1st, 10 miles from the southern flank and surround whatever enemy units were still in the area. The next day forward reconnaissance revealed the enemy was retreating, abandoning their field fortifications. This lack of resistance allowed 6th Army and 4th *Panzer* Army to link up on the 3rd along a broad front, outside Stalingrad, panicking the Soviet Army commanders into retracting their forces into the city proper.[29]

Hoth was not giving up on his objective of a month earlier to capture the high ground south of Stalingrad, and therefore he attacked southeast towards Beketavka and Kuporosnoye with the 14th *Panzer* Division. The success the 36th *Panzer* Regiment achieved in battling through to the Volga here on September 8th, and at Krasnoarmeisk four days before, effectively separated the Soviet 62nd and 64th Armies.

Paulus realized the opportunity presented by this success and ordered a major concentrated assault on the city to begin.[30] The 24th *Panzer* Division along with the 29th Motorised Division received orders to assault the southern part of the city below the Tsaritsa Ravine. Most of the 14th *Panzer* Division remained in the extreme southern portion of Stalingrad protecting Paulus's right flank when this attack began at 0445 hours on September 13th. His objective was to converge two pincers on the central landing stage in the middle of the city, one from the north and another from the south, to envelope the city. This strategy worked well in open tank country, but now that the *Panzer* force was engulfed in city fighting, *Blitzkrieg* tactics were useless. His approach to the problem of urban warfare became methodical, deliberate, and anticipated, applying more and more force on a stubborn dug-in enemy.[31]

The 36th *Panzer* Regiment's orders were to support the infantry and grenadiers of the other two divisions (elements from the 94th Inf. and the 29th Mot.Divs) attacking northeast from the Yelshanka mining district towards the central landing stage.

Heavy Soviet rocket and artillery barrages fired from the east bank of the Volga slowed the attack as 60,000 Soviet soldiers resisted furiously.[32] Although German combat doctrine specified that armoured vehicles should not be employed in street fighting, three years after the urban warfare dilemma the Regiment experienced in Warsaw they came full circle, and the same mistakes made in 1939 were now being repeated again. Distances previously counted in miles were now measured down to the yard.[33]

As the Germans developed a combat doctrine to deal with the city fighting, it was apparent that the cost of using tanks independently of supporting units was to be avoided at all costs. Soviet urban warfare tactics were remarkably effective as they created kill zones in which to separate the grenadiers from the tanks, and attack them from behind. Soviet infantry formations were broken down into small storm groups that conducted guerrilla attacks against the Germans from basement cellars and subterranean hideouts. Losses of officers to Soviet sniping also increased the confusion and led to command and control problems within the Regiment. Only the employment of tanks, *Panzergrenadiers*, assault-guns, combat engineers, dive-bombers, and artillery proved effective in clearing the streets block-by-block and street-by-street.[34]

Vicious fighting developed around the grain elevator and morale within the German units began to deteriorate; talk of making it home by Christmas and avoiding another dreadful Russian winter, were no longer heard. The elevator was finally captured on the 22nd, but only after all the defenders were either killed, captured, or burned alive inside, after they sealed themselves shut in the massive building and fought bitterly to the end. The taking of this structure meant that the whole southern part of the city was now in German hands, although the main railway station continued to hold out as Soviet reinforcements tenaciously defended this and other key positions.[35] On the 25th Paulus reported that the Reich's battle standard now flew over the Communist Party headquarters near Red Square.

The 14th *Panzer* Division was placed in 4th *Panzer* Army reserve (*Kampfgruppe Schmid*) outside the fighting at the end of September. Paulus meanwhile sought more infantry for his final planned attack on the city, and in response to this request transferred the replenished 14th and 24th *Panzer* Divisions (*Gruppe Janecke*), along with the 94th Infantry Division, to 6th Army's control. The Division fell under command of von Seydlitz-Kurtzbach's LI Corps, located in the northern suburbs of the city (Seydlitz was critical of both Paulus's and Hitler's conduct of the battle and was outspoken against the war after his capture).[36]

The planned attack concentrated an enormous amount of force on an 11-mile stretch of northern Stalingrad known as the factory districts. Starting just south of Rynok (the northern most suburb) stood a tractor factory, brick factory, Red Barricades Ordinance Factory, followed by a bread factory and the Red October Steelworks, and finally a maze of buildings in a broad loop of railroad tracks called the Lazur Chemical Works (known as the 'tennis racket'). Against this fortress of stone, steel, and rubble the Germans planned to send in 90,000 men, and 300 tanks![37]

The advance group arrived on October 9th after travelling by way of Woropovono, Pitominik and Gumrak, with a total of 38 tanks.[38] Group Janecke[39] moved against the Red Barricades Factory on the morning of October 14th preceded by *Panzergrenadiers* and heavily supported by pinpoint accurate *Stuka* dive-bombing attacks. This assault began the most savage and bitter battle fought by the 36th *Panzer* Regiment during the war as a detachment of tanks led by Bernard Sauvant, and supported by *Panzergrenadiers* of the 103rd Regiment, succeeded in being the first unit to breakthrough to the Volga that night.[40] By dawn on the 15th a narrow corridor to the river was secure as the attack continued north towards the Tractor Factory, and the Germans moved in on three sides with 180 tanks! The German infantry fanned out along the riverbank as fighting raged in and under the destroyed city, with some units moving forward only half a mile that day (Karl and most of those in the unit were awarded the tank assault badge for this attack).[41]

The LI Corps daily report listed the destruction of 20 enemy tanks and the capture of 1,028 POWs that day. Casualties were mounting for the Soviets and in the first 24 hours of the attack Chiukov, the Soviet commander in Stalingrad, reported that 3,500 wounded men were ferried across the Volga to the eastern side of the river, and that his headquarters was almost overrun.

An attack on the Bread Factory started on the 17th beginning a gruelling one-week battle of attrition for the building. Packets of six or seven tanks assisted the *Panzergrenadiers* in small set piece engagements among the debris-covered streets. Battle conditions were horrendous, artillery ammunition was in short supply, and morale was reaching an all time low.

Manoeuvring over rubble and debris took a heavy toll on the tanks suspension, and even those commander's whose vehicles were not in need of repair, made up any excuse to get out of the fighting.[42] Karl's command section ultimately decided which of these tanks could be re-committed to the battle or held back for repair at the regimental workshop centre, located 25 miles outside the city. His position allowed him access to situation maps and radio broadcasts used and made within the headquarters staff, and he began to form a fairly accurate picture of the catastrophe that was about to befall Stalingrad. Anticipating certain encirclement by the Soviets, he formulated an escape plan and took precautions by loading the section's motorcycle and sidecar into the back of the cross-country truck, loaded with food, fuel, water, ammunition, maps, compass, and the section machine gun.[43]

Hitler issued orders at the end of October to halt all offensive operations on the Eastern Front for winter except those in Stalingrad. Karl immediately put in for the leave time he accumulated since the beginning of the Russian campaign, but was forced to wait until after the battle was deadlocked at the end of October before being granted permission by his officers. The fact that he was allowed to go at all attests to the fact that the city was now nine tenths in German hands, and the remaining pockets were expected to fall very soon. Hitler even boasted during a speech in November that: "we really have already taken the city already, just a few minor pockets of resistance are still holding out".[44]

At the Division rail stop of Woroponovo (just outside Stalingrad), Karl caught the troop train for Germany. North of this town stands the division cemetery

THE DREAM IS DESTROYED   93

begun and maintained by the Division Chaplin, Ebert, during the battle. It contained the graves of hundreds of casualties being brought out of the city daily, and before departing most of those going on leave paid their last respects to fallen comrades here.[45]

Leave was usually for 30 days, with an additional three given for travel to and from Russia. Depending on the rail conditions and partisan activity, travel back to Germany could take days or even weeks. Every man on board the troop train was organized into a self-contained combat unit in each car and required to carry their weapons during travel. At the conductor's order everyone was expected to counterassault any attack on the train by Soviet partisans. Eastern front soldiers were provided greater privileges than men going on leave from other fronts, including extra food, chocolate, and civilian clothes. They were also supposed to be properly fed for two weeks, although Karl undoubtedly was unable to take advantage of this benefit, due to the heavy October battles in Stalingrad.

Travel between Schweinfurt and Stalingrad took at least four days and upon arriving back home, Karl's first order of business was discarding his uniform for civilian clothes. The next three weeks were spent enjoying music, solitude, and bicycle riding in the countryside with Else. During one of these excursions they conceived their first child, Horst. Karl's ultimate aim was to marry Else after the war, so they were delighted later when he found out she was pregnant. Many soldiers realized the advantages of marriage over being single, including extra pay, rations, and greater privilege within their units, but the full extent of their actions were not fully appreciated until three and a half years later, when only those men with children were allowed to evacuate from the Courland peninsula.[46] His timing to take his leave couldn't have been better also, as the most famous Soviet counterstrike of the war was about to unleash against his comrades in Stalingrad.

The Encirclement

Relatively weak Rumanian, Hungarian, and Italian armies held the northern and southern flanks outside of Stalingrad. Due to the alarms being raised by the Rumanians of strong enemy forces building up opposite their northern front, Hitler ordered a restored XLVIII *Panzerkorps* sent to counter the threat.

Mechanized elements of the 14th, 16th and 24th *Panzer* Divisions were told to disengage from fighting in the city; refuel, rearm, and make their way towards the endangered areas.[47] With completion of this order the 36th *Panzer* Regiment fought in all the major sectors during the Battle of

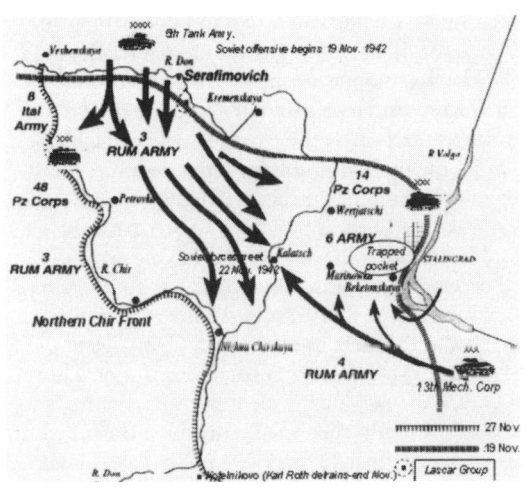

Stalingrad: The Encirclement

Stalingrad, including the southern advance in August, support of the attack on the central landing stage in September, was the first unit to reach the Volga during the assault on the northern factory districts in October, and now in November the defence of the northwest front. The entire fate of 6th Army was entrusted to the decimated tank companies extricating themselves from the street fighting in Stalingrad.[48]

After the vicious battles fought in October most of the 36th *Panzer* Regiment's tanks were in need of repair and fuel before they could make the 60–80 mile advance to the northwest. Therefore, some of the tank companies made for the workshop centre of Aksay, located along the southern Stalingrad rail line.

By November 11th the unit was broken down into the following three battle groups: one tank company (Bremer) and the majority of the workshop company, as well as the headquarters company, remained in the city attached to 'Group Seydel', while the remainder were ordered to provide security for XLVIII *Panzerkorps* (Heim),[49] less one company assigned to division headquarters reserve at Army Group Don (General Major Bassler). Some regimental tank platoons heading towards the northwest were collected by the commander of the VI Army Corps and rushed into defensive positions along his front when the Soviet attacks began. By the time the remainder reported to XLVIII *Panzerkorps* (made up of the tank regiments of the 14th and 22*nd Panzer* Divisions and the 1st Rumanian Armoured Div) in the 3rd Rumanian Army sector, they comprised only 35 tanks, of which only seven were *Panzer* Mark IV's. This meagre force deployed just behind the front opposite Serafimovich and was expected by Hitler to repulse any Soviet attack on the Rumanian positions.[50] Leo Schwarz was assigned to XLVIII *Panzerkorps* and told to report to the Rumanian sector, giving this account of what happened to him on that fateful grey morning of November 19th:

> We were ordered to move out of the street fighting in Stalingrad in November, and support the Rumanians defending the city to the northwest. Our company had only 5 tanks and these were in bad need of repair, with mine being the only one running. The next morning our feet were covered in oil and stuck to the bottom of the floorboard of the tank. An oil line had broke and was leaking all over the inside. I informed my superior officer I was going to find a repair station and have the problem fixed. The first mobile repair section we met was too busy to help and I was waved off. The second repair station also could not help, but I drew luck at the third workshop reached, as these were engine mechanics having the tools and expertise to fix the oil leak problem. They were very cordial, telling me to get some sleep in the maintenance shed while they worked on the vehicle, and that they would wake me when it was ready. The next thing I remembered was a Rumanian soldier shaking me awake, and talking excitedly as he waved a map in my face. I thought it was just a hysterical lost Rumanian soldier and rolled back over to get some sleep. But the soldier insisted, grabbing my things, and pulling me out of bed. He said to me in broken German something about the Soviets, and a big enemy offensive was coming this way. This was November 19th. Just then I heard the tack-tack-tack of the Soviet sub-machine gun, (which had a lower staccato sound then the German equivalent). I ran out the door and was astonished to see the maintenance section that worked on my tank already packed up and ready to move off. They said they repaired the oil line, but that I was on my own now. I yelled for them to give me some gas

because the tank was almost empty. One of the mechanics kicked a jerry can of petrol off the side of his truck as they sped away, and my crew filled the tank in record time. We then sped off, following as close as we could the convoy of vehicles in the maintenance section. Our tank was one of those later incorporated into the 1st Rumanian Tank Division until we were recalled to Stalino to reform the regiment.

When the Soviet Army's grand counteroffensive began the Germans expected a Soviet winter offensive similar to the one the year before, but the strength and timing of the assault took them completely by surprise. The Soviets massed 1 million men, 13,500 guns and mortars, 100 rocket launchers, 900 tanks and 1200 aircraft.[51] The Rumanians fought well for the first two hours against opposing Soviet infantry, but when enemy tank brigades began to pour through their lines they broke in disorganized flight.[52]

The XLVIII *Panzerkorps* was ordered to attack northwest against the greater of the two Soviet pincers pouring over the Don. Elements of the 36th *Panzer* Regiment were the first units to engage the enemy and in two days 35 T-34's were destroyed.[53] The following is an after action report from the 36th *Panzer* Regiment:

> At 1600 the Rumanian regimental commander advised that a Soviet unit was pushing thru towards our positions. Several tanks were put in position but no enemy was observed. Shortly later, enemy tanks were again reported... Tanks were again dispatched, but perhaps German reconnaissance vehicles were mistaken for Soviet tanks.
>
> Shortly after dusk, a battery reported shooting at some tanks, which were apparently not stopped. Two tanks were dispatched. At 1800 a Rumanian officer appeared at regimental headquarters and reported that Rumanian troops were trapped and cut off without supplies. His request for tanks could not be granted because of the growing darkness...throughout the night the battle raged throughout Ssadowoje. To the north and east, as well as in the village, machine-guns and rifles were fired, forcing the regiment to strengthen its guard posts. At dawn reconnaissance showed the area around Ssadowoje to be full of the enemy.

In the process of this Soviet assault, four Rumanian infantry divisions were surrounded near Raspopinskaya.[54] The commander of the encircled group was a well-respected Rumanian General named Mihail Lascar. The Lascar Group held out for five days until surrendering with only 4,000 troops making it back to the safety of 22nd *Panzer* Division. The annihilation of the Lascar Group was an example of errors to befall the larger Stalingrad pocket later on. Told to stand fast by Hitler and that supply was coming by air, and a relief attempt imminent, the only survivors were those willing to disobey orders and breakout on their own.[55]

By this time the second Soviet pincer ruptured the southern flank below Stalingrad, again breaking through the Rumanian Army sector. Five enemy tank corps sent spearheads racing for the Don bridgehead of Kalach with the aim of encircling all the German forces inside the city. The Kalach Bridge was captured intact on November 23rd by a Soviet battle group, severing 6th Army's supply line. That night a link up was made between the two converging Soviet pincers, effectively trapping a total of about 269,000 men inside a 40 by 20 mile cauldron inside Stalingrad.[56]

96 ONCE I HAD A COMRADE

Ju-52 transport planes unload supplies on an ice-covered airstrip. Air re-supply was critical and the only means of relief for the besieged troops trapped inside Stalingard. As long as the airstrips were still operating, some wounded and specialists could be flown out (including the commander of the 36th *Panzer* Regiment, Willi Langkeit). After January 1943, only the small airstrip in the city was still in use, and only occasional parachute drops made. (KA)

With the loss of Kalach, the Germans inside the pocket began to set up a defence line facing west. The 36th *Panzer* Regiment only had one tank unit (Company Bremer) still in the pocket, and to better defend their sector they were given rifles and machine pistols and made infantrymen. The headquarters and workshop companies were located in Karpovka, close to the area of any breakout attempt. In anticipation of a coordinated counterstroke, radio contact was established with other separated units of the division (Group Brese) outside the ring. The belief that Army high command was in control of the situation, and that a relief effort was under way, staved off any alarm or panic within the units. All concerns now turned to preparing for a concerted effort to fight their way out of the pocket.[57]

Outside the ring battle groups of all the German divisions were strung out and splintered by the massive Soviet juggernaut. After failing to sustain a successful counter-attack of the enemy, those tanks still operating with XLVIII *Panzerkorps* were disengaged and brought west over the Chir River. The corps commander and former 14th *Panzer* Division commander, General Heim, was then relieved of command by Hitler, put on trial and imprisoned. He was perhaps the most famous of the 36th *Panzer* Regiment's Division commanders, due to his being made a scapegoat by Hitler for the encirclement of 6th Army at Stalingrad. An excuse was now needed by the Fuhrer to explain why an entire German army was now surrounded and faced with annihilation.[58]

The headquarters of XLVIII *Panzerkorps* was transferred on December 4th and reorganized at Nizhna Chirskaya, a vital bridgehead 25 miles from the closest entrapped unit of 6th Army. The few remaining tanks of the 36th Regiment left on the upper Chir River were incorporated into the 3rd Rumanian Army, and sustained their defence.[59] The entire Don-Chir sector was turned over to the

THE DREAM IS DESTROYED   97

resourceful command of General Walther Wenk and Colonel Karl Hollidt, and was known thereafter as Group Hollidt.[60]

Rear echelon troops and scattered remnants of other decimated units held a tenuous position from the upper Chir River (Group Hollidt), along the Don (XLVIII *Panzerkorps*) to Kotelnikovo (LVII *Panzerkorps*). Confusion reigned as local commanders tried to organize a continuous line of defence. Countless historical passages describe a scene of near hysteria in the rear areas as rumours spread of the Soviet breakthrough. Karl stepped off the troop train into this confusion after returning from leave and only the disciplined supervision of seasoned non-commissioned officers like himself kept the entire Don Front from collapsing.[61]

Initially, enlisted men returning to the front were thrown together into *ad-hoc* formations and committed to battle regardless of training or skill. This practice ceased after heavy losses were incurred and the need for individual skills and experience became more apparent. Local commanders were in dire need of armour and Karl's rank and experience repairing tanks made him a valuable asset.[62] Returning as many combat ready vehicles to service as quick as possible during this critical period earned him a promotion to technical sergeant (*Feldwebel*) on December 1st. Most likely he was placed in the division or corps workshops in Millerovo or Kotelnikovo, where 4th *Panzer* Army located its forward repair and supply depots. His exact location during this time is difficult to account for because of the confusion behind the lines, and the lack of any documented material concerning the placement of troops retuning from leave.[63]

A plan to relieve Stalingrad from the railhead at Kotelnikovo was already under way by the new Don Front commander, Eric von Manstein.[64] Manstein was engaged in the Crimea, culminating with the surrender of the Soviet fortress at Sevastopol. After this success his name was well known at the front and he proved himself capable of leading large formations, thus being a natural choice when Hitler ordered him to prevent a disaster on the Don Front, after Stalingrad was encircled. He immediately consolidated the front lines and planned a relief attempt to link up with Paulus's 6th Army.

The remainder of the 36th *Panzer* Regiment's tanks that were being repaired in Aksay also operated out of Kotolnikovo, under the command of Bernard Sauvant. Group Sauvant, with roughly 18 tanks and an infantry company, had retreated from Abganerovo to Aksay and then fought a calculated withdrawal down the railway line leading into the town. This battalion formed the core around which the future regeneration of the Regiment was derived.[65]

Paulus implored Hitler to be allowed freedom of movement as early as November 20th and almost everyone in the high command agreed that the longer the Army Group stayed put, the less chance they had for a successful breakout. Already 6th Army was dangerously low on food, ammunition, and petrol.[66] The mainstay of the troops diet within the city was a pea soup that was sometimes enhanced by the addition of horsemeat.

Hitler was almost swayed into ordering the retreat until once again the ill-advised Goering stepped in. He said the *Luftwaffe* could supply Paulus with the 550 tons of supplies per day that were necessary to sustain the Army, not taking into account the weather or Soviet fighters. Much to the chagrin and protests of other high-ranking officers, Hitler once again agreed to Goering's proposals. So incensed by the decision to hold fast and be supplied by air, General Seydlitz-Kurzbach demanded Paulus disobey orders and actually issued orders for his divisions to pull back on the northwest tip of the pocket, to make ready for a breakout attempt. This was never done and the 6th Army's last hope was von Manstein's promised relief-attack.[67]

The forces available for this attack consisted of such weak remnants of 4th *Panzer* Army that Manstein requested immediate reinforcements. It took 18 days before the two divisions allotted for the attack arrived in Kotelnikovo.[68] A third division[69] that completed the LVII *Panzerkorps* was diverted away by Hitler and did not arrive in time to make a difference.[70]

The railhead at Kotelnikovo was a vital staging area for the relief attack even though it was 60 miles from Stalingrad. Manstein felt that an attack from this direction crossed fewer obstacles and was less conspicuous. Group Sauvant was now part of a larger force (Pannwitz) that was ordered to provide a protective screen around the Kotelnikovo perimeter. Being one of the only armoured units in the area, it was assigned as an alarm battalion, and kept busy beating back repeated attempts by the Soviets to disrupt German preparations for the counter assault.[71]

Paulus is still today one of the most controversial figures associated with the Battle of Stalingrad. Some believe he only did what he was trained to do, follow orders, and that his army had not the supplies or energy to conduct a breakout. The opposing argument is that he waited too long in authorizing such an operation across the frozen steppe, and the result was the annihilation of 6th Army, and Paulus's surrender on February 2nd 1943. (FACP)

Manstein began his relief attempt on December 12th and dubbed it, "Winter Storm" (*Wintergewitter*). LVII *Panzerkorps* had 230 tanks between the divisions, and following this was a convoy of 800 trucks loaded with food, fuel, and ammunition for the besieged troops inside the pocket. Army Group Hollidt and XLVIII *Panzerkorps* was supposed to coordinate a left jab on the Soviet lines from Nitzne-Chirskaya, to divert Soviet forces from the main punch on the right. But XLVIII *Panzerkorps* had trouble just holding their sector from increased Red Army pressure from the northwest, and couldn't realistically act in an offensive capacity.[72]

As the attack ground forward across the frozen steppe the Soviets rushed in armoured reinforcements. Only twenty miles were gained in two days but this due mostly to the rough terrain, as enemy resistance was marginal at first.[73] On the third day of the assault an attacking force of 400 T-34 tanks was engaged near the town of Verkhne-Kumski, between the Aksay and Mishkova Rivers. That day 32 enemy tanks were destroyed and for the next three the winter tank battles continued. To break the deadlock Hitler finally released the 17th *Panzer* Division, but it was too late. Two bridgeheads were taken over the Mishkova River by December 18th, but 28 miles still separated the relieving force from the encircled pocket. It was Paulus's last chance to breakout towards LVII *Panzerkorps*.[74]

When Manstein's relief attack was twenty miles from the outer ring of the pocket the plan called for a second operation to go into effect, code-named 'Thunder-Clap' (*Donnerschlag*). When the code was given, Paulus was supposed to be ready to breakout towards the southwest, "sector by sector". Even though the LVII *Panzerkorps* still needed to gain ten miles before the code could be given, Manstein implored Paulus to breakout on his own initiative. So adamant was Manstein he flew his intelligence officer, Major Eismann, into the pocket on the 18th to try and convince and coordinate with Paulus. But Paulus said he needed six more days to get the Army prepared to move, and then reminded everyone that as of yet, Hitler had not given his permission to breakout. Paulus obeyed Hitler's stand fast order to the end, sealing the fate of the men trapped in the Stalingrad cauldron.[75]

The following day the Italian and Rumanian armies holding the middle Don area to the northwest of Stalingrad broke under the strain of another major Red Army offensive, code-named 'Saturn'. The poorly equipped satellite divisions folded exactly one month to the day of the original Soviet attack, and now strong enemy forces pressed south towards Millerovo and Rostov, trying to cut off Army Group A in the Caucasus.[76]

Severe pressure launched against Group Hollidt in support of 'Saturn' forced it to bend its left flank in, exposing a gaping hole in the front. The release of XLVIII *Panzerkorps*

Although Manstein was able to accomplish a stunning counteroffensive that retook Kharkov and destroyed the Soviet 6th Army in the spring of 1943, the previous December he failed to break through to the Stalingrad defenders. Hitler relieved him of command in March 1944 (along with von Kleist), after having numerous arguments over tactical and strategic decisions.

to assist the relief attempt now was quite impossible. In fact, 6th *Panzer* Division was disengaged from the relieving attack to fill in for the 11th *Panzer* Division, sent further west to stem the Soviet onslaught. Meanwhile, Manstein kept the remaining divisions of LVII *Panzerkorps* on the Mishkova River, all the while insisting Paulus do everything possible to expand the *kessel* (pocket) to the west and link up with the remainder of LVII *Panzerkorps*.[77]

Manstein called off the relief attempt on the 23rd and reluctantly began to fall back on Kotelnikovo.[78] Karl spent Christmas Eve 1942 staying warm under a tank, and watching the flashes of light from the futile battle being fought 18 miles away. Heinz Neuendorff, an officer of the 108th *Panzergrenadier* Regiment (Brese), was also depressed that Christmas outside Stalingrad. His brother, Peter, was the adjutant of the 36th *Panzer* Regiment, and trapped with the headquarters company inside the pocket. For a month the two bothers communicated over wireless radio expressing a gamut of emotion as the drama wore on. Until all communication was lost, Peter Neuendorff continued to express hope and total preparedness for a breakout attempt by the Regiment. Now on Christmas day 1942 the two brothers said their farewells, as one went on to survive the war, the other dying in Soviet captivity.

With Army Group Don now in full retreat all hope of extricating 6th Army was lost forever, and the worst days of the siege began.[79] The regimental commander of the 108th *Panzergrenadier* Regiment, von Brese, was a good friend of the Neuendorff's and recounted the emotions of the men trapped in the pocket. These letter extracts are from a report he wrote in December 1992 for the fiftieth anniversary remembrance gathering of the Stalingrad tragedy, entitled: *Unsere Kameraden in-und Ausserhalb des Kessels von Stalingrad* ['Our Comrades in-and outside the pocket of Stalingrad'].

A letter from a young officer during the terrible pocket battle, a warning to his father. His father was an *Oberst* on the German staff. Writing of the foreboding he encountered at Stalingrad, and a warning for the future progress of the war:

> I think we can hold on for eight more days until it is all over for us. I don't want to analyse the reasons for or against our situation here. The reasons are useless, but if I can say something to everyone who is in charge of others: They must keep their head up, and be alert that a much bigger hell is approaching the fatherland. The battle at the Volga should be a warning, do not let this omen be cast to the wind.

Another letter to a soldier's wife:

> You are going to be 28 and still very beautiful, I am glad I can still give you this compliment. You will miss me, but do not lock other humans out when I am gone. Let a few months pass, but not longer. Gertrud and Claus our children need a father, and remember you must live for them. Do not fuss over me, you are young and at this age you can forget things.

Another soldier:

> If you could see us, me and my comrades you would think that death incarnate were standing in front of you. If you only see the wounded and sick in front of you, even the strongest natured man would lose hope and fall in with despair.

THE DREAM IS DESTROYED 101

From about 380 men who were once very proud going into battle, we are now only 100 human-like creatures, made out of skin and bones, hardly surviving the hunger and pain. The hunger is so painful we search the pockets of dead Soviet soldiers to look for bread. Here and there we find some flour and cook it without salt to have something at all to eat.

A Major to his wife:

And the relentless battle continues, God only helps the brave. We do not know what is our fate but pray we have the strength to see it through. History will show that the German soldier in Stalingrad fought tenaciously like no other before. After all is over, it is the job of the mother to instil this memory in her children, and not to forget.

Goering's airlift was a dismal failure despite the efforts of the brave aircrews involved. Supplies were falling to dangerous levels with only about 90 tons of materials on average ever reaching the pocket. The Saturn offensive uncovered two major airfields behind German lines forcing the aircraft to carry even more fuel and less tonnage than before, to make the round trip.[80] Because of the shortages, 6th Army soldiers were dying of malnutrition and exhaustion at alarming rates.[81]

Pannwitz was a German commander who commanded Russian Cossacks who had traded sides. Bernard Sauvant's battle group that escaped encirclement at Stalingrad operated with Group Pannzwitz outside of Kotolnikovo in December 1942. (FACP)

Even though the suffering continued, Paulus refused surrender terms on January 9th. The following day a huge Soviet offensive got under way to reduce the pocket. The 36th *Panzer* Regiment and the remnants of 14th *Panzer* Division were forced out of the Karpovka valley towards Pitomnik airfield. By the 14th the airfield fell, effectively ending the airlift campaign with only the smaller field at Gumrak now remaining open.[82] Even though the airlift attempt failed to sustain the garrison, it still saved the lives of 42,000 sick, wounded, and specialists[83] who were flown out before the last airfield inside the city fell.[84]

Kampfgruppe Pannwitz defending Kotelnikovo provided a screen for the remains of LVII *Panzerkorps* to evacuate through the day after Christmas. The Red Army was in the process of beginning a wide encirclement of the town, forcing Hoth to gradually pull back. By the time this retreat stopped, 4th *Panzer* Army was on the Sal River, sixty miles behind Kotelnikovo.[85] Further withdrawals brought Groups Hollidt and Pannwitz to defensive positions on the Manych River, just outside Rostov. Army Group A was still extricating itself from the Caucasus, making holding open the Don bridges here vitally important.[86]

As Paulus's forces were pushed just outside the city centre on January 25th, another ultimatum was given urging surrender. All messages of any importance were sent to Supreme Headquarters for Hitler's personal scrutiny and he strictly forbade any capitulation. Since radio communication was still possible, Paulus was well aware of the strategic consequences he faced. Those still fighting in the pocket were in agreement that resistance was still necessary to draw off as many Soviet divisions as possible (90 Soviet divisions were estimated to be besieging the pocket) and secure the safe escape of Army Group A through Rostov. The surrender terms were rejected again.[87]

In the middle of January, von Brese was with the 108th *Panzergrenadier* Regiment, outside the pocket and wrote the following recollection of those days:

> One day I was sitting on a chair I had fashioned out of a snow bank in front of my foxhole, enjoying a mid-day nap in the sun, when someone kicked my feet. In the sun glare I made out an officer's hat, but I couldn't see his face. The voice told me it was Hauptman von Schaumburg, and he looked similar to a Christmas nutcracker! He had his riding boots and full dress adornments on. I asked him, "What are you doing here?" He answered-"I found out from staff headquarters you were out here and wanted to talk to you. I fly out tomorrow". "To where?" "I finished my division adjutant paper last week, and just received an operation order to join an infantry division in the pocket". "Are you completely mad?" "Do you not know what is going on inside the pocket at Stalingrad?" "Who was the bright individual who issued that order?" "Does your infantry division still exist?" "You shouldn't follow orders that are a death sentence" "Go tell your pilot you are not going to fly in this weather, we are in the middle of January and very soon there will be no pocket. As soon as you arrive you may as well join the P.O.W. march". "I talked with him for about two hours, but to no avail. Since I couldn't see him changing his mind, I prepared him for what to expect inside the pocket. I gave him warm clothes, including a fur hat, driver's greatcoat, and new boots. The last we heard from him he was the regimental adjutant to Oberst von Schlieben, and then we lost contact.

Von Brese goes on to say in this report that the soldiers in the pocket felt betrayed, and the only thing that kept them going was a sense of duty and the will to survive. To bear the load many soldiers found in their troubles faith in God, but others began to despair and loose hope of ever getting any outside help. The younger men began to talk as if God had forsaken them and were angry at the army command, as well as at the enemy. The older men were not so fast to lose hope and two men in particular within the 36th *Panzer* Regiment stood out during this desperate time. Alois Grafner and Valentin Einwich, both members of the workshop company, reassured their comrades that faith in God was all the men had left to believe in. Each made a promise on Christmas Eve that if they survived the ordeal they would erect a monument to God and the Virgin Mary, and to those lost in the battle at Stalingrad in 1942–43. They did not survive the ordeal but friends who saw the drawing of the monument on a piece of cardboard vowed to erect it, and today in the Franconian town of Sommerach the 'Madonna from Stalingrad' monument stands and attests to the brave sacrifices and horrible suffering endured so far away. The inscription on the statue reads from the gospel of John: 'Light, Love and Life. Christmas, Stalingrad, 1942'.[88] These soldiers were two of the

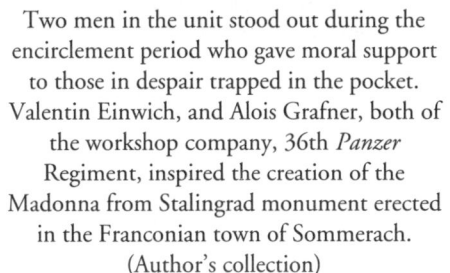

Two men in the unit stood out during the encirclement period who gave moral support to those in despair trapped in the pocket. Valentin Einwich, and Alois Grafner, both of the workshop company, 36th *Panzer* Regiment, inspired the creation of the Madonna from Stalingrad monument erected in the Franconian town of Sommerach. (Author's collection)

The 'Madonna from Stalingrad' memorial is dedicated to the memory of those caught up in the battle, and to those who became prisoners of war. Grafner and Einwich designed the memorial on the back of a piece of cardboard, but when they did not survive captivity, their comrades who kept the drawing of the monument completed it. (Author's collection)

unfortunate men of the Stalingrad pocket to die in Soviet captivity, and of the 90,000 prisoners taken by the Soviets at the end of the battle, only around 5,000 ever made it back to Germany.[89]

After Manstein's relief attempt failed at the end of December and Pitominik airfield was captured, there was no reason to prolong the agony. But Hitler refused to end the tragedy and allow Paulus to surrender, and the fortress fought on for another week.[90] What remained of the 14th *Panzer* Division was set up during the final days of January on the western edge of Red Square, only metres from Paulus's headquarters in central Stalingrad. Due to an order out of his headquarters the Division was to be 'disbanded'. This severely affected the unit's morale because the few supplies that were getting through came from division level rosters. The written off soldiers now had to fend for themselves, and a colonel (Col. Gunther Ludwig, commander of the 4th *Pz.* Art. Rgt., 14th *Pz* Div) with the Division saw no further use for resistance. He secured a truce with the local Soviet commander late on January 30th that originally was only supposed to be a cease-fire until 4 a.m.

Once Paulus's adjutant, General Schmidt, heard of the arrangement he agreed to meet a Soviet representative and surrender his headquarters at 8 a.m. The newly appointed Field Marshal Paulus (promoted by Hitler in the hopes he would realize no German Field Marshal ever surrendered and therefore commit suicide) only surrendered his immediate staff that day, and those still fighting in the northern pocket held out until February 2nd. The once proud German 6th Army, the 14th *Panzer* Division, and the remnants of the 36th *Panzer* Regiment surrendered that day to begin a new life of survival in Soviet captivity.[91]

To achieve a successful counter-thrust and win back the initiative on the Southern Front, Manstein advised Hitler to fall back on the Mius winter line of 1941–42. Only begrudgingly did Hitler permit the withdrawal, even though Soviet pincers were now driving on the Dnepr crossings at Dnepropretovsk as well as on Kharkov and Zaporoshe. Those 36th *Panzer* Regiment tanks still with the remnants of the Rumanian 3rd Army and Group Sauvant, now operating under Group Mieth, were ordered to abandon Rostov and take up positions behind the Mius Line.[92]

The Soviet formations were lured on by the German retreat and began to over extend their resources. Nevertheless, a newly formed SS *Panzerkorps* was disrupted at Kharkov and General Lanz, the commander of the unit defending the city, evacuated it on February 16th (Lanz was later dismissed as the scapegoat for the abandonment of Kharkov, just as Heim was earlier).[93] This went against the express orders issued by Hitler to hold the city as a fortress at all costs. This growing distrust of Hitler's ability to control the battlefield, and the resulting outright disregard of orders by his commanders, was one of the most significant consequences of Stalingrad; the entire German general staff realized the fallibility of their leader, and as a result of the losses incurred in the city so did the German people.[94]

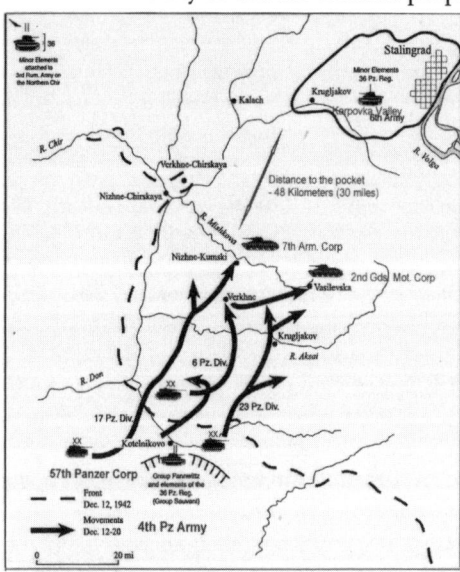

Stalingrad: The Relief Attempt

Hitler decided to visit Manstein at the front on the 17th and stayed for three days to instil his 'not one-foot-back order', demanding the recapture of Kharkov. Manstein assured Hitler that he was about to launch his planned counter-attack, but argued that he needed more time to ensure the timing of the assault was exactly right. The crisis was almost over and the reorganization of the 36th *Panzer* Regiment was also ordered this day, at the assembly area and railhead centre at Stalino. All former tank crews and personnel were recalled from their various units and reformed into two battalions of four companies each.[95]

With the Soviets only 25 miles from the Dnepr River, Manstein

THE DREAM IS DESTROYED   105

launched his first attacks on the 20th. The daring operation was a big success and within two days it was the Soviet 6th Army that was sealed off and eventually annihilated. The Germans were back across the Donets by the end of the month with Kharkov recaptured on March 11th.[96] Aiding in the attack on Kharkov were the Tiger tanks of *Abteilung* (battalion) 503, recently arrived to the southern theatre of operations. Even though the new tanks had teething and other mechanical problems, the high velocity 88mm main gun proved lethal against the T-34.[97]

General Guderian gave a speech in Vinnitsa on March 9th and stated; "the task for 1943 is to provide a certain number of *Panzer* divisions with complete combat efficiency to make limited objective attacks. 1944 must be the year for large scale offensives." Even though Hitler did not heed this advice and planned another large-scale summer offensive at Kursk, he agreed to overhaul the tank divisions. The 36th *Panzer* Regiment was thus sent to France in April to rebuild the 14th *Panzer* Division, and by early summer all the tank divisions on the southern front were reforming and upgrading their equipment.[98]

PART IV
THE NEW 14TH PANZER DIVISION

CHAPTER IX

Rest, Recovery, and Return to Russia

March–December 1943

A new 14th *Panzer* Division was ordered to reform in Brittany, France, in April 1943. Refitting the unit's tanks to pre-Stalingrad levels however proved difficult, because Germany's war production capability could not keep up with the losses sustained on the Eastern Front and in North Africa. The introduction of new designs limited the amount of spare parts available for the older models already in the army's inventory, and only 10 replacement tanks on average were delivered per month to the unit until the end of the summer.[1]

The rebuilding of the 36th *Panzer* Regiment was supposed to be on the design of three tank battalions, but actual combat strength within them existed on paper only. A new general-purpose tank was needed to compete with the Soviet T-34, but the 1st Battalion did not upgrade to the Panther as planned until July, and it was unclear when 2nd Battalion was going to be brought up to full authorized strength either.[2]

The 3rd Battalion authorized by the reorganization plan consisted of a mixed battalion made up of two companies of *Panzer* Mark IV tanks and two of assault guns (*Sturmgeschütz*).[3] This Battalion was originally to consist of Tiger tanks, but it was decided to organize the new heavy designs into independent detachments instead. Combat commanders of the Eastern Front who were consulted, stated that the big tanks operated best in non-integrated units that sometimes became attached to a division.[4]

When the men of the 36th *Panzer* Regiment moved through Germany on their way towards France, Karl secured four days of marriage leave in Schweinfurt. Else and he were married in a church near the city centre on April 4th, with only a few relatives and friends attending the ceremony. Karl wore his army uniform displaying the tank assault badge he was awarded at Stalingrad. Their wedding picture also depicts the fact that Karl was suffering from dysentery and stomach pains, and since Else was almost four months pregnant, she too did not feel well. Even though the reunion was less than romantic, both were thankful that Karl made it out of Stalingrad alive and that he was scheduled for a summer of rest and relaxation, in the sunny wine region of the Loire Valley in France.[5]

The 14th *Panzer* Division took up residence in the area of Angers, a city that once held the strongest medieval fort in France. Local communities on the outskirts of town provided housing to the German units and soldiers who experienced the horrors of the Eastern Front found the climate, scenery, food and champagne a welcome change from the combat environment in Russia. Karl said he and his comrades felt very comfortable billeting in French chateaux and castles, making them feel as if they were on a holiday.[6]

Karl and Else Roth were married in Schweinfurt on April 4th 1943. The photograph reflects that Karl was just returned from Russia and was not feeling well, and Else was five months pregnant by this time. (Author's collection, courtesy E. Roth)

Many of the regimental personnel were allowed to have their girlfriends and wives visit them in France as long as the soldier covered the travel arrangements and expenses. Karl on the other hand told Else not to waste her money, and that if she did travel to Angers he said he would, "put her on the next train back to Schweinfurt". She was not pleased with his response and being upset stopped writing him for a while. Karl apologized and took leave for almost a month in July, travelling by train to Schweinfurt to be with her.

During that summer, non-commissioned officers proved invaluable in forging the new formations into a viable fighting force able to meet the hardships of combat on the Eastern Front. The old hats of the regiment like Karl (awarded the Iron Cross 2nd Class on May 21st) were responsible for training the new soldiers, and a relentless programme was initiated to get the new recruits up to speed. Numerous challenges arose while conducting this training due to the lack of equipment, vehicles, fuel and ammunition shortages that limited live fire exercises.[7]

German troops stationed in France during the war also were responsible to repel any Allied invasion attempt against the continent, and were ordered to lay mines and strengthen the so-called 'Atlantic Wall'. But this Maginot Line of the West was porous, with large areas left undefended. No serious work was done to reverse the situation until after the division was gone, and Rommel took command of Army Group B, in November 1943.[8]

The Allies planned to first cripple Germany's war production capability, before attempting any cross-Channel invasion, and the ball-bearing factories of Schweinfurt provided a tempting target. American war planners thought that a successful raid on the city could reduce German armament production by 30%. The first of 40 bombing raids against the ball-bearing industry got underway on September 17th, and to date was the largest and deepest missions conducted against Germany.[9]

Rest and relaxation was the order of the day during the summer of 1943 in Angers, France, as the 36th *Panzer* Regiment attempted to recover from the German defeats at Stalingrad. Severe losses in North Africa and Russia meant that equipment and replacements were late in coming. Tank crews found themselves without vehicles and new tank models like the Panther were ultimately delayed for almost a year. (Courtesy K. Brier)

British warnings to the Americans that they were going to suffer unacceptable losses if they went ahead with daylight bombing raids, unaccompanied by fighter protection, went unheeded. The resulting air battles became some of the most violent and disastrous of the war. In one day, a total of 60 American planes and 600 airmen were lost on the Regensburg-Schweinfurt raid alone. 80 high-explosive bombs destroyed or badly damaged 663 machines in Schweinfurt, striking the main bearing factory of Kugelfischer. The tank barracks that housed the 36th *Panzer* Regiment's reserve battalions was also hit, along with the city centre.[10]

Karl was allowed leave home a few times that summer but departed Schweinfurt before the bombing raid on the 17th, and birth of his son. Else delivered her baby four days before the attack and was still in the hospital when the air raid hit. The maternity ward was evacuated to the safest place in the hospital, the coal cellar, making beds available for the incoming wounded. Here in the dark,

An American Eighth Air Force bomber drops high explosive and incendiary bombs on Schweinfurt's ball-bearing industry facilities, the beginning of no fewer than 40 such raids during the war. Immediately plans were put in place to break down the ball-bearing factories, dispersing them into the countryside disguised as farm buildings and deep within the forests. This tactic worked well enough that Germany's supply of bearings was never really crippled by the Allied bombing. (FACP)

The tank barracks in Schweinfurt housing *Panzer* Regiment reserve battalions (*Panzerabteilung* 25) was hit along with the city centre during one of the deadliest American air raids of the war, conducted on September 17th, 1943.
(Schweinfurt Archives)

dank, cellar she waited out the bombing, with every explosion kicking up the coal dust in the room. Everyone was choking and suffocating for air, including her new baby, named Horst. Covered with coal dust he developed an asthma problem as a result of the exposure.

As soon as Else was discharged from the hospital she evacuated to the forested area outside of Schweinfurt. Her family owned a small piece of land on a ridge that overlooked what was called the 'Holle', or Hell valley. Here she expected to find some safety from the bombing, but to her dismay found hundreds of the city's

Schweinfurt's other barracks was also struck this day, two miles from the main *Panzerkaserne* on Niederwerner Strasse. (Schweinfurt Archives)

residents camped out in the forest. She did the best she could under the circumstances to find shelter and food for the newborn baby, awaiting an end to the bombing.

The leaders of the German armaments ministry, and the citizens of Schweinfurt, were shocked that such a major effort was made so far into their homeland. Immediately plans were put in place to break down the ball-bearing factories, dispersing them into the countryside disguised inside farm buildings and within the forests. This tactic worked well enough that Germany's supply of bearings never was really crippled by the Allied bombing. Another major raid known as 'Black Thursday' to American aircrews pounded the city again on October 14th.[11]

When the attacks on Schweinfurt resumed, the flak guns were set up and firing very close to Else's property on the ridge, so close in fact some stray rounds actually came down in the area. She was worried for Horst whose respiratory problem was getting worse, and was very scared at the constant sound of the flak guns firing and bombs exploding. At Karl's insistence she was evacuated from Schweinfurt, moving 30 miles northwest to the outskirts of the town of Bad-Neustadt. It was now up to the troops at the front to provide the moral support for those being bombed in the rear.

Because Karl was a non-commissioned officer in the German Army, Else was given transportation and set up with a family in the town. Her first experience under this programme, called '*Mutter und Kind*' (Mother and Child) was not very hospitable. Her host family did not like the fact that German citizens were being dumped into their care, and the locals threw rocks at her windows. She was told to use a well in the city square that was polluted, and food was so scarce she was forced to resort to drastic measures in order to survive that winter. One letter to her

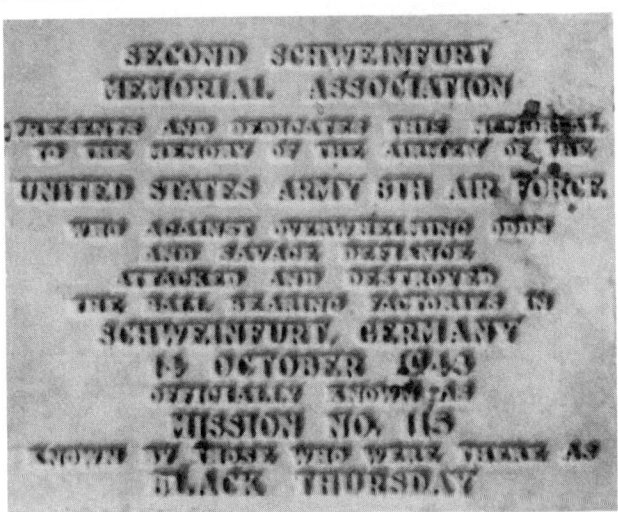

The leaders of the German armaments ministry, and the citizens of Schweinfurt were shocked that such a major effort was made so far into their homeland.. Another major raid known as 'Black Thursday' to American aircrews pounded the city again on October 14th, 1943, the beginning of 40 such air raids.
(Author's collection, courtesy Dan Byrd)

Civilians dig through the rubble of Schweinfurt after the August raids, salvaging anything of use. (Schweinfurt Archives)

husband about these horrible conditions and she could have had the *SS* police sent to the town. But Else bore these difficulties in silence and it paid off for her. Seven weeks later when she was at this well, a local man told her not to use it. He then inquired if she would come and work for him at his farm (the largest in the village) as he was a widower. His oldest son was killed in the military and his youngest son needed caring for. Else accepted and this proved a much better arrangement for her and her son. They were well taken care of here and her sister eventually also joined them, staying until the war was over.

The German high command felt in September that the 14th *Panzer* Division was combat-ready and able to be recommitted to battle. In the beginning of the month, 600 new vehicles were delivered to the Division from units in Norway, and others came from the 25th *Panzer* Division. The arrival of these replacements brought mobility back to the 36th *Panzer* Regiment and a reorganization of all the units in the Division was conducted. Even though some of the best tank crews of the regiment were transferred to help form the *509th Schwere* [heavy] *Tiger Abteilung* (battalion), by the middle of the month they were almost up to full-authorized strength.[12]

Leo Schwarz was selected as a driver and provided a humorous story about the arrival of these new vehicles to the regiment:

> I was ordered to deliver new vehicles to the unit from the railhead-outside of town. Most of the other soldiers were enjoying time off and I was not happy about being on delivery detail, having to drive the new tanks off the trains and then back to their companies. Fortunately we stayed close to the rail station at a hotel, being reimbursed from the military for the expense. On one of my last

trips into town another sergeant talked me into visiting the local French brothel. We started to drink and began to talk to the girls, but this man got so drunk he slapped the madam and also one of the girls. I ran out the door and back to my hotel room before the police arrived! I was fortunate no one recognized me as the other sergeant was arrested and severely punished for the incident.

A last and final reorganization was conducted on October 1st and 2nd and those personnel still on leave were called back to the unit. Orders were then issued to the 36th *Panzer* Regiment to prepare for a move back to Russia, sending a sense of foreboding through old and new soldiers alike. The revitalized 14th *Panzer* Division was officially dedicated on the 6th and another week passed until the Division commander (General Sieberg) was summoned to Hitler's headquarters, receiving his final instructions and ultimate destination. He was told that the fate of Germany was being decided in the fields of the Ukraine, and that the 14th *Panzer* Division was being committed to the defence of the Dnepr River. Three days later the first trains rolled east.[13]

The Germans were routed during the first stages of the massive Red Army offensive against the so-called 'Eastern Rampart' and the Dnepr defence line. The high command falsely believed that this natural and man-made barrier could stem the tide of the mighty Soviet horde approaching from the east. The quality of Red Army tactics was much improved, and most tank units did not even wait for their pontoon bridges or engineers, crossing the river at twenty-six points by using fords or makeshift ferries. Stalin promised the highest reward in the Red Army to the first soldiers to cross the river, and Hitler countered with a proclamation of his

The 3rd Battalion of the 36th *Panzer* Regiment was outfitted with new *Sturmgeschütz* assault guns that were better armoured after Stalingrad, prepare to move to the trains bound for Russia. These assault guns have skirting added to their sides for extra protection against light anti tank weapons.

own, saying that if his troops repulsed the Soviets, they would be awarded the Iron Cross.[14]

By the time the 14th *Panzer* Division detrained in Kirovograd, after being delayed when the rail lines were severed north of the town, the Soviet Army was already in control of the large supply depot at Cremmenchug. Also under enemy control were Bukrin and Zaporozhye, with a major effort underway to break out of the Dnepropretovsk bridgehead.

Hitler insisted that the manganese deposits and bridgehead at Nikopol and the iron ore at Krivoi Rog, be held at all costs. To enable this effort the 14th *Panzer* Division was attached to the XL *Panzerkorps* (1st *Pz.* Army) and ordered to prevent any enemy breakthrough between 8th and 1st *Panzer* Army in the Krivoi Rog sector.[15] Action commenced on the 28th when Group Langkeit (36th *Panzer* Regiment) attacked due east from Kirovograd, towards Dnepropretovsk. Their instructions were to keep open the road and rail lines leading east, and for the next month they became an alarm unit, stopping Soviet penetrations inside the Kirovograd-Dnepropretovsk-Krivoi-Rog triangle.[16]

Most of the combat that followed that month contributed to the tactics developed for the new mixed 3rd Battalion. The assault guns were found to operate best when supporting the tanks in the offence, but proved optimal when used with *Panzergrenadiers* in the defence. The mixed battalion accounted for 211 tanks destroyed up until December 1st, with assault guns accounting for only six of the total.[17]

The great city of Kiev was recaptured by the Soviets on November 6th, after a three-day battle. During this period Karl and his command staff set up their workshop in Krivoi Rog and found tank recovery efforts to be difficult. An officer of the 36th *Panzer* Regiment wrote that in 35 working days 52 *PzKpfw* IV's, and 74 assault guns of the 3rd Battalion were repaired by the workshop company located at Krivoi Rog.

Hitler declared that the fate of Germany was being decided in the Ukraine, ordering the 14th *Panzer* Division back to southern Russia in the autumn of 1943. They were being sent to the 'Eastern Rampart', a fifteen-mile stretch of land on the east bank of the Dnepr River that was denuded of anything the Soviets might use, all destroyed or moved west under Goering's scorched earth policy. (Courtesy L. Schwarz)

I first met Karl Brier in 1998 at a 14th *Panzer* Division reunion. He was able to provide me with a brief interview and also sent photographs taken while he served as a member of the 36th *Panzer* Regiment's workshop company. I had the opportunity to interview Herr Brier again in the summer of 2003, and this second meeting provided many personal anecdotes about the last two and half years of the war, and his photographs were invaluable to the story. Brier before the war was a mechanic and registered electrician with the company Bosch, but in 1941, the social stigma of being a young man and not serving at the front was too great for him, and he joined the infantry. After his training in Ansbach he was sent to North Africa and fought with the famed Erwin Rommel all the way to El Alamein. In November 1942, he was recalled to Berlin (flying aboard the same plane as Rommel) because he was a registered electrician who was to learn the wiring on the newest tanks being developed. In the summer of 1943, in Angers France, he was assigned to the 36th *Panzer* Regiment's workshop company as a mechanic, driver, and electrician. As a mechanic, he operated a generator and was a driver for Major Bernard Sauvant, the 36th *Panzer's* Regimental commander in Courland. He also reported to my wife's father, Karl Roth, at the regimental headquarters level. Therefore, his personal association with my father-in-law, like Leo Schwarz, was important in understanding the type of leader he was. Brier explained that Roth was all business, the professional soldier, and a very stern disciplinarian. He replied that in wartime, you might not always like what you are ordered to do by your officers and NCOs, but the camaraderie of those experiences created a bond between the survivors that lasted well beyond those years. I am indebted to Mr Brier for enabling me to accurately as possible describe the events that unfold in the next few chapters. The last question I asked Brier was what statement he wanted to make in this book. He thought about it for a few seconds and then said, "just tell the truth about the German soldier's sacrifice at the front, that we were disciplined but honourable men".

(Courtesy K. Brier)

The Soviets pressed everywhere along the front, and any immobilized *Panzer* that couldn't be immediately recovered from the battlefield was in danger of falling into enemy hands. The Regiment was responsible for too large a front (95–125 miles) and reassigned constantly inside their area of operations. Making matters worse the heavy hauling equipment promised from army and corps maintenance units never arrived, due to the loss of Kiev, which interrupted rail service south along the Dnepr.[18] The *Panzer Instandsetzungs-Abteilung* (Karl's command section) could not increase the recovery vehicles needed by the workshop company, in spite of a major effort, because they were employed mainly in the areas around Zhitomir and Kiev, along the severed rail line.[19]

Christmas 1943 was relatively quiet for the Regiment set up in Kirovograd, especially when compared to the previous year outside Stalingrad. But the silence was deceiving, because the Soviets were known to be reinforcing and consolidating their positions, preparing for a great winter offensive meant to clear the Ukraine all the way to the foothills of the Balkans.

CHAPTER X

Year of Fate (1944)

The New Year was only five days old when at 6 a.m. the Soviets launched the first phase of their winter offensive against Army Group South. Their objective was to eliminate Kirovograd and drive as far as Uman, threatening the rear supply base for 1st *Panzer* and 8th Army. The 36th *Panzer* Regiment was deployed east of the city and directly in the path of the oncoming Soviet attack. In two days of hard fighting outside Kirovograd, the 14th *Panzer* Division along with two neighbouring divisions (10th *Panzergrenadier* Division and the 376th Infantry Division) fought tenaciously against the overwhelming odds of the 2nd Ukrainian Front.[1]

The 36th *Panzer* Regiment was exhausted after three weeks of combat and continuous use as a fire brigade, stopping enemy penetrations up and down the line. They were forced to fall back abandoning Kirovograd, and by January 10th almost 5,000 troops were encircled in the village of Lelekovka (including elements of the 36th Regiment and 14t*h Panzer* Division). Only through desperate measures, and aided by the 3rd *Panzer* Division, did this group manage to breakout to the west. Resistance grew as more German reinforcements arrived and the Soviets began to outrun their supply trains. So for the time being, no major breakthrough was achieved on the Dnepr Bend.[2]

Numerous arguments arose during this period between Manstein and Hitler about pulling back towards the Bug River, and withdrawing from the Dnepr positions. Manstein argued that an elastic defence system with room to manoeuvre was needed, and if this request was turned down, he expected Hitler to issue reinforcements to hold the line. Hitler promised reinforcements, but he refused to give up any of the Ukraine, not even the dangerous salient centred on the town of Korsun. This bulge stuck like a balcony into the Red Army positions, and Manstein warned Hitler that the two corps now occupying positions inside this area, made a tempting target to the Soviets. Hitler countered that if any successful counter-attack of the Dnepr front were expected, it had to come from this area, and therefore couldn't be abandoned. Thus the stage was set for what was known as the Cherkassy pocket to the Germans, and the Korsun pocket to the Soviets.[3]

A terrific artillery barrage of German lines pre-empted the second phase of the Soviet offensive on January 24th. A successful breakthrough conducted from the Bukrin bridgehead against 1st *Panzer* Army, and another out of Cremmenchug directed at 8th Army, made it possible for the Soviets to send two armoured pincers streaming south, and north, respectively. Two inner spearheads launched from Kanev and Cherkassy closed five days later on the town of Svenigorodka-Schopala, trapping both the XI and XLII Army Corps, a total of about 56,000 men.[4]

There was great consternation within the Regiment about the coming Soviet offensive because the line they were holding was so weakly held. The Division was broken down into mobile battle groups and again used in defensive hedgehog positions. But huge gaps existed between these hedgehogs, and alarm units (Group

36th *Panzer* Regiment combat vehicle strength during the winter of 1944 was at an all-time low. The early thaw in February quickly refroze around their tank treads, cementing them into the ground. Many of the tanks were then abandoned, as the Germans fell back into Rumania during that spring (14th *Panzer* Division emblem located on the right-side hull of this *panzer*). (Bundesarchiv)

Langkeit) were formed to patrol the front and aggressively engage the Soviet spearheads (including elements of the 36th Regiment and 14t*h Panzer* Division).

These advance groups played a key role in stopping the first Soviet assaults, but at noon on the 25th the situation changed.[5] Soviet mechanized attacks splintered the front line and Karl and his command section were separated from the Regimental headquarters. The story is told that he was lost behind Soviet lines for seven weeks, and that they had last seen Karl that winter in a German tank, but that he returned in the spring with a Soviet one! Moving behind enemy lines he played dead, wore Russian clothes while near enemy troops, or travelled by night through the forests. He also befriended a Soviet deserter who became a *hilfilswillige* (volunteer or auxiliary) in the command section.

Most Ukrainian civilians moving west with the Germans were terrified of Stalin or assumed Germany was still going to win the war, and thousands attached themselves to German units as auxiliaries. Karl's volunteer was named Ivan (his real name), and he earned the trust of those in the command section by cooking, driving, interpreting, and hunting for food in the forest. He was a trained engineer and instrumental in getting Karl through the Soviet lines, remaining under his care until the end of the war, when he was evacuated to northern Germany.[6]

Manstein immediately began to plan a counterstroke to blunt the Soviet encirclement and free the entrapped divisions. Orders were issued to XLVII *Panzerkorps* (3rd, 11th, 13th and 14th *Panzer* Divisions) fighting further north, to assemble

Karl Roth was separated for seven weeks behind enemy lines during the time of the encirclement at the battle of Korsun, in January–February 1944. I was told that he was last seen that winter in a German tank, but that he showed up in the spring driving a Soviet one! His story was that he ate and moved with Soviet troops during that time, lived in the forests, all the while keeping his face down, not talking near enemy soldiers, and wore their uniform. Roth returned to German lines with the help of a Soviet defector (whose name was Ivan), and is seen here changing out of his Soviet uniform. Ivan remained with the unit even after the redeployment to Courland that summer, and was evacuated to Germany in April 1945. Roth was missing for so long his superiors sent another half portion of his identification disk to Else again, saying that he was missing and presumed dead. (Author's collection, courtesy E. Roth)

near the southern breakthrough point at Zvenigorodka. At the same time orders were also issued to III *Panzerkorps* (16th and 17th *Pz.* Div's followed by the 1st *Pz. SS Div. Leibstandarte*, and Heavy Tiger Battalion Bake with 34 Tigers and 47 Panthers) to disengage there as soon as possible and head south, forming the second pincer of the counter-attack.[7]

The forces inside the encircled pocket equalled about six full divisions, including combat and support troops.[8] Command of this battle-group fell to the control of General Stemmerman (commander of XLII Corps), and was known as *Kampfgruppe Stemmerman*. He immediately requested air resupply and evacuation of the wounded, reorganized the units inside, and restored order.[9]

The airlift campaign lasted from January 28th until February 20th employing 1,536 planes. This was an enormous effort by the *Luftwaffe* considering only 850 planes were used during the entire Stalingrad encirclement. Priority was given to the delivery of ammunition and fuel to be used during the breakout, with no thought of fighting a protracted siege inside the pocket contemplated.[10] Parachute drops of supplies requested by Stemmerman on the eve of the attack further bolstered their reserves. The Cherkassy airlift was considered a success with supplies so plentiful in the early days of the pocket, the Soviet emissaries sent over with the surrender terms were offered champagne and cigarettes![11]

Unlike the Stalingrad leadership, command and control inside this pocket was cohesive and organized. To prepare further, the forces inside adjusted their positions to provide the closest jump off points to friendly lines. Units were redeployed at night from the front to the rear of the pocket behind an anti-tank gun screen. Kept constantly moving, the troops were not allowed to make permanent defensive positions, and to allow greater mobility all non-essential items were discarded or destroyed. Stemmerman's skilful plan even required a breakout attempt at night, led by point units allowed only unloaded rifles with fixed bayonets.[12]

The relief attack to link up with the pocket began on February 1st with XLVII *Panzerkorps* striking toward Schopala to relieve the pressure on XI Corps. III *Panzerkorps* followed suit on the 4th as planned, attacking from the southwest. The assault had barely gotten under way when a warm front transformed the ice-covered steppe into a sea of mud. The heavy tanks as well as the other vehicles were mired in the morass and the attack ground to a halt. III *Panzerkorps* drove almost twenty miles into the enemy ring and shot up almost 80 tanks, but twice that distance still separated them from the edge of the pocket.[13]

Mud not only delayed the counterstroke, but also the preparedness for the breakout inside the pocket as well. Stemmerman rejected orders to put the plan into effect on the 10th as impossible to comply with, due to the road conditions. Enemy attacks against the pocket and dogged resistance by the Soviets against the relief forces, delayed any coordinated operations with III *Panzerkorps*. Korsun and its airfield were abandoned on the 13th, with the loss of 3,000 wounded falling into enemy hands. The troops moving west out of the city had to be repositioned, further delaying the breakout by three more days.[14]

With XLVII *Panzerkorps* securely blocked by strong Soviet mechanized forces, the responsibility of resuming the advance fell to III *Panzerkorps*. The new attempt began on the 11th, but bogged down three days later as fierce fighting developed in

The chocolate bar contained in these metal boxes was Karl Roth's most favoured item provided in the Combat Package food kit, and survived on them during the early days of the encirclement at Cherkassy. The emergency iron ration consists of biscuits, cold meat, preserved vegetables, coffee, and salt. The Close Combat Package contained chocolate bars, fruit bars, candies, cigarettes, and biscuits. Each member of a mechanized unit received one combat or iron ration, but it could only be consumed by orders from above, and only in emergency situations. Besides my father-in-law's identification disk, and photographs, this box is the only item that remains from the war years. (Author's collection, courtesy E. Roth)

YEAR OF FATE (1944)   123

When I asked my wife during our first meeting what unit her father belonged during the war, she produced this identification disk. It shows his blood type (A), unit (HQ 36th *Pz.* Rgt.), and number within the Regiment (47). Twice, Roth's wife, Else, was presented with half the disc, informing her that her husband was dead. (Author's collection, courtesy E. Roth)

The wristwatch Hitler gave to his troops in 1943–44. A regimental survivor said that during the encirclement at Korsun they were none that grateful when a canister dropped by parachute supposedly holding food, fuel, and ammunition instead contained only wrist watches and medals from Hitler. (Author's collection, courtesy K. Brier)

the town of Lysyanka, twelve miles from the southern edge of the pocket. Manstein realized this was as much as could be done to reach Stemmerman's entrapped forces and the time to urge a breakout had come. Stemmerman, on hearing Manstein's order, cut radio communications with Supreme Headquarters and gave the breakout code of 'freedom' to his commanders. The attack was set for the early morning hours of the 17th.[15]

In coordination with the breakout, more pressure was put on Lyssanka from outside the pocket by 1st *Panzer* Division and the heavy tanks assigned to *Kampfgruppe Bake*. Dr. Bake's Tigers knocked out 130 Soviet tanks on their drive to reach Hill 239, a rendezvous point with the units moving west. A swift flowing stream called the Gniloy Tikich just outside Lysyanka, was a raging torrent that prevented any further progress, stopping them six miles from the nearest point units inside the pocket.[16]

Stemmerman ordered the forces inside the pocket to prepare all day on the 16th for that night's fateful attack. After midnight, three columns moved west in three successive waves, protected by rear guards. At 4 a.m. contact was made between Stemmerman's armoured advance columns (of which *SS Wiking* Division was strongest) and the tanks of III *Panzerkorps* in Lysyanka. But not all the soldiers attempting to breakout were as fortunate as the advance units. When the morning light exposed the infantry and support troops on the open steppe, the Soviets realized what was happening, wreaking havoc on the columns. Panic engulfed these troops as they were pursued by Soviet tanks, and in their haste to get across the Gniloy-Tikich, many flung themselves into the icy water. Many of these soldiers drowned or died of exposure on the opposite bank of the stream. General Stemmerman, who was with the rearguard, was also killed and his body lain out in a barn complete with medals and his orders.[17]

In total over 30,000 men escaped out of the 55,000 trapped at Cherkassy. 5,000 men were killed or captured during the breakout attempt and the remaining died either during the opening battles, or were wounded and left behind. Those who survived were sent to recover from their ordeal at reception camps north of Uman. The Soviets declared after the battle that they crushed all the German forces inside the pocket and that all attempts at piercing their ring were futile. This assumption has since proven false, as more than half the besieged troops managed to successfully break out.[18]

After the debacle at Cherkassy the 36th *Panzer* Regiment's first order of business was to refit their decimated tank companies. They were so weak in armour that the 14th *Panzer* Division was once again a tank division on paper only. Since being committed to battle at the end of October the Regiment lost 44 tanks, 37 assault guns, and 3 flame throwing tanks. This represented roughly three-quarters of their original strength. Also, 1st Battalion was still being refitted with Panther tanks and was not available for combat.[19]

Once the conclusion was reached that no further replacements were forthcoming from Germany intensive repair work began on all the available vehicles. Those tanks not in the best conditions were cannibalised to ensure the fielding of complete combat worthy vehicles. Karl Brier told an interesting story about he and his friend's experience trying to secure a piece of captured enemy equipment:

> An American GMC truck sold to the Soviets was abandoned in no-mans-land and stuck in a field of mud. Moving under the cover of darkness we crossed the field and began working on the vehicle. One of us performed repairs on the truck while the other stood guard. The battery had been shot out, so we left and returned with a spare. The next problem was that the American posts were on the opposite side of the battery! We solved this problem too, but it took all night. As the sky lightened with the arrival of morning the Soviet shelling and firing began. We started up the truck but now found the GMC gear shifter was also different than European models, but we found that when being shot at and shelled by artillery, you can figure things out fairly quickly! Under dangerously close fire we drove the truck out of the muddy field.

This American truck was so well liked in the workshop company it was sent all the way to Courland from Rumania, and was involved in another episode with Brier's friend, Leo Schwarz, near the end of the war:

> I was driving the same American GMC truck [that Brier salvaged] whose differential had broken. We needed an entire new replacement for the differential but

Workshop company soldiers relax during the reorganization period conducted in Rumania in July 1944. After being re-supplied with vehicles and brought up to strength, soccer games, field parades, and paperwork were the order of the day.
(Courtesy L. Schwarz)

the mobile repair section that was in the area did not have the parts for an American truck. I spent the next three days cannibalising the broken down vehicles in the area to get the parts I needed, sometimes under direct fire from the enemy. When I got back to the workshop company I had to report to *Feldwebel* Roth to explain why I was absent for two days. Roth commended me on the repair job and for saving his favourite GMC truck. I was then given supplies and told I was being awarded a badge from Regimental headquarters for bravery under fire!

This recovery work ceased on March 5th when the 2nd Ukrainian Front opened their next major offensive.[20] The Soviet objective was to take Uman and roll up the German defences between the Bug and Dneister, driving all the way to Kishinev if possible inside Rumania. Simultaneous attacks drove a wedge between 6th and 8th Armies, and all available reserves within these units were brought forward to stem the Soviet advance. The Regiment assisted the attempt to relieve the enemy pressure put on their neighbour, the 376th Infantry Division, by dedicating 7 *Panzer* Mark IV's and 3 assault guns to the counter-attack.[21]

Before any counter effort got under way though, the Red Army offensive swept all before it. The Regiment began a 45-mile fighting retreat from Jakaterinopol to behind the Bug River barrier at Pervomeisk. The enemy offered no respite during this retrograde action and kept up constant air attacks and artillery fire. The weather also vacillated between snow blizzards, rain, and mud. The mud in particular slowed mechanized movement and prevented all but horse-drawn *panje* wagons from making any real progress.[22] Karl Brier's recollection of this retreat was that the early thaw refroze around their treads, cementing the tanks into the ground. Many were abandoned where they stood, and the tank crews took with them only the essential items they could carry.

The Soviets reached the Dniester on a 50-mile front and Uman fell on the 10th. At Kaments-Podolsk, 300,000 men of 1st *Panzer* Army again were entrapped. The

Karl Brier photographs his comrades in the workshop company, posing next to their towed mobile field generator. These soldiers wear assorted uniforms including field-grey work uniforms and old style field caps, and black field trousers, accompanied with the long sleeved work sweater and M1942 field cap. He operated and maintained this 25-kilowatt generator, used for power driven tools, powering lights, and recharging batteries. Brier in this photograph is dressed in a black two-piece coverall and field cap.
(Courtesy K. Brier)

principles developed by Manstein during the Cherkassy pocket operation: decisive action, effective air-supply, and sound leadership, again proved instrumental in saving this force from the fate of their Stalingrad comrades.[23]

Even though this encirclement occurred well to the north of the Regiment's defence line on the southern Bug, they were still in a serious position of being trapped themselves before they could move behind the protection of the Dniester. Pervomeisk was reached on the 14th and to save time units of the 14th *Panzer* Division were rail-headed west to the major road and rail junction at Balta. Most crossed the Dniester at Rybnica by the 21st and the bridge over the Bug was destroyed behind them. The Soviet attacks by this time were so great three *Panzer* divisions were moved north out of the Crimea, to prevent Rumania and its oil fields from being overrun.[24]

Supplies at this time were scarce because of the break in supply lines to the rear, and soldiers were hording and stealing from each other's units to get the equipment or material they needed. In Pervomeisk for example, Karl Brier was tried by a military tribunal and found guilty of not securing his *Volkswagen* that was stolen. His sentence was four months in the local prison, but he only lasted four days of incarceration before he was recalled to the Regiment, who were understaffed to begin with and ready to start their retreat once more.

It was around this time that Karl Roth re-emerged from enemy lines after his seven-week separation from the Regiment. He re-entered German lines through an *SS* division and immediately sought out supplies for his men.[25] Personally acquainted with a supply officer in the unit who was from Schweinfurt, he assumed he could find the provisions he needed there. Inside the supply room this *SS* officer had everything imaginable: ham, eggs, meat, wine, champagne etc. But when Karl asked for fuel, food, and ammunition for his men, the officer replied, "didn't you read the sign outside Karl, this is an *SS* supply room, it's not for the regular army". Karl was so outraged he drew his pistol and put it to the officer's head, saying " you are not only going to give me and my men what we need, you are going to pack it for us too!" One can only assume that the stress of being separated behind enemy lines for so long sent him over the edge, to the point of drawing his sidearm on an officer, but the really amazing aspect of this incident was that he got away with it.[26]

The 36th *Panzer* Regiment experienced a leadership change during March, as did all of Army Group South. The commander, Willi Langkeit, was transferred to *Panzergrenadier* Division *Grossdeutschland*, and the new 36th *Panzer* Regiment's commander was Major Bernau.[27] Hitler also replaced both Field Marshals Manstein (Army Group South), and Kleist (1st *Panzer* Army), during this period, stating to the former that, "the time for grand-style operations in the east…was now past".[28]

Heavy and desperate fighting slowed but could not stop the Soviet mobile troops and cavalry forces from seeping in on the exposed flanks. More valuable equipment that could not be replaced was lost, and another retreat ordered. New defensive positions were thrown together on the Cula River, and German troops once again turned to face the Soviet juggernaut.[29]

After crossing the Dniester at Rybniza, the 14th *Panzer* Division deployed northwest to defensive positions near Floresti. The Regiment was so under-strength (the 3rd Battalion could only muster 2 assault guns and 1 self-propelled gun) at this point they lost all offensive capability, with some crews transferring to the Flak Regiment because they had no tanks.[30] The workshop company was still up to strength, but there were no spare parts to repair the vehicles. This meagre force, backed up by the Tiger tanks of the *Grossdeutschland Division*, tried to halt the Soviet advance on Jassy.[31]

The Soviet attacks were beginning to ease after troops were siphoned off for the great attack being planned against Army Group Centre (Operation Bagration). 2nd Ukrainian Front went over to the defensive on May 6th and only minor probes thereafter were conducted against the German lines. After retreating almost 250 miles, the 36th *Panzer* Regiment was pulled off the line to rest and refit.

Until May 10th they underwent repair and training schedules near Jassy and Kishinev. Both were major logistics centres and the troops were well supplied there. Karl and the workshop company were then sent to learn how to repair Panther tanks, which the 1st Battalion was supposed to have received already, supplied by the 15th *Panzer* Regiment. Equipment was still in short supply, but these hardships did not compare with the extreme stress undergone during the retreat the month before.[32]

Karl Brier remembers one of the most humorous incidents that happened near here concerning the appropriation of supplies:

In Rumania, Karl Brier poses in summer uniform atop the flatbed railcar that will take the 14th *Panzer* Division north to the Baltic coast at the end of July 1944. The Division symbol can be made out below the rear window on the command car in the photograph. In movements of entire divisions such as this, the space occupied on the tracks, rather than the total weight shipped, was the important factor, due to intense enemy air attacks along the rail lines. (Courtesy K. Breier)

My friend and I happened to find a stash of light bulbs in a house that were boxed up and tagged to be picked up by the local NSDAP office. We were about to 'requisition' these items when we decided to wait and see what type of vehicle these Nazi officers were travelling in. The new tyres on the truck that arrived impressed us and while the driver was inside gathering the light bulbs, we jacked up the truck and stole them! We then buried the tyres in soft sand for a few days while waiting for the investigation into the incident to finally blow over.

This was a laughable incident, but also dangerous, as they could have been shot or severely punished for this. For example Brier's friend, Leo Schwarz, related how his new tools were stolen near Kirovogrod and he was given three nights of patrolling the lines for the infraction. The man with him (being disciplined for 'accidentally' discharging his pistol and almost killing an officer) decided to drink on the third night out, and Schwarz decided to join him. Never leaving their lines that night, they were almost too drunk to drive back to the workshop company the following day!

An armoured reserve was accumulated near Kishinev on the 10th using the tank regiments of four *Panzer* divisions, two infantry, and one paratroop.[33] They were to defend a precarious bridgehead over the Dniester at Dubossary and contain a 3rd Ukrainian crossing at Tirasopol.[34] The officers of the Regiment prepared for the anticipated enemy attacks from both of these areas by consolidating all their available tanks into one ready reserve.[35]

For the spoiling attack the 36th *Panzer* Regiment was partnered

The order to board the train cars is finally received by Brier and his comrades. Sp-trains (*Sonderpanzerzuge*) or special tank trains carried approximately 20 medium tanks, together with personnel and other equipment. The standard Sp train was composed of about 33 cars. Very heavy tanks such as the Tiger and Panther were transported aboard S-trains, or special trains, that usually carried between four to six Tiger tanks, and six to eight Panther tanks, interspersed with lighter equipment. (Courtesy K. Brier)

with the 103rd *Panzergrenadier* Regiment and both made contact with the enemy on the 13th. Two Soviet pincers were moving westward and the ensuing battle resulted in considerable loss to the regiment, as well as to the Soviets, and by May 30th the 3rd Battalion had only 1 *Pz* Mark IV tank and 2 assault guns operational. Pushing forward with the *Panzergrenadiers* supported by dive-bombers, artillery and rocket launchers, the task force moved forward towards Grigoriopol. By the end of the day the Soviet assault troops who began the attack were not only thoroughly defeated, but in some instances thrown back across the Dniester. After the battle, the 14th *Panzer* Division counted 3,000 prisoners taken and 7 tanks captured.[36]

Occasional flare-ups along the line by Soviet reconnaissance groups brought instant response from the Divisional battle groups. An example of this was the turning back of a major enemy probe north of Jassy on the 30th. During this attack Karl managed to stop the enemy tanks at a river crossing, and was awarded the tank destruction badge in gold. Awarded on August 1st, the decoration symbolized the destruction of five enemy tanks at close quarters.

My wife described the story she remembered her father telling about this incident:

> My father said the foliage along the rivers in Rumania was very thick, causing the Soviet tanks to sometimes approach a river crossing in single file. He was in charge of a small detachment, having only one tank and a few guns. He said he halted the column by ordering his men to fire all of his available weapons at once at the lead tank, knocking it out, and giving the enemy the impression they were more than they seemed. The follow on tanks were then destroyed with artillery, stopping the attack.[37]

YEAR OF FATE (1944)   129

Brier and his crew settle in for a long wait in the rail yard, until it is their turn to ride the tracks north. The summer weather in the southern theatre was welcome, especially after the harsh preceding winter. German railways generally were used jointly for military and civilian traffic, although military trains were given priority. Here a standard army troop train races by Brier and his bored looking team. Fortunately for them, the movement to Courland was uneventful, as they travelled through the hinterland of the Balkans and then into Germany, before continuing to the Baltic. (Courtesy K. Brier)

After this engagement the Soviets resorted back to minor probing and patrolling of the lines, allowing the Germans to cover the front with their infantry. Moving back behind the lines with orders to stabilize their sector, the *Panzer* regiment recuperated from the recent fighting. Fixed positions were erected, minefields laid, and ammunition and supply depots established.[38]

On June 24th, the same day as the massive Soviet offensive against Army Group Centre began the 14th *Panzer* Division was placed into army reserve. They were upgraded and reinforced at Husi in July, southwest of Kishinev. The Panther tanks of 1st Battalion were finally on their way from France, and the 3rd Battalion now had 35 *Panzer* Mark IV's, and 20 assault guns. This was more armour available to the unit since October of the previous year. The only deficiencies were found in the workshop company's lack of towing tractors for the new medium and heavy tanks.[39]

A major Soviet offensive against Army Group South was duly expected and constant preparedness was necessary. Training replacements and integrating the new soldiers kept the non-commissioned officers occupied. In fact most soldiers in the unit were too busy with organizing the new equipment, and were not that concerned when they heard of the attempt on Hitler's life, on July 20th.

But this event had fateful implications for Karl, and the destiny of the Regiment. As a direct result of the failed assassination attempt on Hitler, Guderian was made Army Chief of the General Staff. One of his first orders given was to transfer General Schörner's Army Group from Rumania to East Prussia.[40] Schörner was a stern disciplinarian and fervent Nazi, judged by some historians to be Hitler's most brutal Field Marshal (at the height of the fighting that summer, he issued a directive that any soldier found without orders behind the lines, "was to be executed on the spot"). By April 1944 Schörner was commanding Army Group South in the Ukraine, at which time the 14th *Panzer* Division came under his control.

The most potent divisions of this Army Group (including the 14th *Panzer*) were sent to the Baltic in July, to reinforce the remnants of Army Group North. Guderian intended these forces to be used to protect Berlin from the Soviet onslaught against Army Group Centre, but later events prevented this from materializing. Even General Beck, one of the July 20th conspirators against Hitler, made moving these troops out of the South Ukraine a top priority. He immediately ordered their transfer from Berlin when he heard that the bomb went off, although Hitler survived the assassination attempt, and Beck was subsequently arrested, tortured, and died at the hands of the *Gestapo*.

Nevertheless, Guderian succeeded in convincing Hitler to accept Beck's decision to move Schörner's forces out of the south, once he was appointed.[41] This decision (by Guderian) saved the 36th *Panzer* Regiment from being surrounded in Hungary with Army Group South during the winter of 1945, instead of moving north to the Baltic as they did. Here they fought one of the most heroic struggles of the war on the Courland peninsula, with the fortunate ones escaping to Schleswig-Holstein by ship, and the remainder surrendering to the Soviets on the last day of the war.

The 36th *Panzer* Regiment loaded onto trains in Jassy on August 6th for the trip north, following behind 23rd *Panzer* Division and *Panzergrenadier* Division *Grossdeutschland*. The going was slow but uneventful, as the travel was mostly through the hinterland of Hungary, into Germany, and then through Poland. Being squeezed on two fronts and under constant allied bombing attacks, the infrastructure of the country was falling apart, and the rail lines were crippled. Karl

Depending on terrain and enemy bombing conditions, division railheads were located about 25–50 miles from the front, and established as far forward as possible. All troop movements were under the direction of the Transportation Headquarters master, who controlled the area of one or more Railway Directorates. They issued the orders as to how and when the troops were to be transported. Brier said that the movement was slow through the Carpathian Mountains and on numerous occasions, they were ordered off the main rails and onto side spurs, awaiting other trains and convoys using the same tracks. (Courtesy K. Brier)

General-Major Willi Langkeit began his military career with the 36th *Panzer* Regiment as a battalion commander in 1938. He was acting Regimental commander on December 12th 1942, while fighting inside the Stalingrad pocket. Three days earlier, he was awarded the Knight's Cross. After being evacuated on one of the last flights out of the Stalingrad pocket, he was promoted to command the new 36th *Panzer* Regiment formed in the summer of 1943. He assumed command of the *Grossdeutschland Division* in 1944, fighting in Romania, the Baltic, and East Prussia. Highly regarded as a great leader, Langkeit was respected by those who survived with and served under him. (FACP)

Brier said that at one point the troops detrained and road marched to another railroad depot, beating the train there! And on a few occasions the troops had to literally push the trains onto rail spurs, to make room for others coming in the opposite direction.[42]

Moving into Germany the men in the Division stopped for two days in Dresden, their home-station. Karl and some members of the Regiment secured a few days leave home also. He met up with Else in Bad-Neustadt, seeing his son Horst for the first time, and as fate would have it, the last time until after the war was over.

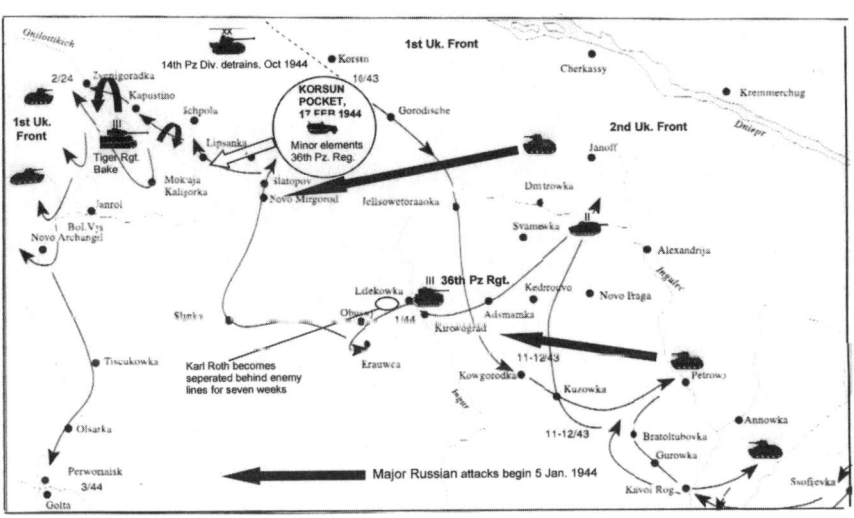

Retreat on the Dniepr

CHAPTER XI

Heroic Stand

Courland (August 1944–May 1945)

The Soviet offensive that began in June and destroyed Army Group Centre (Bagration) also isolated Army Group North against the Baltic, north of Riga. The 16th and 18th Armies were cut off by the 1st and 2nd Baltic Front attacks, and pocketed in Latvia and Estonia. With the assistance of the redeployed *Grossdeutschland* Division, newly arrived from Romania, the Red Army advance towards the coast was held in check.

When the Soviet attacks began, 3rd *Panzer* Army units abandoned their fixed positions and retreated south, jamming the roads to the front. Enemy pockets left behind in the forests after they outran their supply trains began to harass the vehicle columns moving up for the counter-attack. After they detrained in Tauroggen, the 36th *Panzer* Regiment deployed to Kursenai (northwest of Schaulen) and dispatched two companies of tanks to assist the infantry in clearing these areas. The unit then moved forward to prepare for the operation under incessant Soviet fighter, bomber, and artillery attacks. For this reason the Division flak batteries were assigned to operate with the Regiment's armour and infantry companies, providing much needed ground to ground and ground to air support.

In early August the 3rd *Panzer* Army (holding positions in Lithuania) was ordered by Hitler to launch an attack to re-establish contact with Army Group North. This operation, named *'Doppelkopf'* was the last major successful offensive operation the Division and Regiment participated in. The 14th *Panzer* Division was attached to XL *Panzerkorps* with orders to support the heavier attack of XXXIX *Panzerkorps*, towards Mitau (Jelgava).[1] Their first mission was to secure the road and rail lines leading north, but preparations for the operation took longer than expected because of logistics problems that slowed the delivery of food and fuel.

Firepower within the 36th *Panzer* Regiment on the other hand was never stronger (1st Battalion, under Molanari, fielding 73 Panther tanks and the other two battalions having 124 Mark IV's and assault guns between them), being further increased on August 22nd when the 510th *Schwere Panzer Abteilung* (heavy tank detachment) was assigned to the Division. The Battalion, commanded by Major Gilbert, had 20 operational heavy Tiger tanks. The big tanks with their awesome firepower restored much needed morale back to the Regiment six days after they took heavy losses during their advance to the jump off positions for the counter-attack.

The counter-attack finally began on the foggy morning of the 16th. The Soviets were quick in transferring their forces to the main point of the assault and resistance was fierce. Three days later the Regiment was engaged in heavy fighting north along the Ventos canal with 15 enemy tanks knocked out during this engagement, although casualties were high on both sides. The 108th

HEROIC STAND 133

Oberst Willi Langkeit was transferred as commander of the 36th *Panzer* Regiment in Romania, and sent to lead the *Panzergrenadier* Division *Grossdeutschland* in Courland. He is seen here conversing with the crew of a Panther tank while commanding the *Grossdeutschland* Division towards the end of the war. He eventually made it to the West and surrendered to the Allies. (Bundesarchiv)

Panzergrenadiers that were supported by Regimental tank companies suffered the most loss. Their commander, adjutant, battalion commander, and his replacement were all either killed or wounded while dismounted and away from their vehicles.

With XXXIX *Panzerkorps* stalled 22 miles from Army Group North's front lines, a second attempt at breaking through towards Tukums began. With the help of naval gunfire from the German destroyer *Prinz Eugen*, Group Strachwitz, eventually succeeded in making contact with 16th Army units on the 20th and taking the town. Meanwhile, south of this attack the 36th *Panzer* Regiment advanced 60 miles north of Kursenai to the town of Akmene. Here they were told to dig in, hold off all enemy attacks to displace them, repair the damage to their tanks, and wait for reinforcements.

In six days of combat the battle strength of the Regiment was exhausted and due to the dense terrain, the vehicles by this time were broke down and worn out. The new Panther tanks were especially vulnerable to engine, drive gear, and transmission problems, whereas the *Panzer* Mark IV's and assault guns experienced extreme wear on their steering columns and brakes. Much praise was awarded to the repair crews and experienced non-commissioned officers like Karl Roth, who once again improvised solutions to keep as many tanks as possible running.

The lull that settled on the Baltic front at the end of August was not expected to last long. General Schörner reported to Hitler on August 27th that without reinforcements, he did not think 18th Army and Group Narva could hold out, once Soviet attacks resumed. Guderian also advised Hitler to pull the 18 divisions out of the Baltic and reinsert them in East Prussia. So adamant was Guderian, he issued orders on September 6th to begin preparations for such an evacuation. But Hitler heard none of it and the only concessions Schörner received was the transfer of the 14th *Panzer* Division to Army Group North.

The 36th *Panzer* Regiment left the 3rd *Panzer* Army area on the 12th and 13th, moving through Riga towards the east. After some delay due to the Panther tank tracks being too wide for some of the small bridges in Courland, and other routes found, they dug in on the Riga-Vecumi highway (*rollbahn*). Near Erlgi their orders were to prevent any enemy penetrations towards Riga, and to act as an emergency fire brigade to plug the gaps in the line.

The expected large scale Soviet attack on Army Group North began on September 14th. Their objective was to eliminate the German battle groups in Estonia, take the ports, and surround Riga if possible. The 36th Regiment and 14th *Panzer* Division played the critical role during this attack, preventing any further Soviet penetrations towards Riga from Modohn. Near Klapi, a valuable crossroads, the 2nd Battalion with mixed tanks and assault guns was attached to the 108th *Panzergrenadier* Regiment. The 1st Battalion with their Panther tanks assisted the 103rd *Panzergrenadier* Regiment at another crossroads to the northwest.

The Soviet attacks were so strong by the second day Schörner asked Guderian to once again urge Hitler to begin evacuations from Courland, before they were surrounded. Hitler only allowed a slow retreat south and west, from one defensive position to another.

Command and control problems arose during the battle when the tanks of the 36th *Panzer* Regiment and vehicles of 2nd Battalion were mired in swampy ground. Drawing enemy fire, heavy casualties ensued causing the commander to request orders from Regimental headquarters. The Regimental commander (Bernau) replied that he was not responsible for the 2nd Battalion, that they should find a way out of their situation any way possible, and then discontinued radio transmissions! It is interesting to note that this Regimental commander did not last long, and was replaced in October by Major Sauvant, the 2nd Battalion commander of Stalingrad fame. This incident, and the fact the supply situation was still unchanged, severely frustrated the units capabilities of a cohesive defence. Despite these problems, the line held, and the Soviets shifted their attacks to a new sector south of Riga.

Supplies were making their way to the front lines by air transport, ship, and over the land bridge created by 3rd *Panzer* Army at Tukums. But the distribution system used by the army slowed down the delivery to the combat units. Food and fuel came from the 16th and 18th Army depots, whereas spare parts for the vehicles came by way of Riga, and 3rd *Panzer* Army. Once they finally reached the troops fighting at battalion level, the food, fuel and ammunition was transported forward using converted self-propelled artillery guns. Needless to say, many of these big guns became targets of opportunity to Soviet observers.

Karl visited the city of Riga in early September with his command staff and commented on how attractive Courland was, which varied from scenes of sandy beaches to farmland and forests. With German names like Frauenburg and Hasenpoth, he felt at home on the Baltic coast. Most of the population spoke some German and by any means it was an improvement over the hostile Ukraine and

HEROIC STAND 135

Karl Roth enjoyed the change of scenery on the Baltic coast and hospitality of the populace to that over the South Ukraine. He was now promoted to *Stabsfeldwebel*, or Master Sergeant of the Regimental headquarters staff section, in charge of the workshop company. Soon the Regiment had their backs against the sea, and nowhere left to retreat, being isolated on the Courland peninsula until the end of the war.
(Author's Collection-Courtesy E. Roth)

growing uncertainty in Rumania. The danger on this front though was just as real and maybe even tougher, as it seemed the Soviets never ran out of fresh troops to throw at their defences.

Another emergency developed on Riga's southern defensive line when the enemy began attacking north, from Jelgava. Since the 14th *Panzer* was now the sector's fire brigade, they were rushed towards Kekava on the 17th to meet the latest Soviet advance. Their orders were to halt the attacks and close the penetrations by a counter-attack, but disengaging from the present fighting in the eastern sector proved difficult, and was only done in piecemeal fashion. Therefore, the Division committed its regiments into battle in integrated units including pioneers, flak,

As an emergency response unit, the 36th *Panzer* Regiment was to anticipate where along the front the next Soviet blow was going to fall, and then send a battle group to the crisis point and stop it. Panther tanks, mixed in with *Panzer* Mark IV's, assault guns, and Tiger tanks, succeeded time and again at stopping the enemy thrusts and re-establishing the lines. The crew of this Panther uses a range finder to calibrate its gun. (KA)

artillery and *Panzergrenadiers* as they arrived at the new positions. In the next few days they moved from one crisis point to the next battling overwhelming odds. The Soviets attacked with shock groups of heavily mechanized forces, backed up by artillery and air support. As 16th Army's emergency response unit, the *Panzer* group's strategy was to anticipate where the next blow was going to fall, and then send a battle group to the crisis point and stop it. Almost all the crossroads south of Riga and in the Baldone area were flashpoints for these firefights against Red Army tank, assault-guns, and anti-tank gun teams. This fierce fighting sapped the strength of the all ready worn out Regiment with most battalions now down to half strength.

They were encouraged at the end of September when the regiments from 18th Army began to arrive from the northern evacuation of Estonia and the Soviets finally stopped their attacks. The northern groups allowed by Hitler to evacuate by sea and land, made it out of the Soviet trap barely in time. The first elements of III *SS Panzerkorps* reinforced the Regiment on the 23rd, discouraging any additional attempts to take Riga from the south.[2]

The Soviets instead shifted their forces further west, preparing another offensive for October meant to drive all the way to the Baltic sea-coast. A period of calm descended on the front before this attack and the Division was placed into reserve status near Kekava. The Regiment used this period of inactivity to inventory captured vehicles taken in the previous battles around Riga (110 tanks and assault guns were counted, of which only 23 were usable), and to repair damaged equipment.

Meanwhile the enemy built up their forces in the Schaulen pocket area, and unleashed a tremendous offensive against 3rd Panzer Army on October 5th. The 14th *Panzer* Division was instructed that day to leave Riga and march hastily west, to prevent the Soviets from breaking through the land link near Doblen. The Soviets superiority in numbers punched holes in the thinly held line, overrunning the isolated hedgehog positions held by the *Panzergrenadier* Division *Grossdeustchland*. The strength of this division forced the Soviets to avoid taking them on directly, and instead they sent their armoured thrusts towards the sea on both flanks. Riga was abandoned without a fight as the Division tried to move to their new positions supporting 3rd *Panzer* Army. Their progress was hampered by the multitudes of refugees crowding the roads and the inability of the new Panther tanks at keeping up with the faster moving older models.

It was not until noon on the 6th that they reached the town of Autz, where they were scheduled to load onto trains to Preekuln. Once near the town, the sounds of the ferocious battles being fought to the south were heard, and Soviet attacks along the roads intensified. The train transports came under direct attack and although saved from destruction, were not utilized for the move to Preekuln. Because of these heavy assaults the Regiment used side roads to advance the remaining distance to their assembly areas.[3]

Their orders were to link up with the *Grossdeutschland* Division, re-establish a continuous line of defence, and prevent at all costs the capture of the ports Memel and Libau. For Karl Roth and the 36th *Panzer* Regiment, the long months of constantly retreating were over, and with their backs to the sea they began preparing a deliberate defence of the Courland peninsula.

The Six Battles of Courland

The Soviet attack that began on October 5th quickly overran the main roads leading north between Memel and Libau. The enemy, carrying sub-machine guns and riding atop tanks, broke through south of the 14th *Panzer* Division's positions at Skuoda, and all contact with the *Grossdeutschland* Division was now lost. Not being strong enough to engage the enemy at this point, the 14th *Panzer* Division forces already on the scene decided to wait for the 36th *Panzer* Regiment's tanks to arrive.

All the available armour was sent to the southeast sector of the line on October 8th between Skuodas and Preekuln.[4] A defensive line was set up facing east and two companies of combat engineers arrived to fortify the crossroads, erect barbed wire obstacles, and mine the river fords. A string of outposts and strong points developed, but the forested areas were left mostly undefended due to the lack of infantry units available. The enemy took advantage of the situation, infiltrating their own troops into the gaps. By dusk the wooded areas were retaken, but attacks by Red Army infantry forces began again the next morning.

The First Battle of Courland began on the 16th when strong German counter-attacks destroyed large parts of the Soviet spearheads. Even so, during this heavy fighting the 103rd *Panzergrenadier* Regiment located on the southern most point of the line was separated and under heavy pressure. Vigorous attempts to re-establish contact with the lost unit were made, but it was not until an infantry division arrived that they were relieved.[5] The 36th *Panzer* Regiment was further reinforced on the 15th and 16th by *SS* Division *Nordland*. On the northern sector of the line support arrived in the form of tanks from the 502nd Heavy Tiger Battalion and *Panzergrenadiers* from the 7th *Panzer* Division, who closed the gaps here as well.

After eight days of heavy fighting over crossroads for predominant high ground and at river crossings, the enemy attacks were brought to a halt. Hundreds of Soviet soldiers fell just outside their positions as the attacks were stopped with artillery and rocket fire. Horrendous losses were suffered by the Soviets and their goal of taking the all-weather port of Libau was not successful. Karl and his comrades hoped this victory broke the back of the Red Army, as Hitler insisted it must, but the Soviets just dug deeper into their powerful reserves of manpower and prepared another thrust at the Baltic coast.

Leo Schwarz provided his account of an incident concerning one of these Soviet attacks in his interview:

Tiger I tanks like this, attached to the 510 Heavy Tiger Battalion, and assisted by 36th *Panzer* Regiment's tanks, became the fire brigade of the Courland peninsula. The tank carried a mix of high explosive and armour piercing ammunition. (Bundesarchiv)

One of my soldiers was wounded in the shoulder and bleeding badly. I placed the man on top of my tank and we headed for the aid-station. Within minutes we ran straight into a major Soviet assault. I drove the tank at top speed through the first Soviet checkpoint surprising the enemy before they could get a shot off. But soon we saw the first wave of attackers before us and so I drove the tank into a hedgerow next to the road. Once in the ditch and concealed, I told the crew to play dead and not make any noise, and also told the wounded man on the roof the same. The wounded man pleaded for a machine-gun as thousands of enemy soldiers swarmed around us, but I refused, telling him to hold the pain and be quiet. We waited all night until the following morning when an artillery observation halftrack showed up, but was abruptly destroyed in a ball of fire and smoke from a direct hit. An artillery duel then began between Soviet and German gunners, which we used to escape back into our lines, but without our tank. As for the mission we were attempting, the wounded man made it to the aid station later that day, and survived the ordeal.

The Soviet attacks south of Skuodas breeched the security line and reached the sea by the 16th, cutting off Army Group North. The *Grossdeutschland* Division, which the 36th Regiment was trying to link up with, was now surrounded in the port of Memel. They eventually abandoned the city, but were evacuated to fight another day in East Prussia, minus their equipment.

Meanwhile, the 14th *Panzer* Division was ordered into Libau to prevent it from being taken from the southeast. The coast road from Libau to Memel was vital for any future drive to re-establish contact with 3rd *Panzer* Army, and an order was issued for three divisions to try to affect this. The 2nd Battalion, along with grenadiers of the 103rd Regiment, attacked down this road on the 12th and 13th. Along with the 4th and 12th *Panzer* Divisions, they were told to facilitate a link up with forces in the south. Not since the French Campaign of 1940 had the 36th *Panzer* Regiment fought alongside their old comrades, the 35th *Panzer* Regiment from Bamberg. By the second day it was evident that the enemy was stronger than believed and the attack was stopped. Although this remained the only attempt to secure a land link south, the goal of re-establishing contact with the fortress at Memel was not successful.

As the Germans continued their withdrawal from Riga and more units arrived on the Courland peninsula, the enemy attacks began to ease. The Courland Army Group took this opportunity to reorganize their entangled forces, and straighten out their lines. The fortifications were still weak and nightly incursions from the enemy were common. A new mission was ordered for the Division when enemy forces were observed massing for an attack northwest of Vionode. Regimental tanks supported infantry of the 563rd Infantry Division, counter-attacking this assembly area. Strong rocket and artillery fire pre-empted the assault and enemy resistance was broken quickly. But the infantry overextended themselves during the advance and the gap was not closed until the 25th.

Further progress was hampered by the terrain, which consisted of swamps and impassable forests. These obstacles forced the attackers to detour around them, slowing the advance and losing the attacks momentum. Resistance stiffened until the Regiment was under another major Soviet assault by 50 tanks and assault guns. Several breakthroughs at night were successful, but were later contained during the following day. The local tactic was to send the grenadiers in on foot to clear the villages, as the armour provided fire support from the woods.

As the fighting died down, the unit was only able to count 15 tanks as operational and these were being used to tow the other vehicles off the battlefield.[6] After the battle more than 80 Soviet tanks were counted as disabled, and 12 of these were destroyed completely. It was now approaching the end of October and the rain and muddy season brought a cessation to the First Battle of Courland.

The Red Army left the Regiment little time to recover and launched the Second Battle of Courland on October 27th. This struggle lasted about a month, and was directed against the port of Libau, the lifeline for Army Group Courland. 2,000 guns opened the attack and the barrage lasted for an hour and a half. The heaviest blows fell on the Regiment's positions, situated on the middle front between Vionode, Preekuln, and Skuodas. Small, combined arms battle groups were once again formed to provide an all-round defensive hedgehog. But the front line was not defended completely and gaps still existed between these positions. Heavy mechanized Soviet units tore into these soft areas between the lines until stopped by flak, mines, or anti-tank guns. The enemy armour was actually not as threatening as the Red Army infantry, who encroached as close as possible to German lines to avoid the artillery and rocket fire. The soldiers then fought ferociously hand-to-hand in the trenches, getting no sleep for days.

Artillery and rocket fire began again on the 29th, signalling another attack in the same area as before, between the 30th Infantry and the 14th *Panzer* Division. But during this attack the Panther and Tiger tanks of Group Molanari assisted the defence line, destroying some of the new super heavy Joseph Stalin tanks (these monstrous tanks were armed with a 122 mm main gun). Soviet reinforcements

The Tiger went on to become the most famous tank of the war, but repair crews needed special cranes and equipment to work on them, which wasn't always available. The turret of this Tiger is being lowered into the cassis with the use of a heavyweight crane. This repair work was done well behind the combat front due to the special efforts needed and the time consuming work being performed. (Bundesarchiv)

continued to arrive and these reserves exploited the gaps made by the first echelon. But German replacements were also being called forward, including rear area and support troops. Nevertheless the positions around Vionode were abandoned, and the old fortification line held earlier in October reoccupied again.

After a period of inactivity, constant artillery fire opened a new attack on noon of November 19th, along the front between Preekuln and Frauenburg. In the south, Schrunden was also under assault, with several penetrations reported by nightfall. At 4 p.m. that day the 1st Battalion began a counter-attack while attached to the 108th *Panzergrenadiers*. This battle group fought forward beyond the defensive line to the town of Cimmeri, an important crossroads defended heavily by the enemy. In a battle that lasted four hours the tanks and grenadiers overran Soviet fortifications hastily erected in the streets, and cleared the town. They withdrew the following day, and the losses on both sides were excessive, with the Soviets losing 4,000 men and 1,000 prisoners captured. The Germans on the other hand reported 13,000 casualties by the time the Second Battle of Courland was over.

The Tigers of the 510th Heavy Tank Battalion remained in the forest to provide a deadly screen against additional enemy attacks, as a fresh attack began on the 23rd when two columns of Soviet tanks struck down the main road. Most were destroyed in the killing zone that developed in front of the German lines as Tiger, Panther tanks, and anti-tank guns eliminated what few remaining enemy vehicles survived the artillery barrage and minefields. Adverse weather conditions and the strength of the German defence brought a halt to Soviet attacks at the end of November.

Besides a Soviet attack in force conducted from the 1st until the 3rd, the first three weeks of December were quiet. This latest lull was used to reorganize, re-supply, and train replacements. The 36th *Panzer* Regiment reported operational in an inventory report on the 12th: 10 Mark IV's, 13 assault guns, and 20 Panthers.[7] It was estimated another 69 tanks and assault guns were needed to bring the Division up to authorized strength.

When not performing maintenance the soldiers built barricades, bunkers, and strongpoints. By the beginning of year the entire Courland peninsula was one massive fortress line, containing outposts, barricades, and supply depots. Behind this screen the 'Courland Fire Brigade' as it was called, stood by on alert ready to repulse any break-through in the line.[8] They were ordered to new defensive location further north of the railway line near Rudbarzi and the workshop company was sent to Hasenpoth.

Karl Brier was sent ahead to secure billets in Hasenpoth for the workshop company and the Regimental headquarters staff as well. When he reached the entrance to the town he was met by a sentry who denied him entry. This man said the town was already occupied with enough troops and they wouldn't find quarters there. After a while, Brier asked the guard where he was from, and they realized they came from the same town near Stuttgart. The guard then allowed him to pass and complete his mission and they became close comrades. Brier went on to explain that the first thing that happened after an operational move of this sort was that Ivan, the Russian engineer working with the unit, always secured liveable quarters for Karl Roth and the headquarters section. He was well liked and went so far as to hunt down deer in the woods, producing venison stew, and made rabbit fur boots for them. The workshop company spent the rest of their time in the town of Hasenpoth outside Libau, until the war ended

The Soviets began the Third Battle of Courland at first light, on the 21st. The rolling artillery barrage began in the area south of Frauenburg, and along other major points along the line. Three Soviet army groups attempted again to split the 16th and 18th Armies, and take Libau from the east. Infantry and armour assaults (including some American-built Sherman tanks) followed the artillery bombardment, but no major penetrations were achieved, this due mainly to the fast reaction of the *Panzergrenadiers*, whose leaders worked seamlessly to conduct effective counter-attacks with the tanks.

Most of the attacking force was contained by the night of the 23rd and Christmas Eve was relatively calm. The miserable living conditions and also the cold and hunger all contributed to the churches reporting packed conditions during that last Christmas of the war. Karl ironically spent this Christmas in a barn, half occupied with Soviet soldiers. Both sides quietly celebrated their holiday, weary after six years of war, and the following morning went their separate ways.

Using the protection of a deep forest, the mobile repair team uses a halftrack and jib to remove the drive train from a medium Panther tank. When asked what tank Leo Schwarz favoured during the war, he said the Panther for its manoeuvrability and good engine performance. The Panther was also easier to repair than both the Tiger I and the King Tiger II tank. Despite the severely devastated countryside that was laid waste from the continuous fighting, Courland still provided dense forest tracks that were perfect repair areas used by the workshop company. (Bundesarchiv)

The battle was costly up until this point, with one infantry unit reporting they had repulsed 111 enemy attacks in one week! The town of Vanagi for example was fought over for three days, and changed hands seven times.

At the end of December the Soviet attacks switched to the area being held by the Regiment near the rail line to Frauenenburg. Every yard of ground was fought over and each time the enemy tanks and assault guns attacked they were turned back or destroyed. The Third Battle of Courland cost the Germans 513 tanks by the end of December and a staggering 27,000 casualties.

A severely cold winter with heavy snowfall descended across all of northern Europe in the beginning of 1945. As was the case in the Third Battle of Courland, the Fourth began after a few weeks of calm. In the first half of January a few enemy incursions resulted in only a few miles gained into the defensive line, with none breaking through to Libau or Windau. The troops dug in and the Army Group was officially designated '*Kurland*' on the 15th. The fortress line was around 180 miles long, stretching from Schrunden in the south to Tukkums in the north. The line was relatively static now and conditions were more akin to Verdun or the 17th Army's stand in the Crimea. Supplies were only getting through to Libau and Windau by sea, and this route was becoming ever increasingly dangerous to hold open.

Increased enemy reconnaissance always preceded any major Soviet assault, and the Fourth Battle of Courland was no exception. Probes and air attacks against Preekuln began as early as the 21st with double thrusts breaking out on either side of the town four days later. More enemy attacks opened four days after that to the north, down the main road between Schrunden and Frauenburg. For three days the Soviets threw 11 divisions into this sector, forcing the Germans to retire behind secondary positions.

With the infantry and grenadiers under intense pressure to hold the line an order went out to the *Panzer* reserve to restore the situation. The 36th *Panzer* Regiment, the 103rd and 108th *Panzergrenadiers*, and the 510th Heavy Tiger Battalion, set off immediately through a thick snowstorm to counter-attack the Soviet assault. They anticipated the call forward and were already prepared to move out of their containment area when they received the order.

At Purmsati, three miles south of Preekuln they encountered and destroyed 63 vehicles. The Tiger and Panther tanks were both superior to comparable Allied designs and the Tiger in particular frightened the enemy.[9] Many times the actual firepower between the opposing tanks was equal, now that the JS II Stalin tank was available, but German command and control tactics proved more effective in determining success on the battlefield. The American Sherman tank was also encountered more often now, but even the *Panzer* Mark IV outgunned it.

By evening the crisis was over and the Regiment pulled back behind the line to rearm and refuel. An artillery duel ensued between the two combatants as the Germans hurled high explosive shells towards the Soviet lines and they returned fire with *Katyusha* rocket barrages. The sky cleared also, allowing the Red Air Force to fly again. Fighting continued to be heavy and Preekuln was lost during another attempt to take Libau, at the end of January. With roads frozen solid and the troops suffering from severe injuries to the elements, a period of recovery was needed. Despite the heavy losses[10] and more attacks in the north by Tukkums, a message from Army headquarters on the 28th declared the finality of the Fourth Battle of Courland.

During a meeting with Hitler on February 8th, Guderian again brought up the subject of evacuating the Courland Army Group.[11] The conversation devolved into a shouting match between the two and one of the worst outbursts of emotion shown by Hitler during the war. He put the *Reichs* naval commander, Doernitz, on the spot and asked whether the heavy equipment (Tiger and Panther tanks) could be evacuated from the peninsula. When Doernitz answered in the negative, Hitler considered the case closed, whereby sealing the fate of the Courland Army Group to a forlorn and forgotten outpost. The Army Group was now fighting for the same

HEROIC STAND   143

objective as those before them had done encircled at Stalingrad, to tie down as many divisions as possible from being used on the central front, which by this time was the German border itself.

Around the clock British and American bombing raids were pounding the home-front cities, one in particular on the 13th and 14th of February, 1945, that personally affected many of those in the 14th *Panzer* Division. A night raid against the mostly undamaged city centre of Dresden resulted in the most destructive and controversial fire raid of the European theatre. It is estimated that between 35–80,000 people died in the raid, including some Allied POWs. Even though news was travelling slowly from Germany to Courland during this time, the stories arrived of how severe the destruction was in the city, destroying morale within the Division. The soldiers in the 14th *Panzer* Division from Dresden, and those of the 36th *Panzer* Regiment from Schweinfurt, now both shared in the grief of the destruction to their cities.

When the Fifth Battle of Courland began on the 20th the 36th *Panzer* Regiment was seriously understrength since they never received the arrival of the 2nd Battalion that was being converted to *Panzerjäger* tanks in Germany. The quality of the replacements was also lacking, with boys and *Luftwaffe* ground troops now filling the front ranks. Those few tanks remaining in the unit supported the infantry positions northwest of Preekuln. Whereas before they defended a line parallel to the rail line, south of Preekuln, they now covered the crossroads and bridgeheads near Ciruli that protected the main road to Libau. This area was crisscrossed with streams and creeks that were prone to flooding, limiting the success of any armoured attack by either side. Therefore it became necessary for the Soviet infantry and special troops to seize the bridgeheads, enabling the tank support to get through. The Soviet infantry assaults were constant, even after their supporting armour was all but disabled or destroyed behind them. The resulting pockets of enemy soldiers within the line were then cleared out at night, in close quarters fighting.

Members of the workshop company make themselves at home, as best they can while in Courland. Battle conditions on the peninsula during the last six months of the war resembled that of the First World War, including static trench warfare and massive artillery preparations.
(Courtesy K. Brier)

The following day was spent beating off another Soviet relief attack made up of T-34s, Shermans, and JS II tanks. Every anti-tank weapon available was used to fight back the assault, including mines, Pak, howitzers, *Panzerfäuste*, and grenades. An effective counter-attack by the fire brigade was impossible since the tanks had run out of fuel, resulting in a few miles retreat and two major road junctions lost. The Soviet artillery eased up and by the end of February the attacks were finally stopped.

The Fifth Battle of Courland only put a dent in the main defensive line, but inflicted high losses on both sides. By the time it was over up to 70,000 Soviet soldiers were casualties, and they had lost 600 tanks. The Germans reported 5,400 casualties in the 18th Army alone. During all the battles, the lethal efficiency of the *Panzer* reserve regiments in Courland were by now, legendary. This was not only known to those in the Army Group, but to the enemy as well.

A meeting of Army Group commanders in the beginning of March planned a reorganization of the still usable units in the 14th *Panzer* Division. The only reinforcements the 36th *Panzer* Regiment could hope for at this point consisted of the walking wounded being returned by the aid stations from the Fourth Battle of Courland. Supplies and replacements were scarce or non-existent, as more troops were evacuated out of the pocket than were being brought in. Those reinforcements that were provided were boys between the ages of sixteen and eighteen.

The 14th *Panzer* Division was relocated in the middle of March occupying positions between the towns of Gelzi and Padone, (east of Durben). This was a vital sector and any Soviet attack towards Libau had to come this way. The Regiment was only able to report operational on the 15th – 15 assault guns, 28 Panthers, and 15 Tigers. This was the final strength left to thwart yet another attempt by the Red Army to drive along the railway between Frauenburg and Libau, splitting the 16th and 18th Armies.

Dozens of Soviet artillery and rocket batteries fired on the main sectors to be attacked (south of Fraunenburg) on the 18th. Before the smoke cleared, T-34s and JS II Stalin tanks poured down the main road overwhelming the forward outposts. The spring's snowmelt created entire lakes between the roads and the isolated villages and hamlets. This decreased the cohesion between the German units, but also limited the amount of manoeuvring the Soviets achieved.

In the first few hours of the attack, a wedge developed between the two German armies and casualties were high on both sides. As the situation deteriorated, the fire brigade (36th *Pz* Rgt) of the Army Group was again called forward to fill the gaps and halt the attacks. Self-propelled guns and artillery pieces on the high ground fired over open sights at distances of only a few hundred metres. Like in all the previous battles individual close quarters combat followed and personal heroism decided the outcome. The following account by Leo Schwarz illustrates the tactics used in this battle:

> One of my most harrowing moments came while I was a driver for the 36th *Panzer* Regiment's commander, Major Bernard Sauvant. We were set up on a ridge with only five tanks and a few anti-tank guns available. That night we heard lots of commotion and the sounds of vehicle engines in the valley below us. At first light that morning we saw almost 600 Soviet troops accompanied by tanks moving towards a log bridge at the end of the flooded area. This swamp was on either side of the main road and the only way into our lines. I said to Sauvant "Oh my God, look at all those troops! We are surely dead this time". But the commander remained calm and told me "Don't worry, all the farmhouses and buildings were occupied and fortified last night and the flooded fields will channel the Soviet armour into our pre-targeted areas. I relocated the guns last night and we will catch them at the bottleneck on the wooden bridge. As soon as the first Soviet tank tries to cross the bridge we will open up with everything on the lead vehicles." The Soviets were taken by surprise by this tactic and abandoned the tanks on the bridge, many soldiers drowning in the swamp.

Our forces then opened up with machine guns, artillery, and mortars. The resulting fire missions were devastating in such a contained area, although a lack of ammunition forced our barrage to be of short duration. The enemy was caught in the open and it was a turkey shoot as we cut them down, and the flankers moved in.

Sauvant was concerned that the lead tanks were abandoned but not destroyed, and the Soviets would try and salvage them at night. So he decided to blow up the tanks on the bridge, telling me and another soldier [later killed] to follow him. To cut down on noise and not draw the enemy's attention we loaded a motorcycle and sidecar with explosives, heading down a small track that led into the swamp. Once at the edge of the swamp we went into the water, using the remaining wooden beams to get to the bridge. We crept among the abandoned vehicles when suddenly Sauvant threw a grenade into one of the tanks. The resulting explosion and smoke brought instant small arms fire from the remaining enemy soldiers still in the water. I yelled at the Major, saying "These aren't thermal grenades, so don't do that again, I don't want to die out here today!" (Since I was Sauvant's driver we were pretty close and I could get away talking to him like this under the circumstances). We decided to detonate the fuel tanks on the tanks and blew up all three, although drawing enough attention that by the time we destroyed the last one we were under serious Soviet fire.

The combat was close and personal during this period in Courland and many men broke under the strain of the constant attacks and heavy artillery bombardments. The new replacements were nothing but young boys or wounded men being returned to their units with sergeants being promoted into positions they were neither ready nor trained for. But the German resistance was stubborn, costing the Soviets 92 tanks in the first few days of the attack. Just when the fighting was reaching its peak and the line looked as if it was going to break, the Soviets switched their assault to the area north of Fraunenburg. Within seven days the Red Army attack ground to a halt without any breakthrough to Libau achieved.

The Battle of Berlin was about to begin and so the Soviets waited patiently for the obvious outcome there before attempting again to break the Courland Line. This was fortuitous for the Army Group, as another attack with the ferociousness of the last battle could not be withstood. The troops in Courland now had only three choices left open to them – to fight, evacuate, or surrender.[12]

Evacuation and Capitulation

The battle was slowing in intensity during the last weeks of the war and the usual monthly Soviet attack did not materialize. The decimated companies and battalions of the 14th *Panzer* Division were regrouped after being intermingled during the last battle of Courland, and the Soviets continued to probe the lines for weak spots, but never again attempted another major attack. Their overwhelming superiority in men and machines made the outcome of the war inevitable, and they ultimately prepared to starve the Germans out of Courland. A naval blockade of the peninsula meant that more and more of the transport ships trying to reach the ports were sunk, and the Army Group's supply lifeline cut off.

Soviet loudspeakers announced across no man's land the death of Hitler on May 1st, followed two days later with news of the fall of Berlin. Rumours of betrayal and sabotage within the government circulated inside the pocket, and the highest-ranking officer in the Army Group stated that the Courland Army Group should be evacuated to northern German ports. Other rumours went around that the British were slated to clear the Baltic ports, and that they were going to link up with the 18th and 16th Armies, to repel the Soviets! But it was too late for such optimistic talk, and at any rate no more transports were getting through to supply the Army Group, much less to evacuate or save it.

After the Sixth Battle of Courland Karl was concerned about the deteriorating situation within the pocket and prepared for his own evacuation. Elements of the 36th *Panzer* Regiment's headquarters staff, and the 108th *Panzergrenadier* Regiment, moved into Libau harbour to protect the port and load the transports. Karl immediately began searching for a boat and managed to secure a sailboat, stocking it with a map, compass, food and water. His escape plan was to sail to Sweden if possible, and he planned to take his chances out at sea when the time came, and not with the Soviets.[13] According to Leo Schwarz, most of the Soviet officers respected the German Army in Courland, but the average Soviet fighting man was bent on avenging the high losses they suffered during the six attempts at destroying the pocket, and members of the 'Courland Fire Brigade', including those in the 36th *Panzer* Regiment, were especially fearful of individual reprisals against them.

The *Kurland* Army Group had already made detailed plans in February to evacuate the bulk of their troops, trying to put them into action in April and early May. But due to a severe lack of fuel and coal for the transports coming from the harbours of Mecklenburg and Denmark, and also from the high losses being sustained from Allied navies, only a select few soldiers were allowed to leave. This caused an immediate discipline problem for the German Army, and strict measures were implemented to substantiate who was properly authorized to leave. Military and *SS* police units roamed the pocket performing summary courts-martial, executing at will anyone found guilty of abandoning their post. In the port of Danzig for example, hundreds of soldiers were executed and hung from the lampposts, which lined the main street of the city.

In this frightful environment Karl prepared his escape with a few close friends, but was fortunate enough to be told at the beginning of April that he could board a torpedo boat (fast boat) for evacuation to northern Germany. These ships were bigger than the American torpedo boats, and Karl volunteered to shovel coal for the duration of the trip. Only the wounded, specialists, fathers, non-combatants and a few select officers were allowed to evacuate at this time. He was only allowed to board the cruiser because he was a father,

With Hitler now dead, and the Battle of Berlin over, the end for the surrounded Courland pocket defenders was not far off. Here a member of the workshop company receives the news of Hitler's death. (Courtesy K. Brier)

underscoring the importance of the event with Else during his leave from Stalingrad in 1942.

His small sailboat was turned over to his comrades in Libau who reportedly made it to Sweden. And Ivan, the faithful Russian volunteer allowed to stay with the headquarters company, was also evacuated to Germany on the same ship as Karl, residing after the war in Schleswig-Holstein.

Unfortunately there is no recorded document that survives telling us what that ship ride was like, nor did Karl take any photographs. But I was able to interview Karl Brier and get his account of the evacuation, along with the invaluable pictures he took of his voyage a month later:

> My evacuation began when Leo Schwarz and I were permitted to drive a vehicle (VW) to Libau harbour and retrieve a friend from the infirmary. This man was recovering from an appendix operation that was performed only two days before, in the port cities hospital. Once he was discharged we all decided to take our chances at boarding a ship in the harbour. I was carrying a pistol, binocular case, and around my waist were two grenades that I was prepared to use if forced with surrender to the Soviets. At the dock a captain allowed my friends to board a fast ship, telling us the Courland Pocket was forgotten and finished. Unfortunately I was told to report my car to the harbourmaster. As I drove to find the officer in charge, the Soviets began shelling the docks, and an almost direct hit landed right in front of my car. The *Volkswagen* drove into the crater created by the explosion and I bailed out of the vehicle. Being not far from the ship my friends were on, I raced back along the wharf and flung myself onto the boat as it was pulling away from the dock!
>
> We got on the ship and the captain told us to stay in our bunk beds and act sick, as we did not have the proper papers to be on board. To prevent seasickness the captain told us to brace our heads against the pipes at the head of the bunks. We sailed out to sea, and to avoid Soviet ships and planes headed towards Swedish waters. That night we were denied entry into a Swedish port, and we slept out on the deck of a ship meant for 12 crewmembers, that was holding 120 men onboard! The following morning, in international waters, a Swedish flotilla threateningly approached to take us prisoner. Our flotilla commander had arrangements with the British to surrender his crew and ships in Schleswig-Holstein, and he decided to confront the Swedish navy ships even though we had no torpedoes or weapons. He sent out a screen of torpedo boats tethered together as close as possible in a menacing direction. The scare tactic worked and the Swedish flotilla turned and sailed away.
>
> We were held on an Baltic island until accepted for prisoner of war processing by British authorities and granted permission to dock in the port of Kiel. Upon arriving I could hardly believe my ears as I heard the navy band playing a ballad in honour of our successful voyage!

The dissolution of the 36th *Panzer* Regiment was already underway by the end of April and the unit was down to half strength. Only every other outpost was now occupied, as the lines ran through destroyed enemy tanks, burned down forests, and destroyed crop fields. The commanders ordered their troops to destroy all the equipment and leave nothing of use to the enemy. But grenades and demolition munitions were scarce, and many of the vehicles were driven into the swamps as a means of rendering them inoperable. Destruction stations were set up along the route of March into the harbours and all papers, documents and radio equipment deposited there. Strong orders were again issued that no one was to assemble near the wharfs unless already approved for evacuation, and only when a person was authorized to sail were their personal army documents issued to them for the trip.

Karl Roth surrendered himself and his men to British army troops in the port of Flensburg sometime in April. Before he left Libau harbour some of his comrades within the Regiment tried to persuade him to stay, saying they heard rumours that Doernitz (the new German leader), was preparing to send a relief force to save the Courland Army. Karl remembered the same promises made to the Stalingrad defenders in 1943 and handed his pistol over to his commanding officer. All together 25,300 soldiers were evacuated from Libau and Widau alone to Schleswig-Holstein. They hoped for a short period of captivity in allied prisoner of war camps and most were granted this.

An interesting endnote to Roth's surrender story is how Else first found out that he was safe, told from a soldier who was outside her door one day looking for a drink of water. Else told him to come inside and as he was drinking, saw Karl's wedding picture on the mantle. He asked, "Who is that man?" Else told him the photograph was of her husband who was serving in Courland. The man then said, "he's safe, I was the commander of the ship that evacuated him from Courland! Your husband helped shovel coal on the journey" This statement was made hundreds of miles from where Karl was imprisoned, in northern Germany! Their comrades surrendering to Soviet troops were not as fortunate, suffering for years in Stalin's gulags in Siberia, most never to return.

The Germans capitulated on May 8th and soldiers from Tukums in the north to those entrenched around Libau to the south, put out white shirts or underwear to surrender. The cease-fire went into effect officially the following day as 42 generals, 8,000 officers, and 191,000 enlisted men of Army Group Courland marched into captivity. Their Soviet guards were more hospitable to the Germans at first than most expected. The officers were allowed to stay together and the enlisted men able to keep the fuel they possessed and the uniforms they wore. Even so, the

An eerie silence descends over the Courland battlefield after the cease-fire goes into effect on May 9th 1945. (FACP)

Karl Brier took these remarkable pictures of his Courland evacuation on May 5th 1945. The ports and rear areas of the German Army were heavily policed, and only those with authorization and proper documents were allowed to be near the wharfs. Karl Brier and his comrades were especially fortunate to locate a captain who was sympathetic to their hopeless situation and allowed them to board his ship. (Courtesy K. Brier)

This picture shows the historical evacuation to northern Germany aboard the 'fast boats'. The Germans used all types of cargo and passenger vessels for the transportation and evacuation of troops from the Courland peninsula. The depth of water of the embarkation and debarkation ports determined the size of the boat to be used, and many of the Baltic seaports limited cargo ships up to 2000 gross tons. Here a navy fast boat squadron (termed a torpedo boat by the Germans, but larger than the American version) catches up to Brier's ship. The loading and unloading times necessary for a vessel varied with a number of factors, including the size of the ship, planning, port facilities, and the efficiency with which loading was conducted. An entire *Panzergrenadier* regiment of the 14th *Panzer* Division was assigned to help with embarkation detail and security for the port at Libau. (Courtesy K. Brier)

An all out effort was made on May 6th to evacuate as many of the Courland fighters to the West as possible before the cease fire went into effect on the 9th. Mine sweepers, munitions carriers, fishing trawlers, motorboats, transports, civilian vessels and twenty fast boats were ordered to make haste for the ports of Windau and Libau and conduct a last minute Dunkirk-style evacuation attempt. Here a cruiser of the flotilla prepares to overtake Brier's ship. There was constant fear that the flotillas would get attacked from the sea or air, but in the end, over 175 ships rescued 25,300 men from the ports of Libau and Windau alone. Karl Brier, Leo Schwarz, Ivan the Russian, and Karl Roth all arrived in the port of Flensburg, in Schleswig-Holstein.

last ships leaving Libau and Windau were attacked heavily even after the armistice went into effect.

'Fire Brigade Courland' and the remainder of the Army Group North were one of the last bastions of resistance to surrender during the war, and were never defeated in battle. A northern group with elements of the workshop company marched from Hasenpoth to Windau for the surrender. The remainder, including the 14th *Panzer* Division headquarters staff, made their way into Libau. Their heroism concluded the Seventh Battle of Courland and the end of the war itself. The battle group destroyed their last tank on May 9th, a Tiger from Heavy Battalion 510, ushering in an eerie silence that descended across the battlefield.

The End in Schweinfurt

In early April as the American 42nd Infantry Division advanced on Karl and Else's hometown, backed up by the 4th Armoured Division, they met stiff resistance in the outskirts of the city. Wurzburg to the south had not surrendered easily either, with heavy bombers being called in to level that famous academic centre.

Hitler Youth manned the flak guns inside Schweinfurt and old men of the local *Volkssturm* ('People's Army'), defended the strongpoints thrown up hastily to stop the Americans. These fanatical resistance fighters were led by Prussian guards and *SS* men, who couldn't care less about the Franconian towns they oversaw. As casualties began to mount, the two American division commanders decided to take the city from behind, instead of continuing the frontal assault. An infantry and armour pincer attack, moving in from the northwest began on April 8th. A relative of my wife's, Alois Weigand, was an eight-year-old boy in the town of Rannungen on

HEROIC STAND   151

Schweinfurt's Flak 88 guns put up resistance when the Americans arrived and this forced them to flank around the city. In the meantime, the heavy bombers were called in once again, reducing the town to rubble. Here infantry of the 42nd Infantry Division cautiously advance down a street with weapons at the ready. (FACP)

this fateful weekend in 1945, and gave the following personal account of what happened there:

The battle began on April 6th, when German engineers heard the Americans were approaching and detonated all the munitions at their secret forest depot [The Muna Rottershausen], two miles north of Rannungen. The Muna, as it

Comparatively, the town of Neustadt where Else Roth was residing near surrendered without much of a fight, as the white flags and relaxed nature of the American infantry reveals in this picture. (FACP)

was called, produced and stored aircraft ammunition and bombs inside bunkers hidden deep inside the forest that was fed by a major rail-spur between Stuttgart and Berlin. The Allies knew the secret site existed and were searching for months to find its location. I remember that once two low flying Mosquito fighter-bombers attacked a train entering the forest, and the resulting explosion was so great the two British planes were lost as well.

The explosion at the Muna, almost two miles from town shook the ground and blew out all the windows. Two days later, at eight o'clock in the morning, Sunday, April 8th, I was preparing for my first communion (white Sunday) in the town's church. Usually Catholics did not get their first communion until they were ten years old in Germany, but during the war they decided on mass ceremonies because the age of those being drafted to fight was getting so low. The priest hoisted the Catholic white and yellow flag in the church steeple, as was their practice, but some local girls, sensing the Americans were close to town, also put out white flags, immediately drawing the attention of the local *SS* in Schweinfurt.

Within minutes two *SS* military policemen ('chain dogs') on a motorcycle with sidecar entered the town and demanded to know why a surrender flag was waving from some of the balconies. The priest explained they were conducting first communion ceremonies that day, and all he knew was that it was his obligation to fly the flag, and said it would remain up. The two trench-coated policeman were not amused, and reminded the priest he was in violation, got back on their bike, but vowed to return.

At 2 p.m. that day a man rushed into the church in the middle of the second ceremony and exclaimed that the Americans were approaching. The American infantry were steadily advancing from the west and took casualties outside the town of Rottershausen. A ridge to the south of Rannungun was giving the advancing US infantry a difficult time, forcing them to alter their route of attack, which was rerouted into our town. A nun immediately organized the children in the church, and rushed us outside in double file through the vestibule

Another citizen of Rannungen, Elfriede Wenzel, was part of the fire brigade that tried to save the *Rathaus* (city hall) when the fires began. She was killed inside when the Americans entered from the opposite end of the building and opened fire through the door, not knowing she was on the other side.
(Author's collection)

A 12th Armoured Division Sherman tank moves into the centre of Schweinfurt after the initial resistance was overcome. (FACP)

exit. As we stepped out of the door I saw out of the corner of my eye the first shell destroy a farmhouse, decapitating my aunt who was inside. These rounds were not American, instead they were the work of our artillery dug in on a ridge closer to Schweinfurt and the SS policemen making good on their promise that "they would be back". The 88mm flak guns destroyed fourteen farmhouses in like manner during the next two hours.

The other children and I were evacuated to a cellar behind the church to ride out the battle. Being afraid we were going to be burned alive inside the basement, my friend and I ran for his house. By this time the American infantry were entering the town and my mother pleaded with them not to shoot, and that her children were inside the house. The first soldier she encountered replied, "Why don't you hang out a white flag! Where is your white flag!" She immediately ran inside the house and retrieved a white cloth and hung it out.

Another citizen of the town was not so lucky as to be warned first. This young woman, Elfriede Wenzel was part of the fire brigade, and tried to save the *Rathaus* [city hall] when the fires began. She and her fellow fireman entered the structure from a separate entrance behind the church, as the American soldiers entered the building from the front. When the soldiers heard the commotion on the other side of the door, a volley of gunfire fired through it killed her, she becoming Rannungen's second victim that day.

Meanwhile we sought shelter in the barn behind the house, and a German soldier took refuge inside alongside with us, deciding to destroy his weapon before the Americans got there. Just then an American soldier threw open the barn door and seeing the soldier with something in his hands shot him dead in front of us. If this soldier had gotten out of his uniform and hidden his rifle in the hay, as we urged him to do, he probably wouldn't have been killed. But the Americans seemed too scared, tired and weary of house-to-house fighting to ask questions first.

By 5 p.m. that day the battle was over and heavily armed American infantry entered the town. I had never seen so many columns of troops and remember seeing my first black man, an African-American soldier, smoking a cigarette with one leg resting on the town wall. I was overtaken by how exhausted the American troops appeared and was allowed later to carry an infantry commander's carbine up the ridge towards Schweinfurt."

By Tuesday the two American divisions were mopping up the remaining resistance in Swabheim, outside Schweinfurt. Schweinfurt's *Burgemeister* (mayor) committed suicide rather than surrender the town, and his replacement was almost shot by an American commander who demanded at gunpoint to know where in the city the flak ammunition was stored.

Alois remains to this day in the small community of Rannungen, and as fate would have it he bought the farm and lives above the same cellar he sought shelter from during the battle. His vivid recollections of his first communion under artillery fire clearly illustrate the short but tragic fighting that was happening in small and large cities alike all over Germany in the last months of the war.

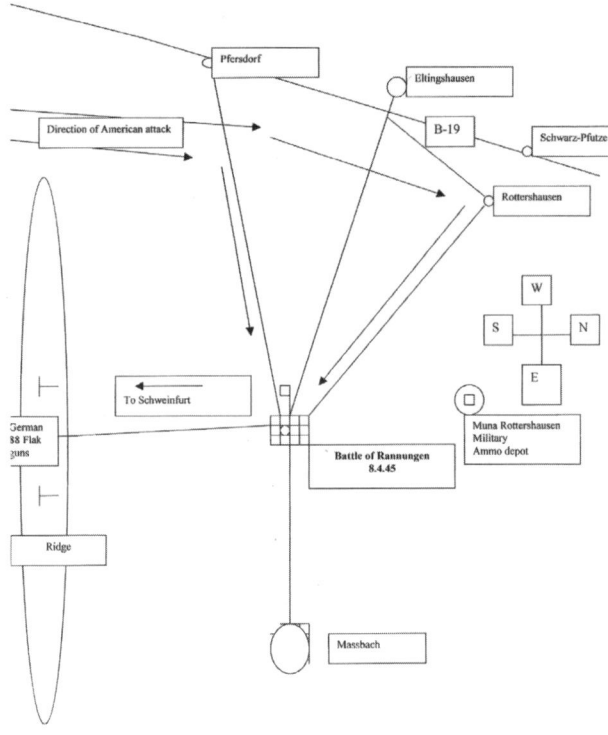

Battle of Rannungen, April 8th 1945.

PART V
CONCLUSION: AFTER THE WAR

CHAPTER XII

The Nightmare is Over

May 1945–Present

By the time the evacuees of Courland arrived in northern Germany they were weary and disillusioned by six years of war. Those soldiers that surrendered in Schleswig-Holstein to the British were then segregated and divided between officers, non-commissioned officers and enlisted men. SS men were further separated for the de-Nazification procedures, and possible legal proceedings for war crimes.

Most of those in the regular German Army were allowed to live and work among the local population in Schleswig Holstein, but were expected to remain there for possibly up to two years. Karl Roth was placed on a farm in the town of Sollerup as an agricultural worker after arriving in the British zone, but because of his second bout with the malaria he contracted in 1944 (causing a rising body temperature, pneumonia and the flu), was allowed to relocate home to Franconia that summer (in the American occupied sector).

Almost all the major cities were bombed beyond recognition with Schweinfurt being especially hard-hit throughout the war. The ball-bearing factories and train station had to be totally rebuilt, and due to the ground fighting in April, the old city centre as well. Karl could hardly believe this was the same city he had last seen the year before.

After Karl Brier evacuated by ship he was almost immediately employed as a driver for the British in Schleswig-Holstein. More than 25,000 troops were evacuated from Libau Harbour to ports in northern Germany. (Note the '*Kurland*' cuff band on Brier's arm sleeve). (Courtesy K. Brier).

Karl returned to a devastated homeland, and having no career waiting for him, faced the personal difficulties of readjusting to a society far different from the one he left. He first worked for a friend that owned a hot and cold-water installation business, but part-time worked at an auto repair shop located directly across from his former tank barracks. The Americans were now occupying the barracks and a maintenance sergeant once sought Karl out at the garage, because he was told that the former *Wehrmacht Feldwebel* working there could repair any military vehicle made. He helped fix a problem on one of the American's new heavy tanks that just arrived in Germany, and was offered monetary compensation after completing his work (probably the M-47 Patton tank). He asked instead if his son could be seen

The destroyed city of Schweinfurt after the battle in April 1945. (FACP)

at the base hospital for his asthma problem, and Else said that the Americans offered them very good treatment and medicine at the facility.

Karl performed roof service for the US Army at the renamed Ledward Barracks, and eventually was employed long-term as a maintenance engineer at one of the ball-bearing factories in Schweinfurt (the *Kugelfischer* plant or F.A.G.).

In the beginning of the recovery period it was all Karl Roth could do to put a roof over his family's head, the city being totally destroyed by the fighting in April

Total devastation lay inside the city. (Schweinfurt Archives)

and the allied bombing raids.[1] He used an ox-cart to drag rubble and wood from the city centre to build his house on land bought from Else's family, situated on the same steep ridge that she sought shelter at during the war. Being highly skilled at masonry, piping, and wiring work, Karl installed the steps, plumbing, electricity and sewer system himself, with only the help of his family and friends.

He chose a quiet lifestyle in the Franconian countryside, keeping in touch with a few close comrades after the war. One of these comrades was a Schweinfurt bus driver whose leg Karl saved while they were serving together in Russia during the war. This man was placed on a stretcher and secured to the hood of a truck to be transported away from the battlefield. Evacuating him at night, total blackout drive was necessary, so Karl used his flashlight to see over a treacherous icy road and guide the truck. Holding on to the bumper of the truck, he directed the driver until they were at the battalion aid station, where surgery was performed, saving the man's limb from amputation.

This incident illustrates what comradeship meant to these men, and gives an example of why the term 'Kamerad' is held in such high esteem by the German veterans and people. It meant an eternal, fraternal brotherhood of men who shared the same souvenirs of pain they carried away from the war. Many never expected to befriend those they did, but found themselves in situations requiring the total trust of each other's abilities. This trust and reliability developed into a deep bond that exists only when formulated under dire life and death circumstances.

Their neighbours on this forested ridge were a Jewish couple, the Rosenkranzs'. They survived the war on the property next to theirs with the help of Else and others in the area who never turned them in to the local SS police. Paul Rosenkranz died in 1961, his wife Clara surviving him by a few years. She gave my

The factories of the Kugelfischer ball-bearing works destroyed in Schweinfurt by the American and British bombing raids. (FACP)

wife Jutta her name in 1957, saying that it meant, "the woman from Judea". Else then took care of her in old age until she passed away, and was surprised to find that Clara deeded her their property, willing her a girl's boarding school also, having no surviving family members. The school was in the former East Germany, and since Karl and Else had no access to the region, they dissolved their ownership in it. Else never really thought that they did anything outstanding by saving the Rosenkranzs' from the Nazis, but just a glance at the number of people persecuted under Hitler's nightmarish reign of terror, and the consequences to those Germans harbouring them, clearly shows how selfless this act was.

As things in Schweinfurt returned to normal the full meaning of the war years resurfaced at different times during Karl's life. Always hidden just below the surface, the rage he held inside for all that he experienced was manifest one night while watching a new film about Stalingrad. This was the black and white film: *Hunde Wollt ihr ewig leben* ('Dogs do you want to live forever' directed by Frank Wisbar, 1958). About half way through the movie a scene depicting a Soviet rocket barrage made Karl leave the room saying, "I don't have to watch this, I was there." And on another occasion during a debate on the conflict he reminded everyone around the dining table that if Hitler had not lost the war, he would still be on occupation duty somewhere in Russia.[2]

The women of Germany played a tremendous role in rebuilding the destroyed cities and towns. Else Roth remembers these times as being very difficult for lack of even the basic necessities, but she mentions that the hard times also brought out the best qualities of the people in those days. This photograph was taken in Frankfurt.
(Courtesy O.W. Byrd)

THE NIGHTMARE IS OVER 161

Once Karl Roth fully understood how many years were lost to the war, the more he was determined to make something out of the rest of his life. My wife says Christmas was very special at her house, and that her father was always grateful for every holiday spent in peace after the war. The other very important event to Karl and Else was voting day. My wife still has a vivid memory of her parents dressed in their finest clothes, her father wearing his best suit and hat, and her mother in her dress, with best hat on also, participating in an election. It meant everything to them to be able to vote for their own representation, something not possible under Hitler.

Every night possible Karl took a solitary walk through the forest with my wife, reflecting on the past and thinking about his lost comrades. He never forgot them and every November 1st (All Souls' Day) he stood at parade rest on his balcony, paying tribute and listening as a band echoed the famous ballad: *'Ich hatte ein Kamerad'* ('I Had a Comrade') off the surrounding forest and valley floor. This song was adopted by the *Luftwaffe* and was almost as popular as *Lili Marlene* by the end of the war. My wife's cousin, who spent 30 years as a sergeant in the American army after the war, was 14 years old in Germany in 1945. Even after all the years she said she still gets shivers down her spine when reading the words to *'Ich hatte ein Kamerad'*.[3]

But a generation as well as a social gap developed between the parents who experienced the war and their children, due in part to the attitude of the survivors. They held that no one but those who endured their horrors and hardships could ever hope to understand them. They couldn't understand how their children could take anything for granted, after the sacrifice and rationing they experienced during the war years. Karl often said at night, just before retiring to sleep, "a bed, a bed, thank God for a bed; people, you don't understand what a bed means". These men who underwent superhuman conditions during their lives and learned to survive them, expected the same effort in life from their offspring.

In comparison the youth post-war sentiment turned against their parent's generation, and they held the opinion that obedience to orders, discipline, and blind service to one's government founded the root causes of the chaos. They couldn't understand how their parents could lead Germany into such despair, and they openly rebelled against family order, questioning the social norms of their society.

Karl Roth's first two children harboured these attitudes of discontent against him and felt unconnected to his service record during the war, without really understanding the causes behind it. I believe this book further helped their sentiment evolve into a deeper understanding of the circumstances that required his sacrifice and commitment.

Many former soldiers also felt guilty about surviving the war when so many of their comrades did not. Karl could only explain his good fortune as an unseen force that always seemed present, guiding and directing his destiny. As a result of these experiences he matured and was aged well before his years. The war was the defining experience of his life, and nothing before or after excluding the birth of his children, had as much impact or meaning.

Karl's attitude after the war for those in power can be compared to the outrage held by many returning war veterans, cynical and contemptuous. He never lost his resentment for Hitler and the Third Reich for wasting the prime years of his and

American bomb assessment teams immediately arrived in Schweinfurt to inspect what damage was actually done from all the bombings on the ball-bearing facilities. (FACP)

his comrade's lives. They felt used and forgotten, made the scapegoats for all the atrocities committed in the war. His character was transformed from that of a carefree youth before the war, able to entertain an entire room of people, to that of a resigned and sceptical man thereafter. Even so, he never lost the principles acquired as a leader of men in the German Army.

My wife said this attitude is best summed up by an action he took one day when she was a young girl. Twice a week a 'Good Humour' ice cream truck would deliver at the guest house in the forest, and on this particular day the driver did not secure the back latch to the door. Out rolled gallons of ice cream which all the kids grabbed excitedly. Jutta took her gallon home and when Karl saw it asked her if she had stolen it. She said no, it fell off the back of the truck, and all the kids took some home. Her father said in a stern voice, " if you did not pay for it, it's not yours to keep" and with that he called the 'Good Humour' company in Schweinfurt and made all the kids return the ice cream, upsetting them and most of the adults in the neighbourhood also! As for the lessons learned from the war, the answer he gave to a former officer who offered him a commission in the new German Army best describes his sentiment. Declining to accept the offer he replied, "what I have learned is that my country is worth dying for, but never again will I fight for a government".[4]

THE NIGHTMARE IS OVER 163

Jutta Roth sits with a playmate in front of the house her father built after the war, located on a steep ridge in a protected forest region in Schweinfurt. He installed the wiring, plumbing, and masonry work himself, and with the help of friends in the area. (Author's collection, courtesy E. Roth)

Paul Rosenkranz was Schweinfurt's clock setter and mechanic. Jewish and an accomplished painter, amazingly he and his wife survived the entire war living on the tract of land in the forest next to Karl and Else Roth's property. He and his wife conducted a dangerous underground railway for other displaced people wanting to leave the city. (Author's Collection, courtesy E. Roth)

Members of the *14th Panzer Division Traditional Association,* including commander Willi Langkeit seen here in the centre, hold a reunion of the 14th *Panzer* Division in the 1950's. (Courtesy K. Brier)

Karl Roth worked as a mechanical engineer for the Kugelfischer ball-bearing factory, and in this photograph celebrates 25 years with the company.
Karl Brier also returned not long after the war to his hometown near Stuttgart, and in 2004 still was operating a service station and garage in the town.
(Author's collection, courtesy E. Roth)

14th *Panzer* Division monument at the Prince Eugen military barracks in Kuhlsheim. (Author's collection, courtesy *Prince Eugen Military Kaserne.*)

Karl Roth is interred at the cemetery in Schweinfurt, along with his mother-in-law, Rosa Schaub. (Author's collection)

APPENDICES

APPENDIX I

Hans Niedt

The Photographic Journal of A Combat Pioneer

In the summer of 2000 I was staying at the house where my wife was raised in Schweinfurt, Germany, and came across a photo album (*Meine Dienstseit*) [My Service Time]. My wife said it was the World War II era journal belonging to her father's stepbrother, Hans Niedt, and that he was a combat engineer. His photographs were interesting in content, but they ended abruptly. I was told by Else my mother in law, that Niedt was supposed to be married in 1943, but that just before his wedding he was killed in a land mine explosion. He performed dangerous secret missions behind enemy lines and his final picture shows him weary and tired. Hans was not the only combat casualty Karl Roth's family suffered during the war, as his other two stepbrothers on his father's side of the family were killed in France as well. (Hans Niedt Collection)

The German Army stressed the importance of horsemanship training as a great majority of their divisions were still using horse-drawn means of transportation. (Hans Niedt Collection)

The motorboat was a broad beamed craft constructed of steel plates with copper nickel rivets. It was transported on a special two-wheeled trailer that the boat was directly launched and recovered from. (Hans Niedt Collection)

Motorboats were mostly used for pushing and towing rafts and bridge sections in bridging operations, reconnaissance of the opposite riverbanks, and barge pulling. (Hans Niedt Collection)

An officer inspects a demolition charge set on a bridge-span. The thoroughness of engineer operations carried out during the war increased steadily. (Hans Niedt Collection)

Once a bridgehead was established pneumatic boats played an important role, either ferrying equipment or acting as bridge supports. Small boat operations were practiced in all kinds of weather including during the winter. (Hans Niedt Collection)

Engineer units often formed small detachments within their unit for special missions. Many of the tactics used for winter warfare were techniques developed by the mountain divisions for the extreme cold. (Hans Niedt Collection)

Primarily division engineer columns used ready-made timber bridges. Here Hans Niedt inspects a heavy trestle structure supported on whole pontoon piers. (Hans Niedt Collection)

Hans Niedt's section takes time out for a short lunch and a quick smoke. (Hans Niedt Collection)

Photograph of Hans Niedt just before he was killed in 1943. (Hans Niedt Collection)

APPENDIX II

Karl Roth's Personal Records

Original military pass book destroyed by enemy action on 8 April 1943

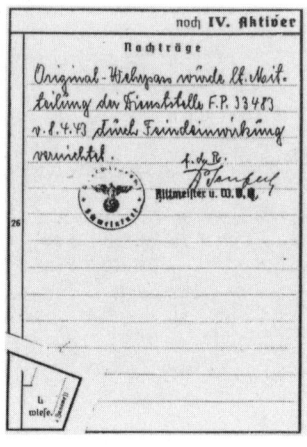

Karl Roth personal statistics page

Missing documents explanation page

Rank and promotions page. From top to bottom: *Gefreiter* – Private, *Obergefreiter* – Corporal, *Unteroffizer* – Sergeant, *Feldwebel* – Tech Sergeant, *Vorhandwerker* – Labourer

Official medals awarded page. From top to bottom: Campaign Victory Cross, Eastern Front Medallion, Tank Assault Badge, Iron-Cross, Second Class, Tank Destruction Badge in Gold, Tank Assault Badge-Silver

KARL ROTH'S PERSONAL RECORDS

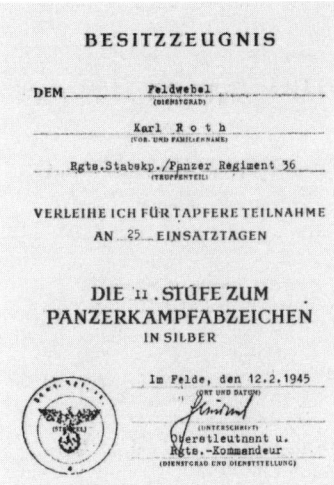

BESITZZEUGNIS

DEM Feldwebel
(DIENSTGRAD)

Karl Roth
(VOR. UND FAMILIENNAME)

Rgts.Stabskp./Panzer Regiment 36
(TRUPPENTEIL)

VERLEIHE ICH FÜR TAPFERE TEILNAHME
AN 25 EINSATZTAGEN

DIE II. STUFE ZUM
PANZERKAMPFABZEICHEN
IN SILBER

Im Felde, den 12.2.1945
(ORT UND DATUM)

(UNTERSCHRIFT)
Oberstleutnant u.
Rgts.-Kommandeur
(DIENSTGRAD UND DIENSTSTELLUNG)

Tank assault badge second class in silver award. (Courtesy E. Roth)

2.) Feldzug gegen Frankreich

A. Der Durchbruch zum Ärmelkanal im Verband der 6. Armee:

1.) 10.–12.5.40 Schlacht bei Maastricht
  a) 10. 5.40 Übergang über die Maas
  b) 11. 5.40 Durchbruch über den Albert-Kanal westlich Maastricht
2.) 12.–16.5.40 Panzerschlacht bei Hannut-Gembloux
  a) 12.–13.5.40 Panzerschlacht bei Hannut
  b) 14.–16.5.40 Durchbruch durch die Dyle-Stellung
3.) 18.–19.5.40 Verfolgungskämpfe über Seneffe u. Dendre
  a) 17.–18.5.40 Verfolgungskämpfe von der Dyle bis zum Charleroi-Kanal

B. Der Durchbruch zum Ärmelkanal im Verband der 4. Armee:

1.) 19.–22.5.40 Kämpfe um den Mormalwald

C. Schlacht in Flandern und im Artois im Verband der 4. Armee:

1.) 23.–26.5.40 Kämpfe zwischen Arras und St Omer
  a) 23.–26.5.40 Kämpfe um den la Bassee-Kanal bei Bethune
2.) 24.5.–1.6.40 Kämpfe bei La Bassee und Lille
  a) 27.6.–40 Durchbruch über den la Bassee-Kanal bei Bethune
  b) 28.–29.5.40 Kämpfe bei Armentieres und Bailleul

French Campaign Record, Operation Yellow. (Courtesy E. Roth)

noch IV. Aktiver

Im Kriege mitgemachte Gefechte, Schlachten, Unternehmungen

Tag, Monat, Jahr	Ortsangabe, Truppenteil usw.
1.) Feldzug gegen Polen:	
1. 9.– 2. 9.39	Kämpfe um die Lyswarta
2. 9. 39	Waldgefecht nördlich Klobuck
5. 9.– 6. 9.39	Kampf um die Widamka-Stellung
8. 9. 39	Stoss über Mozczonow in die Vorstädte von Warschau
8. 9.–14. 9.39	Kämpfe in und bei Warschau
15. 9.–19. 9.39	Angriff und Verfolgung bis zur Weichsel
16. 9.–19. 9.39	Vernichtungskämpfe südl. Wysogrod
15.10.–29.11.39	Verwendung im Heimatkriegsgebiet
30.11.– 9. 5.40	Verwendung im Operationsgebiet der Westfront

Polish Campaign Record, Operation White (Courtesy E. Roth)

Yugoslavian Campaign Record (Operation Punishment). (Courtesy E. Roth)

French Campaign Record (Operation Red). (Courtesy E. Roth)

Russian Campaign Record (Operation *Barbarossa*). (Courtesy E. Roth)

Kharkov Campaign Record (Operation *Fred*. I and II). Stalingrad Campaign (Operation Blue). (Courtesy E. Roth)

APPENDIX III

Orders of Battle and Organisational Charts

14th Panzer Division Unit Organisation

14th *Panzer* Division when formed:
Panzer Regiment 36
Motorised (*Schützen*)-Regiment 103
Motorised (*Schützen*)-Regiment 108
Motorcycle Battalion 64
Panzerartillerie Regiment 4
Panzerjäger Battalion 4
Flak Battalion 4
Panzer Reconnaissance Battalion 40
Pioneer Battalion 13
Signals Battalion 4
Field Medical Battalion 4
14th Divisional Support Units

14th *Panzer* Division when reformed 1943:
Panzer Regiment 36
Panzergrenadier Regiment 103
Panzergrenadier Regiment 108
Motorcycle Battalion 64
Panzerartillerie Regiment 4
Panzerjäger Battalion 4
Flak Battalion 276
Panzer Pioneer Battalion 13
Signals Battalion 4
Field Medical Battalion 4
14th Divisional Support Units

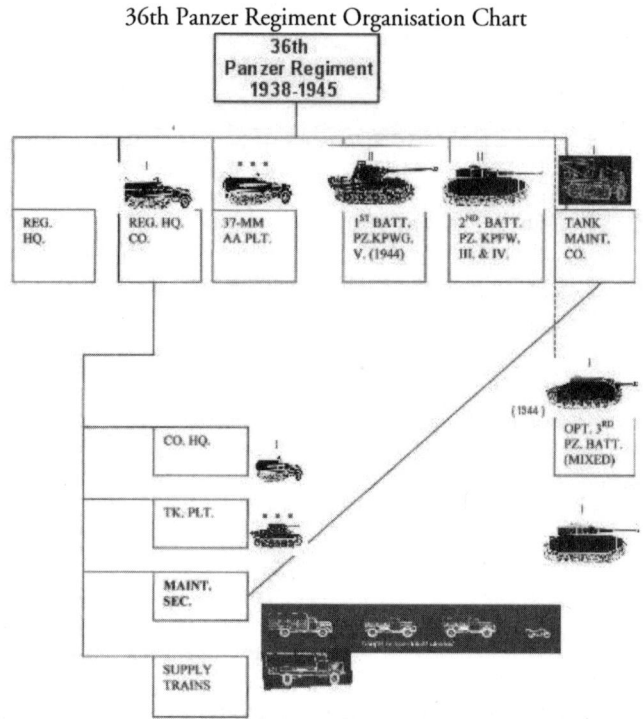

Theoretical Strength of 1944 Panzer Regiment

	Officers	Beamt	NCOs	Troops	Hiwi	Total
Panzer Regiment	8	—	63	97	8	176
I. Abteilung (batt.) (Staff)	7	—	41	111	—	159
Panzer Company (4 companies of 17 tanks)	12	—	228	172		412
Versorgungskompanie (Panther battalion)	5	2	59	188	23	277
II. Abteilung (batt.) (Staff)	7	—	41	111	—	159

ORDERS OF BATTLE & ORGANISATIONAL CHARTS 179

	Tanks	APC	AA Guns	Motorcycles	Cars	Trucks	Half-Track	Other
Panzer Company (4 companies of 22 tanks)	12	—		264	196	—		472
Versorgungskompanie (Pz. Kpfw. IV batt.)	5	2		51	103	20		181
Panzerwerkstattkompanie	3	3		39	164	21		230
Total *Panzer* Regiment	59	7		786	1,142	72		2,066

Beamt: An official or administrator
Hiwi: *Hilfswillige* – Soviet auxiliary

Equipment:

	Tanks	Armoured Personnel Carriers	AA Guns	Motorcycles	Cars	Trucks	Half-Track	Other
Panzer Regiment (total)	151 + 9 command vehicles		10	14	57	70	187	27	39

36th *Panzer* Regiment: Assignments to Higher Formations

1 Sep. 1939	Polish Campaign. XVI *PK* (Hoepner) – 5th *PA* – 1st *PD*, 4th *PD*, 14th ID, 31st ID
10 May 1940	French Campaign. XVI *PK* (Hoepner) – 5th *PA* (Breith) – 3rd *PD*, 4th *PD*, 20th MD, *SS* Div. *Totenkopf.*
5 Apr. 1941	Yugoslavian Campaign. VLI *PK* (v. Vietinghoff) – 8th *PD*, 14th *PD*, 16th MD
22 Jun. 1941	*Barbarossa. Panzer* Group One (v. Kleist) – III MC (Mackensen) – 13th *PD*, 14th *PD*, 1st *SS* Div. *Leibstandarte*, 5th *SS* Div. *Wiking.*
8 Aug. 1941	Attack on Krivoi Rog. XIV MC (v. Wietersheim) – 14th *PD*, 60th ID
16 Aug. 1941	Attack on Dnepropretrovsk. III MC (Mackensen) – 13th *PD*, 14th *PD*, 1st *SS* Div. *Leibstandarte*, 5th *SS* Div. *Wiking.*
10 Sep. 1941	Crossing the Dnepr River. XIV MC (v. Wietersheim) – 14th *PD*, 60th ID
10 Oct. 1941	Attack on Rostov. III MC (Mackensen) – 13th *PD*, 14th *PD*, 1st *SS* Div. *Leibstandarte*, 5th *SS* Div. *Wiking.*

1 Jan. 1942	Winter war on the Mius Line. III *PK*, so understrength it was broken down to form 'Group Mackensen', with amalgamated battle groups forming hedgehog positions to stop the first Russian winter offensive. Each group was designated by its commander's last name. Group Hube – with parts of 14th *PD*, 16th *PD*, 100th LD Group Montfort – 60th *PA* (Renamed from 2nd Batt. 36th *PR*). (Other Divisional Battle Groups – Kohlerman and Special Battalion Grams).
28 May 1942	Kharkov Operation *Fredericus I.* (Volchansk). III *PK* (Mackensen) – 14th *PD*, 16th *PD*, 384th ID
16 Jun. 1942	*Fredericus II.* (Kupyansk). Group Hube – elements of 14th *PD*, 16th *PD*, 44th ID
11 Jul. 1942	Begin Operation Blue. XIV *PK* – 14th *PD*, 22nd *PD*
mid Jul. 1942	Move on Rostov. III *PK* (v. Mackensen) – 14th *PD*, LSSAH, 16th *PD*
30 Jul. 1942	Advance on southern Stalingrad. VLI *PK* – 4th *PzArmee* (Hoth) – 14th *PD*, 16th *PD*, 24th *PD* (arrived late), 29th MD
20 Aug. 1942	Attacking southern Stalingrad. Transferred to 6th Army (Paulus) – 14th *PD*, 24th *PD*, 29th MD, 94th ID
4 Oct. 1942	Attacking the northern factory districts with LI *Korps* (v. Seydlitz) – 14th *PD*, 389th ID, 60th MD
19 Nov. 1942	Operating with the 3rd Romanian Army. 48th *PK* (*Panzer Reserve Heim*), with elements of 36th *PR*, 16th *PD*, 44th ID
19 Nov. 1942	Defending the northern flank of Stalingrad. VIII *AK*, with elements of 36th *PR*
23 Nov. 1942	Trapped in the Stalingrad pocket. XIV *PK* – elements of 36th *PR*, 14th *PD*, 3rd MD, 376th ID, 29th MD
12 Dec. 1942	The relief attempt on Stalingrad. LVII *PK* (Kirchner) – 1st Batt. 36th *PR* (Group Sauvant operating near Kotelnikovo under Group Pannwitz), 6th *PD*, 23rd *PD*, 17th *PD*
12 Dec. 1942	Defending the upper Chir River. VLIII *PK* (Knoberlsdorff), with surviving elements of 36th *PR* not attached to the 3rd Romanian Army.
30 Jan. 1943	Surrendered in the Stalingrad pocket. XIV *PK* – One CO. tanks of 36th *PR*, HQ. and workshop CO., elements of the 14th *PD*
17 Feb. 1943	36th *PR* reformed at Stalino.
25 Apr. 1943	14th *PD* reformed in Brittany (Angers), France.

ORDERS OF BATTLE & ORGANISATIONAL CHARTS 181

27 Oct. 1943	The Dnepr River battles near Kirovograd. XL *PK* – 4th *PD*, 24th *PD*, SS *PD Totenkopf.*
6 Nov. 1943	Northern attacks by Krivoi-Rog. LVII *PK* (Kirchner) – 14th *PD*, 9th *PD*, 11th *PD*, 16th *PGD*, 23rd *PD*, *Pg*D *Grossdeutschland.*
25 Nov. 1943	Deployed near Cherkassy. 6th *AK* (Stemmerman) – elements of 14th *PD*, 6th *PD*, 11th *PD*
5 Jan. 1944	Attack on Kirovograd. VLII *PK* (Vormann) – 14th *PD* (Divisional *Kampfgruppe* Brese), 3rd *PD*, 376th ID, 10th *PGD*
10 Feb. 1944	Relief of the Cherkassy pocket. VLII *PK* (Vormann) – 14th *PD* (with minor elements of 14th *PD* trapped inside the pocket with 42nd *AK* (Stemmerman)), 3rd *PD*, 11th *PD*, 24th *PD* (to be sent in later).
Mar. 1944	Retreat into Romania. Divisional Operational Group Mummert.
14 Apr 1944	Near Roman, Romania. LII *PK* (Kirchner, 6th Army Reserve) – 14th *PD*, 23rd *PD*
15 Aug. 1944	Operation *Doppelkopf.* Attack on Kursenai-Schaulen (near the Venta Canal). XL *PK* (Knobelsdorff) – 14th *PD*, 7th *PD*
01 Sep. 1944	Defence of Modohn. 16th *AK* – 14th *PD*, 24th ID
15 Sep. 1944	Supporting 10th *AK* near Baldone, and 1st *AK* near Kekava. 14th *PD*, GD Div.
23–24 Sep. 1944	Bridgehead of Kekeva, south of Riga. III SS *PK* – 14th *PD*, 11th ID, 11th SS Div. *Nordland,* 225th *PGD*
10 Oct. 1944	Near Preekuln. 10th *AK* – 14th *PD*, 11th ID, 61st ID
22 Oct. 1944	1st and 2nd Courland Battles (near Vianode). 10th *AK* – 14th *PD*, 30th ID
24 Jan. 1945	4th and 5th Courland Battles. *Kurland* Fire Brigade – 14th *PD*, sPzAbt 502 (renamed Jan.), sPzAbt 510, 4th *PD* (evacuated Jan.), 12th *PD*, SS Div. *Nordland* (evacuated Mar.).
1 Mar. 1945	Outside Libau Harbour (Durban). 18th Army Reserve – 14th *PD*, 12th *PD*, 121st ID
8 May 1945	Libau. Last Army Group Reserve – 14th *PD*, 11th ID

AK – *Armeekorps*
GD – *Panzergrenadier* Division *Grossdeutschland*
ID – Infantry Division
LD – Light Division
MC – Motorised Corps
MD – Motorised Division
PA – *Panzer* Battalion
PD – *Panzer* Division

PGD – *Panzergrenadier* Division
PK – *Panzerkorps*
PR – *Panzer* Regiment
PzArmee – *Panzerarmee*
SPzAbt – Heavy *Panzer* Battalion

APPENDIX IV

Panzer Recovery and Repair: The Workshop Company

Designed to support the tanks of the *Panzer* regiment, the workshop company (roughly 230 personnel) formed the backbone of the maintenance system of the German Army. Their main priority was to do everything possible to extricate damaged or stuck vehicles from the battlefield in less than twelve hours, with the tools at their disposal, and get them back up and running again. If the repair work on a vehicle was too extensive for the workshop company, it was then sent to an Army Motor Transport Park *(HeKP)*.

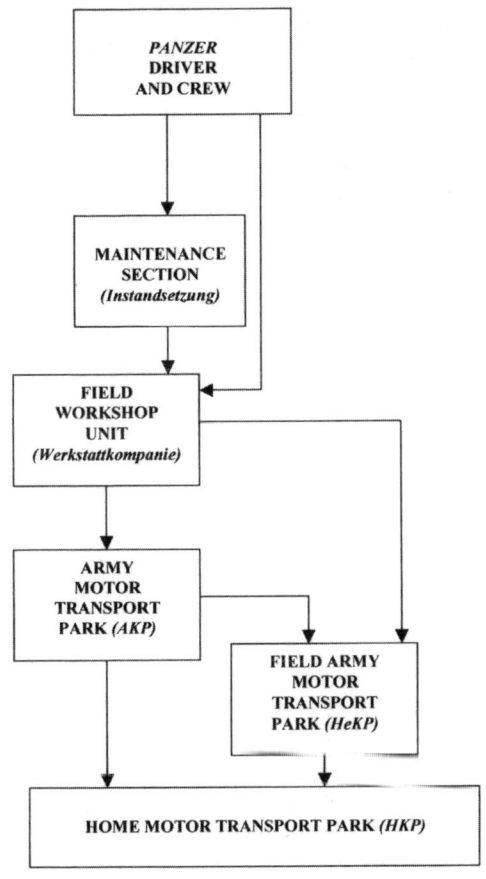

Motor Vehicle Repair and Maintenance Flow Chart. (U.S. War Dept.)

Recovery operations with a Tiger

Leading the mobile field workshop company was a maintenance section (*Instandsetzungsgruppe*) assigned to the regimental headquarters of the *Panzer* regiment. This section, which Karl Roth was assigned, was responsible for carrying out repairs that could take less than four hours time. Their main function though was to report directly to the regimental commander precisely how many tanks were operational, damaged, or total write-offs. This command group of two officers and around eighteen enlisted men kept the records on all the regiment's vehicles and made decisions on which tanks were to be salvaged, repaired in the field, or sent back to collection points as far back as their Home Motor Transport Park (*HKP* in Schweinfurt). Another vital function of the *Instandsetzungstruppe* was to requisition the parts from major supply centres in their operational area, and occasionally transport those supplies back to their unit (in the Soviet Union rail supply was used heavily for this). The maintenance command section was the liaison between the regimental headquarters and the workshop company in the field, and a vital part of the *Panzer* regiment's repair and recovery effort. (Bundesarchiv)

Salvage teams of the workshop company utilized various pieces of equipment and vehicles adapted to recovery operations. This included prime movers between 6 and 18 tons equipped with towing winches to pull vehicles out of the mud, and cranes for removing entire engine assemblies, to specially designed tanks *(Bergepanzer)* for recovery work. Below is the 8-ton version of the *SdKfz. 251/7* medium halftrack, known to maintenance crews as a 'prime-mover'. This was the most successful vehicle series produced by the Germans during the war, and had multiple uses. By 1944 a standard *Panzer* regiment had 27 prime mover halftracks of various configurations. This photograph is part of the Hans Niedt collection (see Appendix I), featuring a combat engineer design. Ground clearance: 44cm.

PANZER RECOVERY & REPAIR 185

8-ton version of the *SdKfz. 251/7* medium halftrack

Maximum road speed 50km/h. Onboard storage: 3 tons of equipment. (Hans Niedt Collection)

APPENDIX V

Regimental Tanks

Pz. Kpfw. I

The first standardized German tank design, produced in 1934, the *Sd Kfz* (special motor vehicle) 101 light tank was armed with two machine-guns (later model C armed with one AT Gun and one MG, but never saw combat) and crewed by two men. The tank weighed between six and eight tons and travelled at an average speed of only 16mph with a range of approximately 95 miles. This tank quickly became obsolete and was relegated to reconnaissance roles and then finally was deleted from the Table of Equipment for the *Panzer* regiment. (AC)

Pz. Kpfw. II

The *Pz. Kpfw.* II, *Sd Kfz* 121 light tank, built between 1934–1936, carried a 20mm gun, MG 34 machine gun, and a crew of three. The commander acted as the gunner and was accompanied by a radio operator, and a driver. It had a road speed of between 15 and 40mph with a range of approximately 130 miles. A large number of the 12-ton tanks were produced before they became obsolete in 1943. In a very much-modified form it reappeared as Lynx reconnaissance tank in Western Europe. A flame-throwing version was also produced, and the modified hull was used as a self-propelled gun carriage. This tank was also phased out quite early in the war and was used only in the anti-partisan and reconnaissance roles. Although highly valued by the maintenance company, *Pz. Kpfw.* II and III recovery vehicles were rare, with only 271 being built during the war. By early 1944 all *Pz.Kpfw.* III's returned for overhaul were then to be converted into *Bergepanzers* (armoured tank recovery vehicles). (AC)

Pz. Kpfw. III

The *Pz. Kpfw.* III, *Sd Kfz* 141 medium tank weighed 24 tons and appeared in many models of the same characteristics. It was first armed with a 37mm gun, and one MG 34 machine gun, until late 1940 when it was up-gunned to the 5cm long barrelled version. Fielding a crew of five, it travelled at approximately between 22 and 35mph (depending on conditions) with a range of 102 miles. The *Pz. Kpfw.* III was also decommissioned although versions mounting the short 7.5cm gun, a commander's vehicle, flame-throwing tank, as a wrecker tank, ammunition carrier, and observation post models were also produced. (Courtesy D. Byrd)

Pz. Kpfw. IV (S)

The *Pz. Kpfw.* IV, *Sd. Kfz.* 161 medium tank with a crew of five, was armed originally with a short 75mm gun and a coaxially mounted MG 34 in the turret. Later models added a MG in the hull as well, along with a re-armed long-barrelled high velocity 75mm. (Courtesy D. Byrd)

Pz. Kpfw. IV (L)

The only original German tank design to stay in service throughout the war, it changed its role as a close support vehicle to a fighting tank displacing the *Pz. Kpfw.* III as the main armament of most *Panzer* regiments. This tank also appeared as a commander's vehicle, observation tank, ammunition carrier, and as an armoured anti-aircraft platform. It travelled at 20–25mph and had a range of 130 miles. The Mark IV was the workhorse of the *Panzer* regiments. (Courtesy D. Byrd)

Pz. Kpfw. V

Regarded as the most successful and best tank of its generation, the *Pz. Kpfw.* V Panther medium tank weighed about 50 tons, and its armour was enhanced by the fact that most of the plates are sloping. Introduced on the battlefield at Kursk in the summer of 1943, its 7.5cm gun, manoeuvrability, high speed (30mph), sloped armour, and good protection made this an awesome and feared weapon. Internally the Panther is arranged with the driver's compartment in front, the fighting compartment in the centre section, and the engine at the rear. The undercarriage is designed to employ double torsion-bar suspension, having the effect of expanding their length. Teething troubles reduced the original strength of the tanks within *Panzer* regiments, but when this problem was overcome it served notably on all fronts during the war. The *Jagdpanther,* a noteworthy variant of the Panther incorporated an 8.8cm gun, and was issued to *Panzer* divisions and independent SP anti-tank battalions. The *Bergepanther* (recovery vehicle) was employed in the workshop companies of the tank divisions along with a commander's version. (Courtesy D. Byrd)

Sturmgeschütz III and IV Assault Gun

The *StuG* III and IV assault gun mounted a 7.5cm gun in a turret-less chassis, was intended as an infantry support vehicle but nevertheless served in *Panzer* regiments and independent brigades. It weighed 22 tons, had a crew of four, and a speed of 20mph. Inclined to be slower than and less manoeuvrable than tanks, they were suited particularly well for attacks on enemy infantry heavy weapons and main points of resistance. The 7.5cm gun the assault gun carries has been modified to fit an armoured halftrack vehicle and an eight-wheeled armoured car. (AC)

Notes

Preface notes

1. Two died in France with the Luftwaffe, and the other in a land mine accident while assigned to a combat pioneer section. (See Appendix I)
2. There is almost no written English language material concerning the Courland pocket, and therefore this work also provides a detailed account of these battles.
3. Including survivor reunion interviews and letters, official unit histories, and combat strength reports.
4. In Thomas L. Jentz's masterfully detailed book *Panzertruppen*, he states that "Panzer-Regiment 2, 24, and 36th had been wiped out in Stalingrad" p.48. Although only a small battle group, there is no mention of Group Sauvant, or the few tank companies that remained attached to the 3rd Rumanian Army, not to mention the 36th Regiment's commander, Langkeit, who was flown out of the pocket and survived as well.
5. "Only a small group of armored personnel carriers and tanks, carrying the generals and senior officers, managed to get away, and they left their troops to the whim of fate." Even though this statement was far from the truth, Shimansky goes on to say, "On February 17th the encircled force was wiped out. Some 55,000 officers and men killed or wounded…" part 69, p.1906.
6. Erich von Manstein writes in his memoir, *Lost Victories*, "By 28th February we knew that between 30,000 and 32,000 men would come out of the pocket." p.517. And Roger Edwards in *Panzer: A Revolution in Warfare* writes, "and…succeeded (Hube) in driving a relief corridor eastwards through Russian forces investing Cherkassy to reach Lissjanska enabling 54,000 men… to escape encirclement;" p.169.
7. "Completely surrounded in the Baltic States, the remnants of the Courland Army were finally evacuated by boat and arrived at Swinemunde at the beginning of April. Of the eighteen divisions only a few boatloads of men, minus equipment, reached Germany." This statement is interesting because one of the largest evacuations that took place, bringing out over 25,000 troops from Libau and Windau harbour alone, did not even begin until May 1st. Heinz Schön, *Die Letzten Kriegstage: Ostseehafen 1945* p.358.
8. I met Arnie Dupuy, the son of Trevor Dupuy, both well-known military historians, when we served together in the same artillery unit

in the Maryland Army National Guard. Mr. Dupuy is now also a veteran of the Iraq War.

Chapter 1 notes

1. Editors of Time-Life Books, *Storming to Power*, p. 134.
2. Ibid., p. 83.
3. Editors of Time-Life Books, *The New Order*, p. 154.
4. Editors of Time-Life Books, *Fists of Steel*, pp. 139–44.
5. Editors of Time-Life Books, *The New Order*, pp. 131–41.
6. Ibid., p.112.
7. Ibid., p. 141.
8. Edwards, *Panzer: A Revolution in Warfare, 1939–1945*, p. 23. A record of inventory directly before going to war in 1939 listed the regiment as having 101 *Panzerkampfwagen* I's, 66 II's, and only 6 of the heavier IV's, (which after 1943 was the only original tank still in production) Total strength was 173 tanks. Jentz, *Panzertruppen, Vol. 1.*, p. 90.
9. Jentz, *Panzertruppen, Vol. I.*, pp. 56–7.
10. Ibid., pp. 23–30.
11. Else Roth, personal interview, Schweinfurt, Germany, October 1998.
12. Edwards, *Panzer: A Revolution in Warfare, 1939–1945*, p. 109.
13. Jutta Roth, personal interview, Phoenix, 1998.
14. Edwards, *Panzer: A Revolution in Warfare, 1939–1945*, pp. 109–10.
15. Interview by author, 14th *Panzer* Division reunion, Kuhlsheim, Germany, 9 October 1998.
16. Edwards, *Panzer: A Revolution in Warfare, 1939–1945*, p. 109.
17. Ibid., p. 109.
18. U.S. War Department, *Handbook on German Military Forces*, p. 69.
19. Ibid., p. 71.
20. Videotape, *Hitler's 1939 Birthday Parade: Germany Celebrates Hitler's Birthday.*
21. *Illustrated World War II Encyclopedia. Vol. 1.*, pp. 11–13.
22. Ibid., pp. 16–20.
23. Fritz, *Frontsoldaten: The German Soldier In World War II*, pp. 160–1.

Chapter 2 notes

1. Else Roth, personal interview, Schweinfurt, Germany, 6 October 1998.
2. Ibid.
3. Scheibert, *Kampf und Untergang der Deutschen Panzertruppe*, p. 18.
4. Delaney, *The Blitzkrieg Campaigns: Germany's 'Lightning War' Strategy in Action*, pp. 47–51.
5. Ibid., p. 55.
6. Ibid., p. 39.
7. Ibid., p. 58.

8 Edwards, *Panzer: A Revolution in Warfare, 1939–1945*, p. 175.
9 Delaney, *The Blitzkrieg Campaigns: Germany's 'Lightning War' Strategy in Action*, p. 65.
10 Jentz, *Panzertruppen, Vol. I.*, p. 96.
11 Editors of Time-Life Books, *The Reach for Empire*, p. 161.
12 Zimmermann, *Der Griff ins Ungewisse* p. 22.
13 Edwards, *Panzer: A Revolution in Warfare, 1939–1945*, p. 177.
14 Delaney, *The Blitzkrieg Campaigns: Germany's 'Lightning War' Strategy in Action*, p. 63.
15 Pitt, "Prelude to Disaster", p. 27.
16 Editors of Time-Life Books, *The Reach for Empire*, p. 162.
17 Delaney, *The Blitzkrieg Campaigns: Germany's 'Lightning War' Strategy in Action*, pp. 70–1.
18 Ibid., p. 72.
19 Karl Roth's official war file, (see Appendix II).
20 Else Roth, personal interview, Schweinfurt, Germany, October 1998.
21 46 *Pz.*. I's, 33 *Pz.*. II's, and 6 *Pz.*. IV's. Jentz, *Panzertruppen, Vol. I.*, p. 104.
22 This number is in dispute, with some historians claiming losses by the Germans to be twice this number.
23 Delaney, *The Blitzkrieg Campaigns: Germany's 'Lightning War' Strategy in Action*, pp. 72–3.

Chapter 3 notes

1 Scheibert, *Kampf und Untergang der Deutschen Panzertruppe*, pp. 17–25.
2 Jentz, *Panzertruppen, Vol. I.*, p. 120.
3 Delaney, *The Blitzkrieg Campaigns: Germany's 'Lightning War' Strategy in Action*, pp. 74–5.
4 Begun in 1929, the string of fortifications ran from Basel, Switzerland, along the frontier with Germany and Luxembourg, theoretically stretching through Belgium and Holland. Barry, "Military Balance", pp. 100–1.
5 Ibid.
6 Vliegen, *Fort Eben-Emael*, p. 25.
7 Ibid., pp. 123–7.
8 Ibid., pp. 33–5.
9 Editors of Time-Life Books, *Lightning War*, p. 40.
10 Vliegen, *Fort Eben-Emael*, p. 35.
11 Ibid., pp. 41–3.
12 Ibid., p. 43.
13 Editors of Time-Life Books, *Lightning War*, p. 40.
14 Edwards, *Panzer: A Revolution in Warfare, 1939–1945*, p. 178.
15 Delaney, *The Blitzkrieg Campaigns: Germany's 'Lightning War' Strategy in Action*, p. 89.
16 Scheibert, *Kampf und Untergang der Deutschen Panzertruppe*, p. 26.

17 Tank inventory on May 10th was 66 Mk I's, 55 *Pz.* II's 26 *Pz.* III's, and 12 *Pz.* IV's. Jentz, *Panzertruppen, Vol. I.*, pp. 120–2.
18 *Illustrated World War II Encyclopedia. Vol. 1.*, p. 148.
19 Delaney, *The Blitzkrieg Campaigns: Germany's 'Lightning War' Strategy in Action*, pp. 88–98.
20 Editors of Time-Life Books, *Lightning War*, p. 72.
21 Delaney, *The Blitzkrieg Campaigns: Germany's 'Lightning War' Strategy in Action*, p. 101.
22 Karl Roth's official war file, (see Appendix II).
23 Editors of Time-Life Books, *Lightning War*, p. 79.
24 Ibid., pp. 76–7.
25 Edwards, *Panzer: A Revolution in Warfare, 1939–1945*, p. 148.
26 Delaney, *The Blitzkrieg Campaigns: Germany's 'Lightning War' Strategy in Action*, p. 107.
27 Ibid.
28 Ibid., p. 109.
29 Ibid., pp. 111–12.
30 Karl Roth's official war file, (see Appendix II). Also see Stein, *The Waffen SS: Hitler's Elite Guard at War 1939–1945*, pp. 76–7.
31 Delaney, *The Blitzkrieg Campaigns: Germany's 'Lightning War' Strategy in Action*, p. 109.
32 Edwards, *Panzer: A Revolution in Warfare, 1939–1945*, p. 178.
33 Karl Roth's official war file, (see Appendix II).
34 Editors of Time-Life Books, *Lightning War*, p. 108.
35 Edwards, *Panzer: A Revolution in Warfare, 1939–1945*, p. 178.
36 Karl Roth's official war file, (see Appendix II).
37 Edwards, *Panzer: A Revolution in Warfare, 1939–1945*, p. 178.
38 Charles, "Invasion of Holland and Belgium", p. 130.
39 Editors of Time-Life Books, *Lightning War*, p. 118.
40 Ibid., p. 120.
41 Karl Roth's official war file, (see Appendix II).
42 Ibid.

Chapter 4 notes

1 Else Roth, personal interview, October 1998
2 Editors of Time-Life Books, *Lightning War*, pp. 134–8.
3 Ibid., pp. 126–7.
4 Ibid., pp. 128–9.
5 Edwards, *Panzer: A Revolution in Warfare, 1939–1945*, p. 174.
6 Ibid.
7 Jentz, *Panzertruppen, Vol. I.*, pp. 142–6.
8 Edwards, *Panzer: A Revolution in Warfare, 1939–1945*, p. 174.
9 Editors of Time-Life Books, *Lightning War*, p. 126,
10 Lukacs, *The Duel*, p. 153.
11 Editors of Time-Life Books, *Lightning War*, pp. 145–51.
12 Ibid., pp. 132–3.
13 Goerlitz, *Paulus and Stalingrad*, pp. 96–97.

14 Editors of Time-Life Books, *Lightning War*, p. 129.
15 Goerlitz, *Paulus and Stalingrad*, p. 94.
16 Richards, "Battle of Britain", p. 234.
17 Editors of Time-Life Books, *Lightning War*, p. 174.
18 Jentz, *Panzertruppen, Vol. I.*, p. 143.

Chapter 5 notes

1   Jentz, *Panzertruppen*, Vol. I., p. 146.
2   Tank inventory at the start of the campaign amounted to: 45 *Pz.* II's, 16 *Pz.* III's, 35 *Pz.* IV (50mm)'s, and 20 *Pz.* IV's. Jentz, *Panzertruppen, Vol. I.*, p. 154.
3   Grams, *Die 14. Panzer-Division 1940–1945*, p. 16.
4   Palmer, "Operation Punishment", pp. 379–80.
5   Grams, *Die 14. Panzer-Division 1940–1945*, p. 18.
6   Blau, *Invasion Balkans*, p. 56.
7   Grams, *Die 14. Panzer-Division 1940–1945*, p. 18.
8   Ibid.
9   Blau, *Invasion Balkans*, pp. 56–7.
10 Grams, *Die 14. Panzer-Division 1940–1945*, pp. 19–21. Also see Editors of Time-Life Books, *Conquest of the Balkans*, pp. 50–1.
11 Scheibert, *Kampf und Untergang der Deutschen Panzertruppe*, p. 45.
12 Jentz, *Panzertruppen, Vol. I.*, p. 157.
13 Scheibert, *Kampf und Untergang der Deutschen Panzertruppe*, p. 43.
14 For information on this subject see Hamburg Institute for Social Research (ed.), *The German Army and Genocide: Crimes Against War Prisoners, Jews, and Other Civilians, 1939–1944*.

Chapter 6 notes

1   Scheibert, *Kampf und Untergang der Deutschen Panzertruppe*, p. 51.
2   Grams, *Die 14. Panzer-Division 1940–1945*, p. 23.
3   Jentz, *Panzertruppen, Vol. I.*, p. 186.
4   Regimental tank strength on the opening day of Barbarossa amounted to: 45 *Pz.* II's, 15 *Pz.* III's (37mm), 56 *Pz.* III's (50mm), and 20 *Pz.* IV's. Jentz, *Panzertruppen, Vol. I.*, p. 192.
5   Grams, *Die 14. Panzer-Division 1940–1945*, p. 23.
6   Edwards, *Panzer: A Revolution in Warfare, 1939–1945*, p. 151.
7   Editors of Time-Life Books, *Barbarossa*, p. 17.
8   *Panzer* Group One consisted of the 3rd and 14th *Panzerkorps*. Grams, *Die 14. Panzer-Division 1940–1945*, p. 23.
9   The 14th *Panzer Div.* stayed under his command until July 1942, when Army Group A broke off and was directed south to secure the Caucasus oil region. Kleist was relieved of command by Hitler in 1944 and after the war was extradited from Yugoslavia to Russia, dying a prisoner of war in 1954.
10 Delaney, *The Blitzkrieg Campaigns: Germany's 'Lightning War' Strategy in Action*, p. 24.
11 Scheibert, *Kampf und Untergang der Deutschen Panzertruppe*, p. 55.

12 Grams, *Die 14. Panzer-Division 1940–1945*, p. 23.
13 Ibid., pp. 23–4.
14 Soon after the 14th *Panzer* Division vacated the city of Lutzk, the death squads of *"Einsatzgruppe C"* immediately went to work executing the Jewish and so-called communists of the population.
15 Ibid., p. 24.
16 Jukes, "Barbarossa: Drive to Kiev", p. 607.
17 Grams, *Die 14. Panzer-Division 1940–1945*, p. 25.
18 Delaney, *The Blitzkrieg Campaigns: Germany's 'Lightning War' Strategy in Action*, p. 44.
19 Grams, *Die 14. Panzer-Division 1940–1945*, p. 26.
20 Delaney, *The Blitzkrieg Campaigns: Germany's 'Lightning War' Strategy in Action*, p. 143.
21 Grams, *Die 14. Panzer-Division 1940–1945*, p. 26.
22 Jentz, *Panzertruppen, Vol. I.*, p. 211.
23 Grams, *Die 14. Panzer-Division 1940–1945*, p. 26.
24 Delaney, *The Blitzkrieg Campaigns: Germany's 'Lightning War' Strategy in Action*, p. 150.
25 Grams, *Die 14. Panzer-Division 1940–1945*, p. 27.
26 Ibid.
27 Grams, *Die 14. Panzer-Division 1940–1945*, pp. 28–9.
28 Ibid., p. 29.
29 Delaney, *The Blitzkrieg Campaigns: Germany's 'Lightning War' Strategy in Action*, p. 152.
30 Editors of Time-Life Books, *Barbarossa*, p. 88.
31 Delaney, *The Blitzkrieg Campaigns: Germany's 'Lightning War' Strategy in Action*, p. 169.
32 Stein, *The Waffen SS: Hitler's Elite Guard at War 1939–1945*, p. 273.
33 Editors of Time-Life Books, *Barbarossa*, p. 122.
34 Grams, *Die 14. Panzer-Division 1940–1945*, p. 30.
35 Ibid., pp. 30–1.
36 Ibid.
37 Editors of Time-Life Books, *Barbarossa*, p. 142.
38 Grams, *Die 14. Panzer-Division 1940–1945*, pp. 30–1.
39 Editors of Time-Life Books, *Barbarossa*, p. 126.
40 Grams, *Die 14. Panzer-Division 1940–1945*, p. 31.
41 Total write-offs at the end of October numbered: 6 *Pz.* II's, 28 *Pz.* III's, and 12 *Pz.* IV's. Jentz, *Panzertruppen, Vol. I.*, p. 211.
42 Editors of Time-Life Books, *Barbarossa*, p. 126.
43 Ibid.
44 Delaney, *The Blitzkrieg Campaigns: Germany's 'Lightning War' Strategy In Action*, p. 170.
45 On Dec. 16th one company each from the 36th (5th Co), 2nd and 4th *Panzer* Regiments formed 'Group Montfort'.
46 Grams, *Die 14. Panzer-Division 1940–1945*, p. 33.
47 Goerlitz, *Paulus and Stalingrad*, pp. 50–1.

48 Philippi, "The Battle for Moscow: The German View", p. 743.
49 Paul Schmidt, Schonegun, personal interview, 1996.
50 Editors of Time-Life Books, *Barbarossa*, p. 166.
51 One of the German army's greatest crimes of the war was evident when the Red Army retook Lozavaya, along a major railroad artery. A squalid camp was exposed containing thousands of dead and dying Soviet POWs. Stein, *The Waffen SS: Hitler's Elite Guard at War 1939–1945*.
52 Clark, *Barbarossa: The Russian-German Conflict 1941–1945*, p. 200.
53 Mackensen was promoted to Chief of Staff of the German Army's cavalry corps in 1933, and his mounted regiments provided the foundation for the first eight *Panzer* regiments. He possessed the
54 Grams, *Die 14. Panzer-Division 1940–1945*, p. 33.
55 Ibid., pp. 33–44.
56 Editors of Time-Life Books, *Barbarossa*, p. 166.

Chapter 7 notes

1   Editors of Time-Life Books, *The Road to Stalingrad*, p. 19.
2   Morozov, "The Kharkov Offensives", p. 960.
3   Ibid., p. 960.
4   Editors of Time-Life Books, *The Road to Stalingrad*, p. 17.
5   Glantz, *Kharkov 1942: Anatomy of a Military Disaster*, p. 171.
6   Editors of Time-Life Books, *The Road to Stalingrad*, p. 19. Also see Glantz, *Kharkov 1942: Anatomy of a Military Disaster*, p. 198.
7   Ibid. Also see Glantz, *Kharkov 1942: Anatomy of a Military Disaster*, pp. 202–5.
8   Morozov, "The Kharkov Offensives", p. 960.
9   Glantz, *Kharkov 1942: Anatomy of a Military Disaster*, p. 220.
10 Karl Roth's official war file, (see Appendix II).
11 Goerlitz, *Paulus and Stalingrad*, p. 180.
12 Editors of Time-Life Books, *The Road to Stalingrad*, pp. 20–1.
13 Grams, *Die 14. Panzer-Division 1940–1945*, p. 45.
14 Ibid.
15 Editors of Time-Life Books, *The Road to Stalingrad*, p. 21.
16 Clark, *Barbarossa: The Russian-German Conflict 1941–1945*, p. 203.
17 Editors of Time-Life Books, *The Road to Stalingrad*, p. 21.

Chapter 8 notes

1   Grams, *Die 14. Panzer-Division 1940–1945*, p. 46. Reported operational on June 20th, 14 *Pz.* II's, 41 *Pz.* III (short), 19 *Pz.* III (long), 20 *Pz.* IV (short) and 4 *Pz.* IV (long) for a total of three battalions of 98 tanks. Jentz, *Panzertruppen, Vol. I.*, p. 237.
2   Clark, "Stalingrad: The Most Vicious Battle of the War", p. 1047.
3   Ibid., p. 1049.
4   Tarrent, *Stalingrad: An Anatomy of an Agony*, pp. 37–8.
5   Grams, *Die 14. Panzer-Division 1940–1945*, pp. 46–7.
6   Ibid.

7   Ibid., pp. 47–8.
8   Ibid.
9   Ibid., p. 49.
10 *Oberst* Willi Langkeit was a battalion and then regimental commander who was airlifted out of Stalingrad on Jan. 19th and eventually commanded the *Grossdeutschland* Division in 1944. Grams, *Die 14. Panzer-Division 1940–1945*, p. 66. For a full description see McGuirl, Thomas & Remy Spazzano, *God, Honor, Fatherland*, p. 190.
11 Ibid.
12 Clark, "Stalingrad: The Most Vicious Battle of the War", p. 1049 (see map inset).
13 Hoth was a skilled commander of almost every campaign of the war being a *Panzerkorps* commander (XV) in Poland and France and 3rd *Panzer* Army during the advance on Moscow in 1941. Later he was the 17th Army commander in the Crimea until being assigned to the 4th *Panzer* Army for Operation Blue in 1942. The 14th *Panzer* Division was under his command from July 1942 until they were transferred to Paulus and the 6th Army in October of that year. His most famous action was when he led and attempted to reach the besieged garrison of Stalingrad during Manstein's failed relief operation, dubbed 'Winter storm'. Paulus refused to disobey Hitler's orders and affect a link up with Hoth dooming the relief operation. Hitler eventually dismissed Hoth after the loss of Kharkov in 1944 and he was captured by the Allies, released, and died in 1971.
14 Jukes, *Stalingrad: The Turning Point*, p. 28.
15 Edwards, *Panzer: A Revolution in Warfare, 1939–1945*, p. 180.
16 In the start of the campaign the XLVIII *Panzerkorps* originally comprised the 24th *Panzer* and two motorised divisions, but on July 30th it had the 14th *Panzer* and 16th Mot Div's, and the *29th* Mot. Div. During the advance on Stalingrad it comprised the 14th and 24th *Panzer* Div's, and the 29th Mot. Div.
17 Tarrent, *Stalingrad: An Anatomy of an Agony*, pp. 39–44. Also see Editors of Time-Life Books, *The Road to Stalingrad*, p. 62.
18 Grams, *Die 14. Panzer-Division 1940–1945*, p. 49.
19 Ibid., pp. 50.
20 Ibid.
21 Ibid.
22 Tarrent, *Stalingrad: An Anatomy of an Agony*, p. 44.
23 Clark, *Barbarossa: The Russian-German Conflict 1941–1945*, p. 216.
24 Grams, *Die 14. Panzer-Division 1940–1945*, pp. 50–1.
25 Ibid., p. 55. Also see Tarrent, *Stalingrad: An Anatomy of an Agony*, p. 44.
26 Tarrent, *Stalingrad: An Anatomy of an Agony*, pp. 54–5.
27 Ibid., p. 62.
28 Ibid.
29 Ibid.

30   Clark, *Barbarossa: The Russian-German Conflict 1941–1945*, p. 223.
31   Tarrent, *Stalingrad: An Anatomy of an Agony*, p. 74.
32   Ibid.
33   Ibid., p. 76.
34   Ibid., pp. 76–7.
35   Jukes, *Stalingrad: The Turning Point*, p. 81.
36   The regiment reported operational on 9 Oct 1942./ 11 *Pz.* III short, 21 *Pz.* III long, 1 *Pz. Mk* III 7..5, 6 *Pz.* IV short, and 6 *Pz.* IV long, with 4 command vehicles.
37   Tarrent, *Stalingrad: An Anatomy of an Agony*, p. 84.
38   Grams, *Die 14. Panzer-Division 1940–1945*, p. 54.
39   With elements of the 389th Inf. Div., 305th Inf. Div., and elements of the 14th *Panzer* Div.
40   Sauvant was another battalion leader promoted to regimental commander. He earned the German Cross in Gold during the advance on Stalingrad and his tanks helped capture the Tractor Factory, for which he was awarded the *Ritterkreuz*. His was the largest group of survivors from the 36th Regiment operating together outside the pocket.
41   Jukes, *Stalingrad: The Turning Point*, pp. 97–8. Also see Tarrent, *Stalingrad: An Anatomy of an Agony*, pp. 84–7.
42   Editors of Time-Life Books, *The Road to Stalingrad*, pp. 88–92.
43   Jutta Roth, personal interview, 1998.
44   Tarrent, *Stalingrad: An Anatomy of an Agony*, p. 87.
45   Grams, *Die 14. Panzer-Division 1940–1945*, p. 54.
46   Else Roth, personal interview, 1998.
47   Clark, *Barbarossa: The Russian-German Conflict 1941–1945*, p. 247.
48   According to an operational report on Nov. 19th, 6th Army reported the 14t*h Panzer* as having: 1 *Pz.* Mk III (short), 21 *Pz.* Mk III (long), 7 *Pz.* Mk III (75mm), 1 *Pz.* Mk IV (short) and 6 *Pz.* Mk IV (long) a total of
49   Heim began the war as Chief of the General Staff assigned to the XVI Motorised Corps From 1940–42 he was on the General Staff of 6th Army, until replaced and made commander of the 14th *Panzer* Division in July. He held this position throughout the vicious street fighting in Stalingrad up until the end of October, when he was fatefully reassigned as commander of the XLVIII *Panzerkorps* protecting the weak Rumanian northern flank outside Stalingrad. Even though seriously under strength and vastly outnumbered, his Corps (with elements of the 36th *Panzer* Regiment assigned) attempted to stem the Soviet onslaught. After an unsuccessful counter-attack they were ultimately broken up and pushed aside when the Soviet attacks began on November 19th. Hitler immediately recalled Heim to Berlin and wanted to have him shot. Only with the help of Keitel, Hitler's Chief of Staff, was his life spared. Once the weakness of XLVIII *Panzerkorps* was made apparent to Hitler, Heim was placed back in good standing and

reassigned to command the fortress port of Boulogne in France. He surrendered the port to the Allies against Hitler's orders in 1944 and was released from British captivity in February 1948.
50 Goerlitz, *Paulus and Stalingrad*, p. 199. Also see Tarrent, *Stalingrad: An Anatomy of an Agony*, p. 107.
51 Wieder & Graf von Einsiedel, *Stalingrad: Memories of Hell*, p. 23.
52 Ibid. Also see Tarrent, *Stalingrad: An Anatomy of an Agony*, p. 104.
53 Grams, *Die 14. Panzer-Division 1940–1945*, p. 57.
54 Tarrent, *Stalingrad: An Anatomy of an Agony*, p. 104.
55 Goerlitz, *Paulus and Stalingrad*, pp. 202–3. Also see Tarrent, *Stalingrad: An Anatomy of an Agony*, p. 119.
56 Editors of Time-Life Books, *The Road to Stalingrad*, p. 109 (see map inset).
57 Heinz Nuendorff, personal letter to the author, 1999.
58 Goerlitz, *Paulus and Stalingrad*, p. 203.
59 Mellenthin, *Panzer Battles*, p. 173.
60 Tarrent, *Stalingrad: An Anatomy of an Agony*, p. 131.
61 Ibid., pp. 132–3. Also see *World War II Magazine*, Vol. 12, No. 4, November 1997.
62 Center of Military History U.S. Army, *DA Pam. 20–201,. Military Improvisations During the Russian Campaign. Small Unit Actions During the German Campaign in Russia 1998*, pp. 41–2.
63 An entry in a Department of the Army pamphlet does state that furloughed troops returning to the front were stopped at Kamensk-Shakhtinski on the Donets and organized into an immediate reaction battalion. Ibid.
64 Manstein played one of the most important roles during the Stalingrad period by restabilising the Don Front and preventing a Soviet encirclement larger than the one that was achieved. A First World War veteran, he remained in the army and was head of instruction, training, and war-games in the new German Army. A brilliant staff officer, he was instrumental in promoting the Ardennes plan for the invasion of France and his energetic zeal in conducting operations at the front as a Corps commander during this campaign resulted in a promotion to lead *Panzer* troops during the Barbarossa offensive (even though he had no prior experience with armoured troops). Although he was able to accomplish a stunning counteroffensive that retook Kharkov and destroyed the Soviet 6th Army that spring, he failed to break through to the Stalingrad defenders the prior December. Hitler relieved him of command in March 1944 (along with von Kleist), after having numerous arguments over tactical and strategic decisions. Hitler's reasoning was that the time for large-scale operations was now over. After being captured by the Allies in 1945 he was sentenced to eighteen years in prison but was released in May 1953.
65 Grams, *Die 14. Panzer-Division 1940–1945*, pp. 88–97. Also see Tarrent, *Stalingrad: An Anatomy of an Agony*, p. 134.

66 Ibid., p. 61.
67 Tarrent, *Stalingrad: An Anatomy of an Agony*, pp. 141–2.
68 The 6th *Panzer* Division from France and the 23rd from the Caucasus region.
69 The 17th *Panzer* at full strength.
70 Tarrent, *Stalingrad: An Anatomy of an Agony*, p. 158.
71 Ibid., p. 155.
72 Ibid., pp. 152–9.
73 Ibid., p. 159.
74 Editors of Time-Life Books, *The Road to Stalingrad*, p. 125.
75 Tarrent, *Stalingrad: An Anatomy of an Agony*, pp. 166–72. Also see Editors of Time-Life Books, *The Road to Stalingrad*, p. 126, and Goerlitz, *Paulus and Stalingrad*, pp. 259–60.
76 Ibid., pp. 157–63.
77 Sadarananda, *Beyond Stalingrad: Manstein and the Operations of Army Group Don*, p. 48.
78 Tarrent, *Stalingrad: An Anatomy of an Agony*, p. 167.
79 H. Neuendorff, personal letter to the author, 1999.
80 Wieder & Graf von Einsiedel, *Stalingrad: Memories of Hell*, pp. 50–1.
81 Tarrent, *Stalingrad: An Anatomy of an Agony*, pp. 180–1.
82 Editors of Time-Life Books, *The Road to Stalingrad*, p. 136.
83 Willi Langkeit was one of these men flown out of the pocket on the 19th, later to command the 36th *Panzer* Rgt.
84 Goerlitz, *Paulus and Stalingrad*, p. 272.
85 Tarrent, *Stalingrad: An Anatomy of an Agony*, p. 171.
86 Sadarananda, *Beyond Stalingrad: Manstein and the Operations of Army Group Don*, p. 63.
87 Tarrent, *Stalingrad: An Anatomy of an Agony*, pp. 212–13.
88 Heinz Nuendorff, personal letter to the author, 1999. Also see Wieder & Graf von Einsiedel, *Stalingrad: Memories of Hell*, pp. 66–7.
89 Editors of Time-Life Books, *The Road to Stalingrad*, p. 141.
90 Wieder & Graf von Einsiedel, *Stalingrad: Memories of Hell*, pp. 100–6.
91 Ibid., pp. 307–12.
92 Editors of Time-Life Books, *The Road to Stalingrad*, pp. 164–6.
93 2nd *SS Panzerkorps* with *Leibstandarte, Das Reich, Totenkopf* and *Panzergrenadier Div. Grossdeutschland*. This was the first time the *Waffen SS* Divisions operated as an independent corps and saw the arrival of the Tiger tank in notable quantities.
94 Editors of Time-Life Books, *The Road to Stalingrad*, pp. 167–8.
95 Ibid., p. 174.
96 Ibid., pp. 178–9.
97 Scheibert, *Kampf und Untergang der Deutschen Panzertruppe*, p. 165.
98 Clark, *Barbarossa: The Russian-German Conflict 1941–45*, pp. 314–15.

Chapter 9 notes

1. Grams, *Die 14. Panzer-Division 1940–1945*, pp. 120–1.
2. Consisting of mostly *Pz.* IV long and short gun variants.
3. Originally consisting of a HQ company and four *Sturmgeschütz* companies, this changed in July to two tank companies and two assault gun companies. The battalion reported operational in October 1943: 49 *Pz.* IV (long)'s, 44 *Sturmgeschütz* and 7 *FlammPanzer* tank. Jentz, *Panzertruppen, Vol. I.*, p. 68 & p. 109. Grams, *Die 14. Panzer-Division 1940–1945*, p. 121.
4. Jentz, *Panzertruppen, Vol. I.*, p. 64.
5. Else Roth, personal interview, May 1998.
6. Grams, *Die 14. Panzer-Division 1940–1945*, p. 122.
7. Ibid., p. 123.
8. Tute, Costello & Huges, *D-Day*, pp. 44–51.
9. Caidin, *Black Thursday: The Epic Story of the Schweinfurt Raid*, pp. 4–23.
10. Ibid., p. 25.
11. Else Roth, personal interview, May 1998.
12. Grams, *Die 14. Panzer-Division 1940–1945*, p. 125.
13. Ibid.
14. Utkin, "Battle For The Dniepr", pp. 1463–9.
15. 14th and 24th *Panzer* Div's.
16. Grams, *Die 14. Panzer-Division 1940–1945*, pp. 126–33.
17. Jentz, *Panzertruppen, Vol. II.*, p. 122. For a detailed battle report see pp. 116–24.
18. Ibid., p. 123.
19. Ibid., p. 122.

Chapter 10 notes

1. Grams, *Die 14. Panzer-Division 1940–1945*, p. 150.
2. Ibid., pp. 153–5, 171.
3. Manstein, *Lost Victories*, p. 502.
4. Ibid., pp. 515.
5. Grams, *Die 14. Panzer-Division 1940–1945*, pp. 166–7.
6. Else Roth and Paul Schmidt, personal interview, summer 1996.
7. Buchner, *Ostfront 1944: The German Defensive Battles on the Russian Front*, p. 21.
8. Including 5th Mountain Division, 72nd Inf. Div., 88th Inf. Div., Corps Attachment B with 112th Inf. Div., 255th Inf. Div., 332nd Inf. Div. (all divisions in regimental strength only) 5th *Panzergrenadier* Div. *Wiking*, SS Storm Brigade *Wallonie* and minor elements of the 14th *Panzer* Div. (mostly grenadiers).
9. Buchner, *Ostfront 1944: The German Defensive Battles on the Russian Front*, p. 23.
10. Of the total 2,026 tons landed or dropped, 1,247 were of ammunition. Buchner, *Ostfront 1944: The German Defensive Battles on the Russian Front*, p. 39.

11 Ibid., pp. 33–4, 39.
12 Ibid., pp. 23, 30, 37.
13 Ibid., p. 22.
14 Ibid., p. 31.
15 Ibid., pp. 27, 33.
16 Ibid., pp. 36–7.
17 Editors of Time-Life Books, *Scorched Earth*, p. 74.
18 Shimansky, "The Red Army's Drive to Rumania", p. 1906. Also see Buchner, *Ostfront 1944: The German Defensive Battles on the Russian Front*, p. 69, and Editors of Time-Life Books, *Scorched Earth*, p. 74.
19 Grams, *Die 14. Panzer-Division 1940–1945*, pp. 181–2.
20 Ibid.
21 Ibid., p. 182.
22 Ibid., pp. 183–9.
23 Edwards, *Panzer: A Revolution in Warfare, 1939–1945*, pp. 159, 169.
24 Grams, *Die 14. Panzer-Division 1940–1945*, pp. 192–5.
25 This was probably 3rd *SS Div. Totenkopf* or *Panzergrenadier* Div. *Grossdeutchland*. Both units were operating on the Lower Bug with the 14th *Panzer* Div.
26 The 36th Regiments supply officer, Paul Schmidt, verified this story during an interview at his house near Mainburg in 1998, as he was the one who had to explain things in Karl's defence. A side note to the story is that this *SS* officer was Karl's neighbour after the war in Schweinfurt, although they rarely ever talked after this incident.
27 Grams, *Die 14. Panzer-Division 1940–1945*, p. 191.
28 Manstein, *Lost Victories*, p. 544.
29 Ibid., p. 199.
30 Grams, *Die 14. Panzer-Division 1940–1945*, p. 204.
31 Ibid., p. 222.
32 Ibid., p. 219.
33 14th, 3rd, 13th, 17th *Panzer* Divs. and the 294th, 320th Inf. Divs. with the 2nd Parachute Div. assigned.
34 Buchner, *Ostfront 1944: The German Defensive Battles on the Russian Front*, p. 242.
35 Ibid., p. 210.
36 Grams, *Die 14. Panzer-Division 1940–1945*, pp. 213–15.
37 Jutta Roth, personal interview, 2000.
38 Grams, *Die 14. Panzer-Division 1940–1945*, p. 221.
39 Ibid., pp. 223–4.
40 Schörner went with them and continued his terror of the rear area troops. His famous quote at this time to a subordinate officer was "you will report to me by this evening what commanders you have had shot, or are having shot, for cowardice in front of the enemy". As far as his loyalty to duty he abandoned his command (of the largest body of German troops still fighting) at the end of the war in Hungary, changed into civilian clothes and flew to Austria, where he

surrendered to the Americans. He was later turned over to the Soviets and was imprisoned until 1955. He must have had some rapport with his captors, as he was on a wanted list at the end of the war, but despite this was released and died in Germany in 1971.

41   Ryan, *The Last Battle*, p. 75. Also see Lucas, *The Last Year of the German Army: May, 1944–May1945*, p. 203.
42   Ibid., pp. 224–6. Also see personal interview with Karl Brier, Kuhlsheim, Oct. 1998.

Chapter 11 notes

1   39th *Panzerk*orps with: *Gossdeutschland Div.* 4th, 5th and 12th *Panzer* Divs. and two *Panzer* brigades.
2   HQ troops, 11th SS *Panzergrenadier D*iv. Nordland, the 11th Inf. Div and the 225 *Panzergrenadier* Div.
3   Information for this chapter see Grams, *Die 14. Panzer-Division 1940–1945*, chapters 18 & 19, and from Haupt, *Kurland: Bilderchronik der Vergessenen Heeresgruppe*, Chapters 1, 2, & 3.
4   The battalions were assigned to the 103rd and 108th *Panzergrenadier* Regiment's.
5   The 11th Inf. Div.
6   It took three medium tanks to tow a Panther and three Panthers to tow a Tiger!
7   Reported as being repaired: 1 *Pz.* Mark IV, 3 assault guns, and 20 more Panthers.
8   36th *Panzer* Rgt., the 14th *Panzer* Div., and the 510 Heavy Tiger Batt.
9   Leo Schwarz, who served on a Panther and Tiger tank, stated that the former was effective up to 1600 metres, while the latter could achieve a range of 2000 metres.
10   *Panzergrenadier* Reg. 108 lost one-third of its officers.
11   Another argument at the end of March over the same subject resulted in Guderian's forced retirement.
12   Information for this section see Grams, *Die 14. Panzer-Division 1940–1945*, chapters 20–3. Also see Haupt, *Kurland: Bilderchronik der Vergessenen Heeresgruppe*, chapters 4–8.
13   Else and Jutta Roth, personal interview, 1998

Chapter 12 notes

1   Tiger Co Kummersdorf was sent to bolster the defence of Schweinfurt defenders, one of the last *Panzer* units available.
2   Else Roth, personal interview, 2001.
3   Jutta Roth, personal interview, 2002.
4   Information for this chapter see Fritz, *Frontsoldaten: The German Soldier in World War II,* Chapter 9.

Bibliography

Archival Material

The National Archives: Guides to German Records Microfilmed at Alexandria, VA. No. 41. Records of German Field Commands: Divisions (Part 1) No. T–315, Rolls 1–303. No. 63. The 14th *Panzer* Division: Rolls 656–9.

Interviews and Letters

Hans Braun, letter dated November 29 1998.
Hans Braun, General Butler, Erwin Jungkuntz, Heinz Neuendorff, Leo Schwarz, & Klaus Voss, interviewed at the reunion of the 14th *Panzer* Division at Kuhlsheim Military Kaserne, October 1998.
Karl Breir, October 1998 and July 2003.
Von Brise & H. Neuendorff, "Unsere Kameraden In- Und Ausserhalb Des Kessels Von Stalingrad", December 1992.
Heinz Neuendorff, letter dated August 2000.
Else Roth, 1988–2003.
Paul Schmitt, 1996.
Leo Schwarz, April 2004.
Karl Voss, letter dated December 1998.
Alois Weigand, The End in Schweinfurt, July 2003.

Printed Sources: Books

Allied Intelligence, *German Order Of Battle 1944: The Directory of Regiments, Formations and Units of the German Armed Forces*, Mechanicsburg, PA, Greenhill Books, 1994.
Anon *Illustrated World War II Encyclopaedia. Vol. 1.*, Orbis Publishing Ltd., H.S. Stuttman Inc., 1972, 1978.
Blau, George E., *Invasion Balkans*, Shippensburg, PA, Burd Street Press, 1997.
Buchner, Alex, *Ostfront 1944: The German Defensive Battles on the Russian Front*, Atglen, PA, Schiffer Military/Aviation History, 1995.
Caidin, Martin, *Black Thursday: The Epic Story of the Schweinfurt Raid*, New York, NY, E.P. Dutton Publishing Co. Inc., 1960.
Clark, Alan, *Barbarossa: The Russian-German Conflict 1941–1945*, New York, NY, William Morrow and Co. Inc., 1965.
Center of Military History U.S. Army, *Historical Studies: DA Pamphlet 20–291, Effects of Climate on Combat in European Russia*, Washington D.C., February 1952.
Center of Military History U.S. Army, *DA Pam. 20–201,. Military Improvisations During the Russian Campaign. Small Unit Actions During the German Campaign in Russia 1998*, Washington D.C., August 1951.
Delaney, John, *The Blitzkreig Campaigns: Germany's 'Lightning War' Strategy in Action*, New York, NY, Sterling Publishing Co. Inc., 1996.
Del Re, Gerhard & Patricia Del Re, *World War II Trivia Quiz Book: Answers to Your Questions About World War II*, New York, NY, Barnes and Noble Books, 2001.

Editors of Time-Life Books, *Barbarossa*, Richmond, VA, The Time Inc. Book Company, The Third-Reich Series, 1990.
Editors of Time-Life Books, *Conquest of the Balkans*, Richmond, VA, The Time Inc. Book Company, The Third-Reich Series, 1990.
Editors of Time-Life Books, *Fists of Steel*, Richmond, VA, The Time Inc. Book Company, The Third-Reich Series, 1988.
Editors of Time-Life Books, *Lightning War*, Richmond, VA, The Time Inc. Book Company, The Third-Reich Series, 1989.
Editors of Time-Life Books, *Scorched Earth*, Richmond, VA, The Time Inc. Book Company, The Third-Reich Series, 1991.
Editors of Time-Life Books, *Storming to Power*, Richmond, VA, The Time Inc. Book Company, The Third-Reich Series, 1989.
Editors of Time-Life Books, *The New Order*, Richmond, VA, The Time Inc. Book Company, The Third-Reich Series, 1989.
Editors of Time-Life Books, *The Reach For Empire*, Richmond, VA, The Time Inc. Book Company, The Third-Reich Series, 1989.
Editors of Time-Life Books, *The Road to Stalingrad*, Richmond, VA, The Time Inc. Book Company, The Third-Reich Series, 1990.
Edwards, Roger, *Panzer: A Revolution in Warfare, 1939–1945*, New York, NY, Sterling Publishing Co. Inc., 1989.
Fleischer, Wolfgang, *Deutsche Kampfpanzer im Einsatz 1939–1945*, Wölfersheim-Berstadt, Podzun-Pallas-Verlag, 1995.
Fritz, Stephen G., *Frontsoldaten: The German Soldier in World War II*, Lexington, KY, University Press of Kentucky, 1995.
Glantz, David M., *Kharkov 1942: Anatomy of a Military Disaster*, New York, NY, Sarpedon, 1998.
Goerlitz, Walter, *Paulus and Stalingrad*, Translated by Col. R. H. Stevens, New York, NY, Citadel Press, 1963.
Grams, Rolf, *Die 14. Panzer-Division 1940–1945*, Wölfersheim-Berstadt, Podzun-Pallas-Verlag, 1986.
Hamburg Institute For Social Research (ed.), *The German Army and Genocide: Crimes Against War Prisoners, Jews, and Other Civilians, 1939–1944*, translated from the German by Scott Abbott with editorial oversight by Paula Bradish, New York, NY, The New York Press, 1999.
Haupt, Werner, *Kurland: Bildchronik der Vergessene Armeegruppe 1944/1945*, Wölfersheim-Berstadt, Podzun-Pallas-Verlag, 1984.
Jentz, Thomas, *Panzertruppen*, Atglen, PA, Schiffer Military History Publishing Co., 1996, 2 vols.
Jukes, Geoffrey, *Stalingrad: The Turning Point*, New York, NY, Ballantine Books, 1968.
Koch, Fred, *Waffen und Fahrzeuge der Heere und Luftstreitkräfte, Band 172: Laufwerke und Ketten Deutscher Kampfpanzer 1935–1945*, Wolfersheim-Berstadt, Podzun-Pallas-Verlag, 1998.
Kollatz, K., *Der Landser, Erlebnisberichte zur Geschichte des Zweiten Weltkrieges, nr 2095: Sturmgeschütze am Fiend. 1941. Die Sturmgeschützabteilung 191 in der Anfangsphase des Krieges gegen die Sowjetunion*, Rastatt, Germany, Pabel, 1998.
Lucas, James, *The Last Year of the German Army: May 1944–1945*, London, Arms and Armour Press, 1994.

Lukacs, John, *The Duel*, New York, NY, Ticknor and Fields, 1990.
Manstein, Erich von, *Lost Victories*, Novato, CA, Presidio Press, 1982.
Mellenthin, F.W., *Panzer Battles: Chief of Staff to the 4th Panzer Army*, Norman, OK, University of Oklahoma Press, 1977.
Nafziger, George F., *German Order of Battle World War II: Panzer, Panzer Grenadier, Light and Cavalry- Divisions - Vol. 1*, Privately Published, 1994.
Rossino, Alexander, *Hitler Strikes Poland*, Lawrence, KS, University Press of Kansas, 2003.
Ryan, Cornelius, *The Last Battle*, St. James Place, London, Collins Pub., 1966.
Sadarananda, Dana V., *Beyond Stalingrad: Manstein and The Operations Of Army Group Don*, Westport, CT, Praeger Publishers, 1990.
Scheibert, Horst, *Kampf und Untergang der Deutschen Panzertruppe*, Wölfersheim-Berstadt, Podzun-Pallas-Verlag, 1973.
Scheibert, Horst, *Nach Stalingrad-48 Kilometers: Der Entsatz Vorstoss der 6 Panzer Division, Dezember 1942*, Heidelburg, Scharnhorst Buchkameradenschaft Gmbh., 1956.
Schon, Heinz, *Die Letzten Kriegstage: Ostseehafen 1945*, Stuttgart, Motorbuch Verlag, 1995.
Stein, George H., *The Waffen SS: Hitler's Elite Guard at War 1939–1945*, Ithaca, NY, Cornell University Press, 1966.
Tarrent, V.E., *Stalingrad: An Anatomy of an Agony*, Barnsley, Pen and Sword Books Ltd., 1992.
Tute, Warren, John Costello & Terry Huges, *D-Day*, London and Sydney, Pan Books Ltd., 1974.
U.S. War Department, *Handbook on German Military Forces*, Baton Rouge, LA, Louisiana State University Press, 1990.
Vliegen, Rene, *Fort Eben-Emael*, Kanne, Belgium, Association pour l'etude, la conservation et la protection du fort d'Eben-Emael et de son site (abbreviated to F.E.E.), 1993.
Wieder, Joechim & Heinrich Graf von Einsiedel, *Stalingrad: Memories of Hell*, London, Arms and Armour Press, 1993.
Zimmermann, Hermann, *Der Griff ins Ungewisse*, Neckargemund, Kurt Vowinckel Verlag, 1964.

Printed Sources: Articles

Anon, "Stalingrad und Stuhlweissenburg: Weihnachten im Kreig bei der 23. Pz. Div.", *Alte Kameraden*, No. 12, 19. Jahrgang, December 1971.
Barry, Maj. Gen. R.H., "Military Balance", *The History of the Second World War*, Marshall Cavendish USA Ltd., 1973.
Charles, Jean-Leon, "Invasion of Holland and Belgium", *The History of the Second World War*, Marshall Cavendish USA Ltd., 1973.
Clark, Alan, "The Most Vicious Battle of the War", *The History of the Second World War*, Marshall Cavendish USA Ltd., 1973.
Grams, R., "Co. Forester, 1942", *Traditionsgeimeinschaft-Mitteilungsblatt des Verbandes ehemaliger Angehöriger der 14. Pz. Div., 23rd Pz. Div., 36th Pz. Rgt.*, December 1971.
Grams, R., "Co. Hofstetter", *Traditionsgeimeinschaft-Mitteilungsblatt des Verbandes ehemaliger Angehöriger der 14. Pz. Div., 23rd Pz. Div., 36th Pz. Rgt.*, No. 3/18, Jul 1971.

Greenberg, L., "Army with No Way Out", *World War II Magazine*, Vol. 6, No. 1., May 1991.
Guttman, J., "Polish Artillerymen on the Eastern Front", *World War II Magazine*, Vol. 14, No. 5, January 2000.
Jukes, Geoffrey, "Drive to Kiev", *The History of the Second World War*, Marshall Cavendish USA Ltd., 1973.
Lew, C., "Armament", *World War II Magazine*, Vol. 12, No. 6, February 1998.
McTaggert, P., "Winter Tempest in Stalingrad", *World War II Magazine*, Vol. 12, No. 4, November 1997.
Mitteilungsblatt der Traditionsgemeinschaft der ehem. 14. Pz. Div., Dec 1979, May 1981, July 1983, Nov 1985, Nov 1989, May 1991, Mar 1992, Aug 1994, Dec 1996.
Morozov, Col. Vasili, "The Kharkov Offensives", *The History of the Second World War*, Marshall Cavendish USA Ltd., 1973.
Palmer, Alan, "Operation Punishment", *The History of the Second World War*, Marshall Cavendish USA Ltd., 1973.
Philippi, General-Major Alfred, "The Battle For Moscow", *The History of the Second World War*, Marshall Cavendish USA Ltd., 1973.
Pitt, Barry, "Prelude to Disaster", *The History of the Second World War*, Marshall Cavendish USA Ltd., 1973.
Richards, "Battle of Britain", *The History of the Second World War*, Marshall Cavendish USA Ltd., 1973.
Shimansky, A. N., "The Red Army's Drive to Rumania", *The History of the Second World War*, Marshall Cavendish USA Ltd., 1973.
Smith, R., "Walther Wenck", *World War II Magazine*, Vol. 5., No. 4, November 1990.
Utkin, Grigory, "Battle for the Dniepr", *The History of the Second World War*, Marshall Cavendish USA Ltd., 1973.
Zabecki, D., "Invasion of Poland: Campaign that Launched a War", *World War II Magazine*, Vol. 14, No. 3, September 1999.

Internet Websites

Bundesarchiv: Potsdamer Str. 1. 56075 Koblenz. Online. Available HTTP: http://www.ghi-dc.org/guide5/archfrg.html
Chapter 4; The Pocket West of Cherkassy-The Inside View. Online. Available HTTP: http://www.army.mil/cmh-pg/books/WWII/20234/20-22344.html, pp. 1–13.
Ich hatte ein Kamerad: German Military Songs in WWII. Online. Available HTTP: http://www.feldgrau.com/songs.html
Niehorster, Leo G. (1998) *German World War II Organizational Series*. Online. Available HTTP: http://www.uwm.edu/people/jpipes/36pzreg.html
Rosander, Magnus *World War II Website*. Online. Available HTTP: http://ww2photo.mimmesrwell.com/tanks/tankme.html
Wisbar, F.(Director) (1958) *Hunde, wollt ihr ewig leben*. Online. Available HTTP: http://us.imdb.om/Title?Hunde,+wollt+ihr+ewig+leben+(1958)

Videotape

Hitler's 1939 Birthday Parade: Germany Celebrates Hitler's Birthday.

To the Bitter End: The Final Battles of
Army Groups North Ukraine, A, Centre,
Eastern Front 1944–45
Rolf Hinze
208pp   Hardback
ISBN 1 874622 36 1

Hitler's Last Levy: The Volkssturm
1944–45
Hans Kissel
224pp   Hardback
ISBN 1 874622 51 5

Related titles published by Helion & Company

A selection of forthcoming titles

For Europe: The French Volunteers of the Waffen-SS
Robert Forbes   ISBN 1 874622 68 X

Panzer Lehr Division 1944–45 (Helion WWII German Military Studies volume 1)
Edited by Fred Steinhardt   ISBN 1 874622 28 0

The Knight's Cross Holders of Panzerkorps Grossdeutschland (Including its Sister Units: Panzer-Führer-Begleit Division/Panzer-Führer-Grenadier-Division/Panzer-Grenadier-Division Brandenburg/Panzer-Grenadier-Division Kurmark)
Ralph Tegethoff   ISBN 1 874622 93 0

Kursk in Normandy: Operation Goodwood, July 1944
Perry Moore   ISBN 1 874622 73 6

HELION & COMPANY
26 Willow Road, Solihull, West Midlands, B91 1UE, England
Tel 0121 705 3393   Fax 0121 711 4075
Website: http://www.helion.co.uk